GOODBYE, GOOD MEN

GOODBYE, GOOD MEN

HOW LIBERALS BROUGHT CORRUPTION INTO THE CATHOLIC CHURCH

MICHAEL S. ROSE

Since 1947

**REGNERY
PUBLISHING, INC.**

An Eagle Publishing Company • Washington, DC

Library of Congress Cataloging-in-Publication Data

Rose, Michael S., 1969-
  Goodbye, good men : how liberals brought corruption into the Catholic Church / Michael S. Rose.
    p. cm.
Includes bibliographical references and index.
  ISBN 0-89526-144-8
  1. Vocation, Ecclesiastical. 2. Liberalism (Religion)—Catholic Church. I. Title.
  BX2380 .R67 2002
  262'.14273—dc21
                        2002006033

Published in the United States by
Regnery Publishing, Inc.
An Eagle Publishing Company
One Massachusetts Avenue, NW
Washington, DC 20001

Visit us at www.regnery.com

Distributed to the trade by
National Book Network
4720-A Boston Way
Lanham, MD 20706

Printed on acid-free paper
Manufactured in the United States of America

10 9 8 7 6 5 4 3 2

Books are available in quantity for promotional or premium use. Write to Director of Special Sales, Regnery Publishing, Inc., One Massachusetts Avenue, NW, Washington, DC 20001, for information on discounts and terms or call (202) 216-0600.

Contents

Introduction

In the months before this book went to press, Catholics throughout the United States were scandalized by one revelation after another about sexual abuse among the Catholic clergy. First came word of the notorious crimes of John Geoghan, a defrocked priest of the Archdiocese of Boston who stood accused of more than 130 counts of sexual molestation in a thirty-six-year spree. He has thus far been sentenced to eight years in prison. If Geoghan's recidivist crimes weren't awful enough, the following week the archbishop of Boston, Bernard Cardinal Law—under mounting pressure from the Massachusetts attorney general—revealed the names of other priests or former priests of his archdiocese who had been accused of sexual misconduct with minors. Then a Missouri man alleged that Bishop Anthony J. O'Connell had sexually abused him while he was a seminary student. He also filed a federal racketeering suit accusing the Catholic Church in the United States of a pattern of illegal activity— a systematic cover-up of sexual crimes by Catholic priests.

The sexual crimes were horrible enough, but most shocking was this pattern of cover-up—the fact that Church officials knowingly protected repeat sex offenders and routinely reassigned them to posts that gave them access to new victims. Commentator (and Catholic) Patrick J. Buchanan likened the situation to Mafia dons providing safe houses for their henchmen. Such an analogy isn't off the mark considering that Bishop James Quinn of Cleveland, in response to the racketeering suit, suggested that Church leaders should hide records of abusive priests at the Vatican embassy, which has diplomatic immunity against subpoenas.[1] Arthur Austin, who had repeatedly been sexually abused by a priest in Boston, put it in stark terms: "If the Catholic Church in America does not fit the definition of organized crime, then Americans seriously need to examine their concept of justice."[2]

Despite the media feeding frenzy, Church officials still hesitated to "come clean." Although Boston's Cardinal Law released the names of the offending priests to law enforcement officials, he would not reveal to the media the number of priests involved. Only by examining court documents and speaking with local law firms did the *Boston Globe* discover that the archdiocese had settled sex abuse claims against *at least* eighty priests during the previous decade alone. That number would later swell to nigh a hundred.

Law's attitude seemed characteristic of far too many American bishops, who often seem to believe that they and their priests are answerable to no greater authority than themselves. Indeed, we are finding that what happened in Boston is routine in many dioceses; similar grave problems have been revealed in Philadelphia, Los Angeles, St. Louis, Brooklyn, Milwaukee, Cleveland, and Pittsburgh, to name just a few. The fact is, orthodox Catholics[3] are demanding honest and forthright action from the Church's shepherds.

The big question now is: Why is this happening? The extent of the sex abuse scandals and the accompanying payoffs and cover-ups has mystified many of the faithful, who are simply at a loss to understand how this could have occurred and why it was swept under the rug for so long.

I researched and wrote this book over the past two years, interviewing more than 150 people, as a professional investigative journalist for the Catholic press, without any idea that the Boston debacle and its many ramifications would blow up just as *Goodbye, Good Men* was going to press. Although I did not set out to write a book about clerical sex abuse, what I discovered provides at least part of the answer to the burning question: How could this have happened?

Goodbye, Good Men presents documented evidence that the root of this problem—the cover-up and the sexual scandals themselves—extends down to the very place where vocations to the priesthood germinate: the seminary. Too often men who support the teachings of the Church, especially the teachings on sexual morality, are dismissed for being "rigid and uncharitable homophobes," while those seminarians who reject the Church's teaching or "come out" as gays to their superiors are given preferential treatment and then ordained to the Catholic priesthood. A corrupt, protective network starts in many seminaries where gay seminarians are encouraged to "act out" or "explore their sexuality" in highly inappropriate ways.

No doubt, for the average American, Catholic or not, much of the material presented in this book will come as a surprise—even a shock. Nevertheless, as one recently ordained priest confided in me after reading the prepublication manuscript, the revelations herein have long been known within the inner circles of the Catholic Church—among bishops and priests especially. The problem in vocations offices and in seminaries is a profound spiritual problem, a sickness of untold proportions. This is a book that seeks first to identify that sickness, or at least a portion of it, in hopes that the pathogen can be removed and the body healed. In short, many have hijacked the priesthood in order to change the Catholic Church from within.

The trouble starts in the seminary, and gross sexual immorality and the protective network formed around that immorality is only one of the major issues that needs to be forthrightly addressed by the shepherds of the Catholic Church, as *Goodbye, Good Men* reveals. The fact is that many qualified candidates for the priesthood have been turned away for political reasons over the past three decades. Systematic, ideological discrimination has been practiced against seminarians who uphold Catholic teaching on sexuality and other issues; dissenters from Catholic teaching—including teaching on homosexuality—have been rewarded.

Goodbye, Good Men exposes this corruption: the deliberate infiltration of Catholic seminaries by what Andrew Greeley has dubbed the "Lavender Mafia," a clique of homosexual dilettantes, along with an underground of liberal faculty members determined to change the doctrines, disciplines, and mission of the Catholic Church from within. Through the seminaries, liberals have brought a moral melt-down into the Catholic priesthood. If the sex scandals that have rocked the Catholic Church are to end, the individuals responsible for this moral meltdown must be rooted out. Only then will the "dark shadow of suspicion" be removed from "all the other fine priests who perform their ministry with honesty and integrity and often with heroic self-sacrifice."[4]

Finally, a note on anonymity: Some of my sources have asked to remain anonymous for obvious reasons—priests, because they fear retribution from their bishops or brother priests; and current semi-narians, because they believe their frankness would jeopardize their chances of being recommended for ordination. As you read on, you will come to understand that one critical remark could mean "nonendorsement" (in other words, expulsion from their seminary). Some former seminarians and those who have not yet been accepted into a formation program also chose to remain nameless to maximize their chances of being accepted into a diocese or religious order. When a pseudonym is used the name will appear the first time with an asterisk like this: John P. Jones.* There are many other men I in-terviewed for background purposes only. They did not even want their comments to be published anonymously, for fear that their identity would be known to their superiors by the mere details of their particular situation.

Michael S. Rose
Cincinnati, Ohio
April 2002

CHAPTER 1

A Man-Made Crisis

Why Archbishop Curtiss Said the Priest Shortage Is "Artificial and Contrived"

It seems to me that the vocations "crisis" is precipitated by people who want to change the Church's agenda, by people who do not support orthodox candidates loyal to the magisterial teachings of the Pope and bishops, and by people who actually discourage viable candidates from seeking priesthood and vowed religious life as the Church defines these ministries.
—Elden F. Curtiss, Archbishop of Omaha

As early as 1966, just a year after the close of the Second Vatican Council, Jesuit Father Robert E. McNally predicted an impending priest shortage. He believed that an imminent vocations crisis would devastate the Catholic priesthood. In fact, he stated that this shortage would become so acute that "in the course of the next century the Catholic priesthood might almost disappear."[1] This was a startling prediction, coming as it did at the tail end of America's "golden age of the priesthood,"[2] during the same year that seminary enrollment peaked in the United States. Nevertheless, statistics bear out at least the first part of McNally's prophecy: There are far fewer men studying for the priesthood at the dawn of the twenty-first century than thirty years before. From 1966 to 1999, the total number of seminarians dropped from 39,638 to 4,826.[3] And from 1965 to 1998 the number of graduate-level seminarians (those ordinarily within four years of ordination) dropped from 8,325 to 3,158, while priestly ordinations during that same time period dropped from 994 to 509 per year.[4]

Since the 1970s, when it became obvious that vocation numbers were plummeting, U.S. Catholics have been bombarded with shrill warnings that a severe shortage of priests will soon deprive them of the sacraments. The doomsayers are with us to this day, prophesying, despite evidence to the contrary, that the priest shortage will continue to worsen until, as McNally predicted, the priesthood is nearly extinct.[5]

How is the "vocations crisis" to be explained? Why, since the Second Vatican Council, has the Catholic Church in the United States seen fewer and fewer young men devoting themselves to the sacrificial life of the priesthood? The decline has been blamed on a multitude of factors, including materialism, practical and philosophical atheism, skepticism, subjectivism, individualism, hedonism, social injustice; parents who don't want their sons to be priests; and the commonly perceived "unrealistic expectation" of lifelong celibacy. The failure to properly instruct Catholic youth in the faith is another important factor.

There is one instrumental component to the problem, however, which has received little attention until recently. In a 1995 article, Archbishop Elden F. Curtiss implicated vocations directors and others directly responsible for promoting vocations as having a "death wish" for the male, celibate priesthood. The article, first published in the archbishop's diocesan newspaper, the *Catholic Voice*, was reprinted in *Our Sunday Visitor* for national distribution. Curtiss, the archbishop of Omaha, Nebraska, made a startling observation based, he said, on his experience as a former diocesan vocations director and seminary rector:

> It seems to me that the vocation "crisis" is precipitated
> by people who want to change the Church's agenda, by
> people who do not support orthodox candidates loyal
> to the magisterial teaching of the Pope and bishops,

and by people who actually discourage viable candidates from seeking priesthood and vowed religious life
as the Church defines these ministries. I am personally
aware of certain vocations directors, vocations teams
and evaluation boards who turn away candidates who
do not support the possibility of ordaining women or
who defend the Church's teaching about artificial birth
control, or who exhibit a strong piety toward certain
devotions, such as the rosary.[6]

In other words, the very Church officials with immediate responsibility for promoting and fostering vocations are turning away qualified candidates for the priesthood. Moreover, this problem is not
confined to a few such persons, but pervades nearly the entire system
for recruiting and training new priests. In short, the priest shortage
is caused ultimately not by a lack of vocations, but by attitudes and
policies that deliberately and effectively thwart true priestly vocations.

Curtiss quickly made headlines across the country, declaring the
resultant priest shortage to be "artificial and contrived." The same
people, he wrote, who have discouraged priestly vocations then turn
around and promote ordination of married men and women to replace the traditional vocations they themselves have aborted. They
exploit the dearth of vocations that they have helped create, to advance their efforts on behalf of a "reenvisioned priesthood" which
consciously rejects the Church's definition of the office for the Latin
rite as a ministry to be exercised exclusively by celibate males.

Turning away candidates who explicitly and proudly accept the
Church's teaching, especially regarding the ordained priesthood, has
been likened to "a Marine recruiter turning away prospects because
they profess a love of America."[7] The conclusion then is that there
is no shortage of vocations; in actuality, there are plenty of young
men who exhibit what Curtiss calls "orthodoxy"—loyalty to the
teachings of the Church—who are not admitted to holy orders,
specifically because of their orthodox beliefs. The result is a "crisis"
of ideological discrimination.

Curtiss also points out that in dioceses which support orthodox candidates there is no vocations crisis but an increase in priestly vocations.
In a follow-up article published in *Social Justice Review,* Curtiss explained that when dioceses and religious orders are unambiguous
about the priesthood as the Church defines this calling, when there is
strong support for vocations, and a minimum of dissent about the
male, celibate priesthood, then there are documented increases in the
number of candidates who respond to the call. Speaking of his own
Omaha archdiocese, he wrote that he is encouraged by the "dynamic
thrust for vocations to the priesthood" and "clear indications of increases in the coming years."[8] He explained the reasons for Omaha's
success:

> Our vocation strategy is drawn from successful ones in
> other dioceses: a strong, orthodox base that promotes
> loyalty to the Pope and bishop; a vocations director and
> team who clearly support a male, celibate priesthood
> and religious communities loyal to magisterial teach-
> ing; a presbyterate [i.e., the priests in a given diocese]
> that takes personal ownership of vocation ministry in
> the archdiocese; two large Serra clubs in Omaha that
> constantly program outreach efforts to touch potential
> candidates; more and more parents who encourage
> their children to consider a vocation to priesthood and
> religious life; eucharistic devotion in parishes with an
> emphasis on prayer for vocations; and vocation com-
> mittees in most of our parishes that focus on personally
> inviting and nourishing vocations.[9]

The archbishop also cited the successful vocations numbers of
Lincoln and Arlington,[10] two dioceses led, at the time, by bishops
who also supported orthodox vocations. Father James Gould, then
vocations director for the Arlington diocese[11] in northern Virginia,
echoed Curtiss when he explained their formula for success:
"unswerving allegiance to the Pope and magisterial teaching; per-

petual adoration of the Blessed Sacrament in parishes, with an emphasis on praying for vocations; and the strong effort by a significant number of diocesan priests who extend themselves to help young men remain open to the Lord's will in their lives."[12]

Curtiss might equally as well have pointed to any number of other successful, orthodox dioceses across the country. His own Archdiocese of Omaha, considered one of the most conservative in the Midwest, ordained an average of seven men (fifty-six total) per year from 1991 to 1998 for a population of just 215,000 Catholics. Compare that to the much more liberal diocese of Madison, Wisconsin (with a slightly larger Catholic population), which ordained a *total* of four men during the same eight-year period.

In the orthodox Rockford, Illinois, diocese, Bishop Thomas Doran ordained 8 priests in 1999, the highest number of ordinations there in forty-one years. Arlington ordained 55 men to the priesthood in the years 1991–98 under Bishop John Keating. In 1985 Keating had 90 diocesan priests. A decade later he had 133, nearly a 50 percent increase. And, under orthodox leadership from Bishop John J. Myers, the Diocese of Peoria,[13] with a Catholic population of just 232,000, ordained 72 priests in the years 1991–98, an average of 9 each year. In comparison, the Milwaukee archdiocese under the leadership of Archbishop Rembert Weakland, with a Catholic population three times that of Peoria, ordained just 2 priests in 2001, while Detroit, with a Catholic population of 1.5 million (almost seven times that of Peoria), ordained an average of just 7 men each year from 1991 to 1998.

Other archdioceses such as Denver and Atlanta have turned their vocations programs around by actively supporting orthodox vocations and promoting fidelity to Church teaching, while emphasizing the traditional role of the priest as defined by the Catholic Church. Atlanta now has sixty-one seminarians, up from just nine in 1985. Denver boasted sixty-eight seminarians in 1999, up from twenty-six in 1991. In addition to Denver's archdiocesan seminarians, twenty more were studying for the Neocatechumenal Way and nine for other orders. All will serve the Archdiocese of Denver when ordained.

Orthodoxy begets vocations. This is proved by the successes of the dioceses just mentioned. The converse is also true: Dissent kills vocations. It is merely common sense that says people generally do not want to give themselves to an organization whose leaders constantly bemoan its basic structures. Young men are normally not going to commit themselves to dioceses or religious orders that dissent from Church doctrine. "They do not want to be battered by agendas that are not the Church's and radical movements that disparage their desire to be priests," Archbishop Curtiss wrote.[14]

Those dioceses that have promoted dissent from the magisterial teachings of the Church have seen the sharpest decline in vocations and are now experiencing the predicted dire priest shortage. The Archdiocese of Milwaukee under the leadership of Archbishop Rembert Weakland is reputedly the most liberal and least orthodox *archdiocese* in the United States. Milwaukee in the 1990s consistently had a small number of seminarians, a third of the number of some dioceses a quarter its size. Weakland, of course, has long sounded the alarm about the dire priest shortage. In 1991 he issued a pastoral letter to Milwaukee Catholics telling his flock that he would ordain married men to the priesthood, subject to Rome's approval. The Vatican was disturbed by Weakland's public statement and reprimanded the archbishop for his "out-of-place" comments. A few years later he again expressed his doubts about the male, celibate priesthood: During the summer of 1995 he was a cosigner of a statement addressing the role of the American bishops conference in its relationship with Rome. Weakland, the only archbishop to sign the statement, expressed his disapproval of *Ordinatio Sacerdotalis*, Pope John Paul II's 1994 pastoral letter which reiterated that the Catholic Church does not have the ability to ordain women to the priesthood. Weakland and his cosigners stated: "The recent apostolic letter *Ordinatio Sacerdotalis* was issued [by the pope] without any prior discussion and consultation with our conference. In an environment of serious question about a teaching that many Catholic people believe needs further study, the bishops are faced with many pastoral problems in their response to the letter."

Only three other diocesan bishops—the remainder were auxiliary bishops—signed onto the statement, which was highly critical of the

Vatican: Bishops Walter Sullivan of Richmond, Virginia, Raymond Lucker of New Ulm, Minnesota, and Kenneth Untener of Saginaw, Michigan. These three dioceses have likewise experienced a shortfall in priestly ordinations. In 1998, Lucker had only fifty-five active diocesan priests to serve his eighty-one parishes, and only nine men, including both college and graduate theology seminarians, studying for the priesthood.[15] Untener, formerly a seminary rector in Detroit, had only seventy-nine active diocesan priests for his 110 parishes with only four seminarians for a Catholic population of 140,000.[16] Saginaw averaged fewer than one ordination per year during the 1990s. Sullivan's numbers in southern Virginia are miserable too, especially in contrast with Richmond's sister diocese of Arlington to the north. In the early 1990s, San Francisco under Archbishop John Quinn and Chicago under Joseph Cardinal Bernardin had equally abysmal records.

When Curtiss's initial article was published in *Our Sunday Visitor*, it set off a flurry of reactions, both positive and negative. The most telling responses came from a number of vocations directors who rejected the Curtiss thesis outright. The *National Catholic Reporter* (*NCR*), a weekly lay-run newspaper published in Kansas City, Missouri, was the first to reply. On October 20, 1995, the *NCR* issued a special report intended to refute Curtiss's claims. Yet the article did more to confirm the archbishop's analysis than to refute it. Staff writer Pamela Schaeffer interviewed several vocations directors whose comments effectively substantiated Curtiss's observations. Father Robert Flagg, vocations director for the Archdiocese of Boston, admitted that he has problems with prospective seminarians who have "preconceived thoughts about the Church" or who are "rigidly locked into positions."[17] Flagg's statement left many wondering whether the magisterial teachings of the Church would be considered "preconceived thoughts" or if commitment to the male, celibate priesthood would be a sure sign of "rigidity." Father John Klein, vocations director for the Archdiocese of Chicago, similarly admitted that he believes young men who desire to "hold on to something" are unsuitable for ordination. He compared the priesthood to a rollercoaster ride: "If you keep your hands inside the car you enjoy the ride. But if you try to hold on to something you're going to get hurt."[18]

Other vocations directors interviewed for the *NCR* piece say they were left feeling "puzzled, pained, and undermined" by the Curtiss report. Challenging his conclusion, they consistently cited "rigidity" as opposed to "orthodoxy" as the cause of rejecting candidates for the priesthood. Boston's Flagg said he looks for candidates who can "move with the Church." Chicago's Klein reiterated that point, saying that the future of the Church is "tremendously exciting but unpredictable."

Privately, reported Schaeffer, vocations directors complained that the dioceses that are not experiencing a vocations shortage are accepting men with a "rigidly conservative view of the Church," in some cases candidates rejected by their home dioceses. Flagg bragged that all but one of the priests ordained for Boston that year were from the archdiocese. The other was from Vietnam, he explained.

Arlington's Father James Gould, responding in *Crisis* magazine, rejected Flagg's charge, noting that only six of Arlington's forty-two seminarians that year were not native to northern Virginia. He also defended the practice of considering candidates who were rejected by their home dioceses: "There are some vocation directors keeping good candidates out. When questioned about the ordination of women or married clergy, if the candidates answer in support of the Church, they are often rejected."[19]

Schaeffer admits to which camp she belongs when she concludes her article by quoting University of Wisconsin sociologist Richard Schoenherr, himself an ex-priest, who says, "There are indeed many people who think the exclusively male, celibate priesthood that served the world well in the past is no longer viable."[20] Statements such as Schoenherr's serve only to underscore Curtiss's essential point.

■ ■ ■

During the Jubilee Year 2000, I devoted much time and energy to interviewing dozens of seminarians, former seminarians, recently ordained priests, seminary faculty, and vocations directors. The 125 seminarian interviewees represent some fifty dioceses and twenty-two major seminaries (some of which are now closed). Each interviewee described himself as more or less representative of the "orthodox seminarian" to whom Archbishop Curtiss had alluded. These are men who are loyal to the teachings of the Church, look to the pope as their spiritual father and leader, pray the rosary, and embrace the male, celibate priesthood. They have no interest in supporting agendas that are not the Church's. Their testimony, often supported by documentary evidence, is remarkably consistent.

They describe the various obstacles deliberately being placed in the way of authentic priestly vocations, leading to the orthodox seminarian's early dismissal or voluntary departure, assuming he is admitted to a seminary program in the first place. These most commonly include:

- a biased application screening process
- unethical psychological counseling
- faculty members and spiritual directors who focus on detecting signs of orthodoxy among seminarians
- a practical moral life of some students and faculty that is not compatible with the Christian standard
- endorsement of homosexual practices and agendas
- promotion of ideas and teachings which undermine Catholic belief in the most fundamental doctrines of the Church
- open contempt for proper liturgy and traditional devotions
- spiritual or psychological manipulation and abuse

It certainly must be acknowledged at the outset that not every candidate who enters a seminary has a genuine vocation to the priesthood. The seminary is a place designed to help a man discern this vocation. Many eventually leave their studies because they have determined that a priestly vocation is not theirs. Others are rightly dismissed from the institutions due to irregularities that would indicate the candidate is not suited for the priesthood: sexual perversions, addictions, mental or emotional problems, incompetence, unwillingness to accept Church teaching, or lack of social or personal skills.

Yet we are not talking here about a procedure designed to winnow out false vocations, but rather a system designed to frustrate genuine vocations because the candidates are perceived by those in control of the vocations apparatus as threats to their agenda. Those in positions of authority at many seminaries are motivated by a desire to "re-envision" the priesthood and to redefine Church ministry according to their own model. That model usually includes women priests, lay-run parishes, secularized worship, and a "soft" approach to Church doctrine—in other words, a desacralized, politically correct Church.

In the face of this "determined effort," in the words of Archbishop Curtiss, on the part of these entrenched dissenters to discourage or-thodox vocations, the U.S. hierarchy has for the most part shown a sin-gular lack of resolution, preferring to tolerate manifest injustices rather than wrest back control of the process of priestly formation from those who have used their power over it to the Church's detriment.

The disaffected orthodox seminarian is rarely supported in his grievances; he is often labeled as a troublemaker or a reactionary zealot, "rigid" and unfit for the priesthood. Once dismissed from a seminary he is typically blackballed from others, effectively lumped in with those who are potential sex offenders. Thus, once dismissed, he finds it difficult, though not always impossible, to be accepted into another seminary, diocese, or religious order.

The network of seminary rectors, psychologists, and priest-makers is a small and tight one. Communications are rapid and ef-fective in purging the orthodox man from the seminary system. When the orthodox seminarian applies to transfer to another dio-cese, he is invariably asked if he's ever been in seminary before. That's fair enough. If the answer is affirmative, a call is immediately placed to the previous seminary, and a negative evaluation from rector, psychologist, and/or spiritual director is received. This ap-plies not only to the seminarian who was formally expelled, but also to the one who left on his own initiative out of frustration or disgust. The problem here is with the *unjust* evaluations and dismissals.

Unfortunately, so many of the seminarians who are treated un-justly and are literally abused—emotionally and spiritually—leave with their tails tucked between their legs. They leave as faceless men who have little or no recourse for the injustices they have suffered. Many believe they have authentic callings to serve the Church as priests but feel they have nowhere to turn. Others who once felt

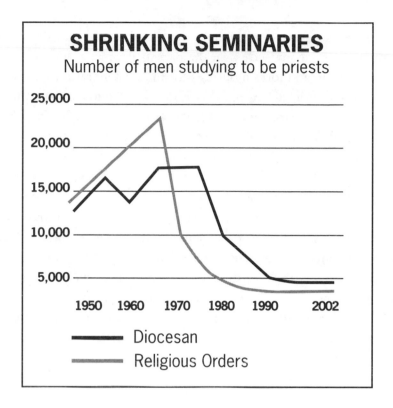

SHRINKING SEMINARIES
Number of men studying to be priests

Diocesan
Religious Orders

called to the priesthood trust the judgments of the biased seminary formation staff who tell them they are not suited for the priesthood. In some cases this is true and becomes obvious to the seminarian. But in all too many cases the young man leaves confused, not really knowing why he isn't suitable for the priesthood but accepting that conclusion all the same. Others leave scandalized yet embarrassed to tell their friends and family—those who had been praying for them—just why they left a Catholic seminary. Many end up with sullied reputations when others conclude that they must have failed or were rejected for psychological or emotional reasons.

■ ■ ■

This book was written to bring to light abuses in U.S. Catholic seminaries over the past three decades so that those outside the seminary subculture might understand what is exacerbating the vocations crisis in this country (as well as in others). It was written with the hope that it will encourage reform of the many seminaries that are in dire need of reform. It was written in hopes that it will rouse the laity to demand greater accountability on the part of the institutions charged with educating and forming priests for future generations.

At the same time, *Goodbye, Good Men* will point out the unmistakable signs that this deplorable situation is at last beginning to turn around. Young men who are now, at the dawn of the twenty-first century, entering seminaries across the country are much more orthodox in their outlook than seminarians of twenty or thirty years ago. Their numbers are slowly increasing too. More and more dioceses and seminaries are straightening out their programs, realizing that seminarians have a much more intense spiritual focus than in recent decades. There is reason to hope that dioceses and religious orders can and will surmount the vocations crisis without "reenvisioning the priesthood," and without creating a "new model of Church" in which Catholic priests are reduced to sacramental ministers. But many problems need to be forthrightly addressed, and many changes need to be made.

CHAPTER 2

Stifling the Call

How for Some Men the Road to Ordination Is Cut Short Before It Really Begins

I realized by Saturday night that I could not trust the people I had met to help me discern whether I had a vocation to the priesthood or not. I was very aware that I would not be able to cope with living and studying in such an atmosphere of dissent and disobedience.
        —Kevin Rowles, former prospective seminarian

Even before a young man is ready to apply to a seminary there are numerous forces within the Church that work against the possible priestly vocation he may be discerning. The feminization of the liturgy, poor catechesis, unmanly priests, and the many sexual scandals involving Catholic clergy are four common deterrents, among others, for the discerning young man.

Each is a scandal in its own right inasmuch as each places undue impediments in the way of one's path to fulfilling his God-given vocation. This is not the place to elaborate much on the poor state of the liturgy and catechesis, but suffice it to say that these are very real deterrents for the healthy young man who wants to serve the Church through the ordained priesthood.

More directly relevant to the subject at hand is the scandal of a lack of male role models in the Church. Many of the men who have recently entered seminaries in North America and Europe, and presumably elsewhere, have looked directly to Pope John Paul II for a living role model in the Church. A superb one indeed—some predict one day he will be known as one of the greatest saints the Catholic Church has ever produced—the Holy Father is by virtue of his office someone quite displaced from the daily lives of these men, who one expects would have looked to local priests for guidance and encouragement in pursuing holy orders and for a tangible role model in how to grow in holiness.

Pope St. Pius X said it well when he wrote of the necessity of holy priestly role models: "In order for Jesus Christ to reign in the world, nothing is so necessary as the holiness of the clergy, so that with their example, word, and knowledge they might be a guide for the faithful."[1]

It is by example and personal influence that dedicated, pious, intelligent, well-formed priests will attract tomorrow's candidates to the priesthood. The fact that this is not happening in many places is little disputed even among the most zealous advocates of the status quo.

Such positive role models need to be everywhere in Catholic life—in the parishes, the colleges, the seminaries, and even in chancery[2] offices. They must especially be in the vocation offices among the clergy whose job it is, day in and day out, to encourage and foster possible vocations to the priesthood for their diocese or religious order. Vocation directors, past or present, such as Father James Gould of Arlington, Father Marty Heinz of Rockford, or Archbishop John J. Myers (formerly director of vocations and later bishop for the Diocese of Peoria) of Newark offer excellent examples of this; they provided the younger generation with positive role models of hardworking, committed priests who strive for personal holiness and seek to preach the Gospel as the Church teaches. Their sacrifices are obvious, and the results they have generated among seminarians—both in quantity and quality—are abundantly in evidence.

Alas, the Catholic Church in the U.S. and in many other western nations is not by and large blessed with an abundance of such positive priestly role models in the parishes, colleges, seminaries, or vo-cations offices. Very often the contrary is true. Father Joseph Illo, vocations director for the Diocese of Stockton, California, attests to this fact from an "inside" point of view. "What makes the priesthood difficult today," he explained, "is not the long hours or changing cul-tures, which priests of all ages have endured. It's our low morale, caused by the betrayal or stupidity in our own ranks. It's seeing priests watch daytime TV. It's hearing priests justify unnatural vices. It's living with priests who prefer getting a little drunk before supper rather than praying the breviary together."[3]

Such "betrayal and stupidity" is legion, even among the clergy who staff certain vocations offices. John Sillasen of San Bernadino, Cali-fornia, has contemplated studying for the priesthood for the past thirty-five years. Sillasen, who is now in his fifties, relates that he "looked into the priestly vocation several times in several places, never getting the right feeling" about the dioceses he would be serving, based on his interaction with priests who, he said, seemed effeminate if not homosexual and were far from supportive of the Church uni-versal. "I could sense some grave problem even before I became aware of the big problems in the Church today," he explained.

After hearing a speech delivered by Bishop Gerald R. Barnes, who spoke of the severe and escalating priest shortage in the diocese, he said, "I felt repelled at the prospect of approaching the Diocese of San Bernadino out of interest in a vocation to the priesthood." One of the problems, related to the lack of proper male role models in the priesthood of that diocese, he explained, is that when Barnes intro-duced the director of the "vocations team," it was a nun.

Father Eduard Perrone of the Detroit archdiocese has been very encouraging of priestly vocations in his inner-city Detroit parish, to which many young orthodox men are attracted from outside his parish boundaries. Perrone points out simply that these aspiring priests, young men who are committed to the faith, "want to save souls, be in touch with the Mass; they want to preach and convert es-pecially." "But when these young men go to Mass at their local parish," he added, "what they too often get is a nightclub atmosphere that is cushy and comfortable, with a tinkling piano in the background. They might have a good laugh, but these young men don't witness any discipline in the cultural sense. It's hard then for the faith to take root. The young man, who in better surroundings might be inspired to pursue his vocation, might think, 'Well, Father is kind of a nice guy, but that's not for me. The priesthood is for someone who wants to talk to old ladies. Me, I want to be a doctor or a sportscaster. I don't want to waste my time.' "

For those who are inspired enough at least to investigate a vocation to the priesthood, many are turned off quickly when introduced to the vocations program and seminary. Some dioceses, for instance, have "come and see" discernment weekends for prospective seminarians. Those interested in the priesthood are invited to experience seminary life by living at their local seminary for two or three days. Unfortunately, too many prospective candidates quickly discern that something is terribly wrong with the seminary. A prospective seminarian at Sacred Heart Seminary in Detroit, for example, reported that during a discernment weekend in the mid-1990s, prospective candidates and seminarians sat together to watch a "childish Rated-R movie" about teenage girls priming themselves for sexual liaisons. Expecting to experience a highly spiritual environment conducive to prayer, worship, and study, the young man experienced an environment that was none too inspiring, if not repelling in the spiritual sense.

Others, who are now ordained priests, confirmed this assessment of the movies shown at these discernment weekends, explaining that these weekends were placed in the hands of current seminarians, "who did not always make appropriate integration between faith and choices."

Father Andrew McNeil,* now a priest in a midwestern archdiocese, visited Cincinnati's seminary as a prospective seminarian in the late 1980s. He saw enough on a Sunday afternoon tour to eliminate any desire he might have had to apply there. "Two seminarians took

---

* As mentioned in the Introduction, when a pseudonym is used to protect a source, his name will appear the first time with an asterisk.

me and my father on tour of the dormitory area at the seminary; it was just after noon on a Sunday, and one of the first things I noticed is that horns had been drawn onto a portrait of Archbishop [Daniel] Pilarczyk; and then when a seminarian stumbled out of his room—apparently he had just awakened—to retrieve a bottle of whiskey from a cooler in the hallway, I kind of figured this place wasn't exactly what I was looking for."

Others are turned off by the treatment they receive from the seminary faculty or administration. Paul Sinsigalli was twenty-five years old when he was first accepted into St. John's College Seminary in Boston. He had applied and done all the interviews without telling his family and friends of his intentions. He was secretive, he said, because he feared that too many people in his life would be unsupportive, if not discouraging, of his vocation. Once he was accepted, he announced he was going into the seminary, and the discouragement he feared became a reality. "What, are you nuts?" was the typical response he received. "Literally every person I ran into was unsupportive," Sinsigalli lamented.

Seeking some encouragement, he called the seminary. He asked Father Bill Spade, the new dean of St. John's, if he could make an appointment to talk over his vocation. "I went in to see him," recounted Sinsigalli, "in order to explain things to him and maybe get some reassurance, to keep me on track since I wasn't getting any encouragement elsewhere." During this first meeting with the dean of the college, Sinsigalli was shocked. "This guy was not at all nice," he recalled, "let alone encouraging."

"Why do I want to be involved with this guy?" Sinsigalli wondered. The net result of the meeting with Spade was that he felt "repulsed by the whole situation." If the dean of the college couldn't be understanding of a guy who wanted to be a priest but just needed a bit of encouragement when his vocation was challenged by everyone around him, he reasoned, he wouldn't give his life over to study for the priesthood—at least not yet. "If he's going to be a jerk to me when everyone else is telling me I'm crazy, why should I do it?" Sinsigalli remembered thinking.

The same problem is manifest in the British Isles. According to Kevin Rowles, "In England the 'weeding out' of orthodox men starts from day one," he explained. In 1992 Rowles, from Middlesex, was discerning a vocation to the priesthood. He met with the vocations director of a large English archdiocese, who advised him to attend a vocations retreat at the local seminary.

"I walked out of this retreat in disgust at what was going on there and never took the matter of a vocation to the priesthood any further," he admitted. Rowles recounted that during the retreat, which he described as "profane," the half dozen participants were asked to listen to, and meditate upon, a recording by American soul band Kool and the Gang. The song, he said, was "clearly about love between a man and a woman," which he thought an odd subject of reflection for those aspiring to the priesthood and religious life.

They were then subjected to several exercises conducted by a nun from the Sisters of Loretto. The most memorable, recounted Rowles, was a painting session. "We were asked to imagine being a tree and what it felt like. We were then asked to imagine God being a tree. And then Sister asked us to open our eyes and paint a picture of two trees, one of which was meant to be God, another ourselves," he said.

"I find it strange," he wrote in a letter to the vocations director after the retreat weekend, "when one thinks of the great spiritual wealth that the Church has at her disposal, that these sources should be used to try and help us to see where God has acted in our lives and where He is leading us."

One of those helping the retreat participants discern their vocations that weekend was a young woman novice whom he knew only as Linda. A brief conversation with Linda revealed that the novice was very interested in being a priest. "Here I was at a retreat and a young woman who wants to be a priest is supposed to be helping me discern *my* vocation," recalled Rowles, who thought the whole situation to be bizarre at best.

On Saturday of the retreat, as Rowles described it, the Mass was offered in the seminary study instead of the chapel. "A low coffee table made out of rough logs and covered in a green Egyptian hieroglyphic fabric" was used as a makeshift altar. Rowles said he was put off by the aberrations in the liturgy, which included the priest's vesting in an "Indian prayer robe," the participants' passing a pottery bowl of consecrated hosts around to each other for Communion distribution, and playing the same Kool and the Gang song immediately after Communion.

Later that evening, the retreat participants were invited to a wine and cheese party, where Rowles was further put off by the drunkenness of the seminarians, who performed a *Salve Regina* which he said was "very distasteful."

"The final straw," however, said Rowles, was Night Prayer. Instead of praying the proper Night Prayer as prescribed by the Church, the seminarians played recordings of John Lennon's song "Imagine" and George Harrison's "My Sweet Lord." The Lord to which Harrison refers in this song is Lord Krishna, and the record clearly has a Hare Krishna/Hare Lama chant. A key line in Lennon's "Imagine" is: "Imagine . . . no religion. . . ."

At that point Rowles left the retreat, disgusted with the seminary, the vocations director, and the diocese. "I realized by Saturday night that I could not trust the people I had met to help me in discerning whether I had a vocation to the priesthood or not," said Rowles. "I was also very aware that I would not be able to cope with living and studying in such an atmosphere of dissent and disobedience."

Savvy young men can learn much in very little time by observing seminary liturgies. Gregory Pearson* attended a discernment weekend at Cincinnati's seminary at the Athenaeum of Ohio in the mid-1990s. Attending the Mass there at the seminary, he was dismayed to find that liturgical abuses were the order of the day. "There was no kneeling during the Mass," remembered Pearson, "and the archbishop himself was the main celebrant. I approached him for Communion to find that the bread used for the sacred hosts was leavened; it was like pita bread." If the archbishop himself was there at the Mass, reasoned Pearson, it must mean that the archdiocese condoned such liturgical abuse. He decided that weekend that it would be difficult to serve an archbishop and an archdiocese that couldn't abide by even simple and relatively undemanding liturgical laws. "What else are they disobeying?" he wondered.

■ ■ ■

Another problem is the profound scandal of sexual improprieties by too many priests in recent years. Public betrayals of priestly vows do interminable damage to the image of the priesthood. These incidents are held up as evidence that the Church should reconsider her position on the celibate priesthood. They are also discouraging to young men considering the priesthood, who begin to believe that they too will not be able to uphold the celibacy requirement, or simply know that they do not want to be perceived as homosexual.

Worst of all have to be the unremitting instances of child sex abuse (mostly of teenage boys) among Catholic clergy, including bishops, adding to the problem of priests who present themselves as unmanly and effeminate. It is worth repeating here that obviously not all, nor most, priests are pedophiles, homosexuals, or even effeminate, but far too many have been exposed as sexual predators, as AIDS sufferers, and as perpetrators of horrible crimes to be insignificant to the subject of vocations. It is the purpose of this chapter only to provide evidence, first, that this is a serious problem that is severely damaging the image of the priesthood and, second, that such problems often quash a young man's drive to pursue his priestly vocation.

At the time I was researching this subject, several cases drew media attention. First was the resignation of Bishop Keith Symons, who stepped down as the leader of the Palm Beach, Florida, diocese after acknowledging he had molested five young men in three parishes. That same month, in June of 1998, "Christoph Cardinal Schönborn, archbishop of Vienna...acknowledged that charges of sexual misconduct with seminarians leveled against his predecessor, Hans Hermann Cardinal Gröer, were true."[4] This admission came after several years of obfuscation on Gröer's part.

The next year another American prelate, Bishop Patrick Ziemann, resigned from the head of the Santa Rosa diocese in California. Ziemann, who served previously as an auxiliary bishop to Roger Cardinal Mahony in Los Angeles, admitted publicly to an ongoing sexual relationship with a priest who sued him and the diocese for $8 million in damages. According to a Catholic News Service report, the suit charged Ziemann "with sexual battery, alleging that he coerced sex from the priest in return for keeping silent about the reasons for the priest's dismissal from St. Mary of the Angels in Ukiah, Calif."[5] The priest, Father Jorge Hume Salas, had been dismissed from his parish for severe financial improprieties.

It was also revealed that Salas was recruited from Costa Rica to work in the Santa Rosa diocese's Hispanic community, and many questions were raised about his preparation for the priesthood prior to his ordination in California. His seminary education could not be confirmed, hinting at the possibility that the priest was recruited by Ziemann for reasons other than Salas's desire to serve the Church.

At the same time, another legal case in northern California was receiving heavy publicity in the media. John Bollard, a Jesuit scholastic from 1988 to 1996,[6] filed a "discrimination in the workplace" lawsuit in San Francisco federal court alleging that three of his Jesuit supervisors—Father Andrew Sotelo, Father Anton Harris, and Father Thomas Gleeson—subjected him to "unwanted verbal and physical conduct of a sexual nature," creating such a "hostile, intimidating, and offensive environment" that he could no longer remain in the order.[7]

In an August 14, 1997, interview with San Francisco's KGO-TV, Bollard explained his charges in finer detail. The harassment began in 1990–91 at St. Ignatius High School, when two fellow faculty members, Harris and Sotelo, sent him greeting cards depicting sexually aroused naked men. Bollard showed one of the pornographic Christmas cards to KGO reporter Dan Noyes. One of the priests had written inside: "Thought this might stir up some theological thought. Hope all goes well. Love T."[8] Sotelo, explained Bollard in the interview, not only sent him pornographic pictures but also invited him out to San Francisco gay bars.

After Bollard left St. Ignatius, where he was teaching religion, the sexual harassment followed him to the Jesuit School of Theology at Berkeley, where he continued his seminary studies. Bollard told Noyes that while there, Gleeson, then president of the school, propositioned him: "He said to me that if I wanted to be friends with him, I shouldn't be surprised if it became sexual and that he himself was most interested in mutual masturbation."[9] Father Gleeson went on to serve as acting secretary of formation for the Jesuits worldwide.

Bollard also explained that when he appealed to Father John Privett, who was then the chief administrator of the Jesuit's California province, he received a very insincere apology from him suggesting indifference to the sexual misconduct of his fellow Jesuit priests.

After the affair became known publicly through media publicity of the court proceedings, one unnamed Jesuit commented to *San Francisco Faith* that "there are some Jesuits who are so distressed by this that they could never recommend the order to a young person interested in religious life.... Young people interested in papal teaching are no longer attracted to the order."[10] His claim is backed up by statistics. In 1965 eighty novices entered the California Jesuit province. In 1997 only three entered the same province, one of the largest in the United States.

Another student at Berkeley's Jesuit School of Theology clarified the problem of homosexual acceptance in the order: "The attitude of the Jesuits here is 'We need to affirm the gay life,' "[11] noting that Jesuit seminarians could receive credits for "gay spirituality" courses offered by the Graduate Theological Union, of which the Jesuit school is a member.

Although Bollard left the Jesuits in 1996, media coverage of his "discrimination in the workplace" lawsuit resurfaced and intensified in 1999 when on May 9 of that year he appeared on *60 Minutes*, interviewed by Morley Safer. The subject of the interview was geared toward whether Bollard had grounds to assert "sexual harassment" charges against the named Jesuits. It is worth noting that the fact that several Jesuits were accused of making unwanted sexual advances against a Jesuit seminarian was taken for granted. (In 2000, after a court upheld the validity of a sexual harassment case against a religious order, the Jesuits decided to settle with Bollard.)

In addition to the Bollard case, the homosexual flavor of the modern Jesuits has received heavy publicity in recent years. Commenting in the *American Prowler*, George Neumayr writes that the "once-formidable society is now a corrupt club for homosexual dilettantes and anti-papal dissenters."[12] In the *New York Review of Books*, Garry Wills, who was once a Jesuit scholastic himself, quotes a young Jesuit who complains that "several of my former Jesuit friends would mention the large number of gay Jesuits and the impact that had on community life as being a big reason they left. As a relatively young Jesuit who is heterosexual, I believe I am in the minority, and that raises questions."[13] And Peter McDonough and Eugene C. Bianchi, in their 2002 book about the American Jesuits, *Passionate Uncertainty*, report on the general consensus among present and former Jesuits that a dominant gay subculture flourishes within the order.

The next big media bomb probing the subject of homosexual priests came just a few months later via the *Kansas City Star*'s multi-installment article on AIDS among Catholic priests. The *Star* presented evidence that more than three hundred priests have died of AIDS since the mid-1980s. The Missouri newspaper concluded that the report translated into an annual death rate of about four per ten thousand—four times the rate of the general population. The news report specifically cited the case of Bishop Emerson Moore, auxiliary bishop of New York, who died of AIDS in a Minnesota hospice in 1995.

Although the Catholic League for Religious and Civil Rights alleged that notable statisticians had discredited the results of the *Star*'s survey of three thousand priests, the fact remains that, considering the Catholic Church teaches that homosexual relations are immoral, three hundred priests dying from AIDS is far too many *not* to warrant attention from the media.

Previous news reports in the *Village Voice*, *New York Post*, and *National Catholic Reporter* had reported on similar evidence of AIDS among Catholic priests. In fact, as early as February 1987, the *St. Paul Pioneer Press* published an article also claiming that the incidence of AIDS among priests seemed to be almost four times higher than among the general population.

In 2000, similar verification of rampant homosexuality in the priesthood came from the rector of Cleveland's seminary, Father Donald B. Cozzens, in his book *The Changing Face of the Priesthood*. Cozzens appears to present such evidence largely for political reasons, in support of his desire that the Church should make celibacy optional for priests and seminarians. By his reasoning, if the Church would allow priests to marry, the priesthood would attract far more heterosexual men to the Catholic seminaries. Yet Cozzens stops short of explaining how the presence of married men would stop homosexual priests from engaging in illicit sexual practices.

Cozzens does, however, introduce another pressing topic of concern when he writes that "[f]or more than fifteen years now priests have reeled at allegation after allegation brought against Catholic clergy for sexual misconduct with teenage boys, and in some cases, with children."[14]

The sexual predator problem among the priesthood in the U.S. is appalling. In 1993, for example, after a spate of such scandals erupted one after another, Philip F. Lawler, editor of *Catholic World Report*, wrote that "during the past ten years, at least 500 American Catholic priests have been accused of sexual assaults on children. One bishop has been publicly charged with pedophilia, and rumors swirl around hundreds of parishes. The scandal of sexual abuse has spawned a new genre of investigative journalism, as books, magazine articles, and television newscasts probe into new allegations, and wonder about the credibility of the American clergy."[15]

Since 1993 the problem has only escalated as new accusations are revealed each month, in a seemingly endless barrage of terrible publicity for the Catholic priesthood. Incontrovertibly, no scandal could better destroy the image of the priesthood than that of pedophilia. Consequently, the priesthood is now seen by many as a haven for sex offenders, especially since it has been shown that many dioceses deny the allegations and cover up the evidence by moving priests around from parish to parish, as was proved again in 2002 with the controversy in the Archdiocese of Boston.[16] The net effect, aside from the many hundreds, if not thousands, of victims who suffer often for a lifetime, is a demoralized priesthood and a major deterrent to those who aspire to wear the Roman collar.

Also in 2000, a case of cybersex misconduct shook the Church in northern California. Father Carl Schipper, a priest of the San Francisco archdiocese and academic dean at St. Patrick's Seminary in

Menlo Park, California, was arrested following a six-month investigation, for soliciting sex with minors over the Internet and distributing pornographic materials online. The San Jose police department's sexual assault unit had posed as young boys on the Internet when Schipper proposed a sexual liaison with someone whom he thought was a thirteen-year-old boy. Schipper pleaded no contest and was sentenced to six months in jail.

The spiritual and psychological disorder of a priest such as Schipper has effects that go well beyond himself and his innocent victims. One wonders how seminarians at St. Patrick's are treated by such a man who plays a supervisory role in the education of future priests.

It is also worth noting—not incidentally—that after Schipper was placed on administrative leave from the seminary, Archbishop William J. Levada called Father Gerald Coleman, S.S., from his sabbatical to return to St. Patrick's. Coleman has been criticized by many for "advancing the homosexual agenda" in the Church through his much publicized writings and research. He, for example, has spoken about the "importance" of seminarians recognizing and accepting their sexual orientation: heterosexual, homosexual, or bisexual. Writing on the topic of California's Proposition 22, an initiative to provide that only marriage between a man and a woman would be recognized in California, Coleman opined that he could "see no moral reason why civil law could not in some fashion recognize these faithful and loving [homosexual] unions by according them certain rights and obligations, thus assisting [homosexual] persons in these unions with clear and specified benefits."[17]

In the wake of devastating revelations in the Archdiocese of Boston at the beginning of 2002 that more than eighty Boston-area priests have been accused of sexual abuse of children—mainly teenage boys—many American bishops in places like Los Angeles, Philadelphia, Pittsburgh, and St. Louis, apparently fearing investigative reporters and embarrassing lawsuits, began to disclose that dozens of priests in their own backyards have been accused of similar sexual crimes. In nearly all of these cases, the diocese had settled out of court with the victims, paying out millions of dollars of what amounts to "hush money." Thus, because of the turn of events in 2002, many priest abusers were dismissed from active ministry.

Even bishops did not escape this wave of scrutiny. Bishop Daniel Ryan of Springfield, Illinois, for example, resigned "for reasons of health" after a lay group of Catholic activists exposed the bishop as having carried on homosexual relationships, including one with a teenage male prostitute, for years.

On March 8, 2002, the *St. Louis Post-Dispatch* revealed that Bishop Anthony O'Connell, who had replaced child sex-abuser Keith Symons as bishop of Palm Beach, Florida, sexually abused a teenage seminarian when he was rector of St. Thomas Aquinas Seminary in Hannibal, Missouri. Former seminarian and ex-priest Christopher Dixon revealed to the press that he was abused for years by three priests at the seminary. Dixon told the *Post-Dispatch* that after being repeatedly molested by one priest at the seminary, he turned for help to O'Connell, who, he felt, "was someone he could trust."[18]

Bishop O'Connell admitted to having abused Dixon for four years, strangely saying that he regretted being so "naïve." He resigned his bishopric the same day—the second homosexual bishop in three years to resign from the Palm Beach diocese for sexually abusing teenage boys.

These are only a few of the more high-profile cases that have been given serious attention in the national media. Bishops and priests responsible for the formation of seminarians too often give bad examples by their perfervid flouting of the sexual morals enunciated clearly by the Church they have vowed to serve. It is a scandal of untold proportions, at least a hundred times worse than what the media have already uncovered in the United States.

Much more attention will be given to the issue of homosexuality in American seminaries in Chapter 4, which will examine its numerous ramifications for the orthodox seminarian. Suffice it to say here that the bad example of priests in everyday life, and the scandal of sexual misconduct that continues to besmirch the image of the priesthood, has no little negative effect on the young man who aspires to the priesthood in the Catholic Church.

CHAPTER 3

The Gatekeeper Phenomenon

How Good Men Are Often Screened Out During the Seminary Application Process

I left depressed. I wanted to live in Gospel poverty; I wanted to forsake wife and children to preach the teachings of Christ; I wanted to feed the poor with bread and eternal Truth. Yet all this vocations director cared about was the acceptance of their redundant political agenda.
   —Timothy O'Keefe, former applicant to an East Coast religious order

Once the orthodox man has discerned that he would like to test his vocation in the seminary, he applies to a diocese or religious order, naturally expecting that his suitability for the priesthood and aptitude for graduate study in theology will be amply assessed. Father Donald Cozzens explains this process of assessment: "Serving now as rector of a seminary and chair of the admissions committee, I know our [admission] decisions are supported with more information and documentation than was the case a generation ago. Letters of recommendation, psychiatric, and psychological assessments, criminal records checks, standardized tests, and a series of interviews make up the ordinary drill for admissions to priestly studies today."[1]

Aside from the unmistakable fact that this screening process is a necessary and often difficult task, what the aspiring priest usually does not expect from this initial process is the unnatural obstacles—those which are not directly relevant to ascertaining the candidate's suitability for the priesthood—that many dioceses and religious orders place in the path to admission. These obstacles often deter at an early stage the orthodox applicant from continuing to follow his call to the priesthood, either by way of discouragement or by outright rejection.

"Far too often," wrote Thomas Fath in *New Oxford Review*, "one hears that the persons performing the initial interviews have a modernistic bias about the qualities a priest-to-be should have."[2] He cites as one example Quigley Seminary in Chicago, which he claims was closed due to its "screening out candidates loyal to the Magisterium"—that is, the Church's official teaching office. According to Fath, the message was, "in effect, 'We have enough priests with an Old Church philosophy; what we are looking for is priests who have a vision of what the New Church should look like.' " There were simply too many young men, added Fath, "who maintained that they had been turned away because they were perceived as 'Old Church.' "[3]

To this end, in some dioceses or religious orders the applicant is subjected to a political litmus test on the subject of "what the Church *should* be." Often this means that the applicant mustn't let on that he accepts Church teaching on issues of authority and sexual morality lest he be dismissed as "rigid" or "dysfunctional." One of the most critical questions posed to potential seminarians, as Archbishop Curtiss indicated, is whether the applicant approves of the ordination of women to the priesthood. This puts the orthodox seminarian in a difficult position. If he reveals that he agrees with the magisterium that the Church does not have the ability to ordain women, he is liable to be dismissed from further consideration. If he lies and says he is "open" to the idea, then he compromises himself—not the ideal way to begin studies he hopes will lead to the priesthood.

According to Father Karl Arguilers,* a priest now serving a midwestern diocese, "Back in 1986 I was getting flack from the vocations director for my hometown diocese in New York State because I did not support the ordination of women, nor was I going to support Charles Curran,[4] who was making headlines then."

Although often it is the vocations director, usually a priest, who conducts the initial interview, it is common that an assistant, often a religious sister, serves as what some call the "inquisitor." In other cases, bishops have allowed "troubled women religious—many of whom had already left their orders—to occupy the top positions in their vocations office and seminary administrative posts."[5] In either case, said Father Bob Oravetz, former regional director for the vocations-promoting group Serra, "One way to detect a diocese that does not put much effort into recruiting vocations is by finding out if they have a woman as the vocations director. Often they are assistants or associates to the priest who is supposed to be the director, but the liberal nun does the actual legwork, such as interviewing potential candidates."

John Sherman,* now a nationally respected radio commentator, remembers that when he applied to study for the priesthood in the Archdiocese of Portland, Oregon, "our assistant vocations director was a liberal nun. She was the only one who was in full-time vocations ministry."

A few years ago, Dr. Garvan Kuskey, a California dentist, attended a Serra Club dinner party. About three-quarters of all area priests were in attendance as well as several seminarians from St. John's Seminary in Camarillo, California. "My wife and I had a lengthy and frank conversation with three of the men about to be ordained," Kuskey recalled. "I asked all three whether it was true, as I had previously heard, that the nun in the vocations office had the final word as to who got in the seminary and who did not." It was the opinion of all three men, he said, that this was indeed the case. "They said that if you didn't get past Sister, you did not get into the seminary."

Kuskey also inquired of them whether it was true that the most crucial question asked by the nun vocations director was whether the applicant approved of the ordination of women. "All three affirmed that this was true," he remembered. "They had all been warned about this question before they went for their interviews. They said they had been advised to say they did not have any strong feelings one way or another, but that they were 'open' to the idea of ordaining women." All three men, said Kuskey, added that they were unequivocally opposed to women's ordination.

One popular if incredible account rendered by numerous seminarians is that during their interview with a nun assistant in the vocations office, the phone rings or there is a knock at the door. Sister answers and begins to engage in an animated conversation, in the course of which she states enthusiastically that she fully expects to be ordained to the priesthood in a matter of years or otherwise makes it clear that she is a proponent of women's ordination.

This account (related from various corners of the nation and with some minor variation in details) is too common for these various nun vocations directors to actually be carrying on an authentic conversation. This is apparently the type of staged intimidation applicants to the more liberal dioceses must endure—if they would like to proceed. Sister is obviously trying to gauge the applicant's reaction. Many say "no thanks" right here at the beginning, believing that the nun's actions are a reflection of the diocese they are seeking to serve. Other inquisitors are not so dramatic, yet the results are essentially the same. It is a psychological game that often proves harmful to vocations, and that is exactly the point.

In similar instances applicants are asked how they might respond to a hypothetical pastoral situation. For instance: If you were assigned to a parish in which the pastor was contravening Church law in the administration of his parish, what would you do? Or, if a man confessed to you that he and his wife have been using artificial contraception, and that they will continue to do so, would you give him absolution? Another popular question: What would you do if you were celebrating Mass at your new parish and a laywoman came up to concelebrate with you before the Eucharistic prayer?

Aside from the peculiarity of the questioning, such probing again puts the orthodox applicant at risk. How can he respond honestly without offending the vocations inquisitor who wants to establish the applicant's "flexibility" or "open-mindedness," as it is often termed, at the expense of Church teaching and discipline?

But this interview is only the beginning of a battery of evaluations and tests that are often specifically designed to weed out applicants who will not be suitable for a particular formation program. In many cases this process is an honest one. Again, properly screening applicants for the priesthood is obviously of grave importance to the Church. Yet, unfortunately, this process is too often abused, and those who are sent away are those faithful to the teachings of the Church, especially those who properly accept the traditional role and discipline of the priest, including lifelong celibacy. The process presents an unnatural impediment that can be called the "gatekeeper phenomenon."

At the same time, despite the rigorous hoops one must jump through in order to enroll in a seminary program, all too many sexual deviants easily advance. There is no need to rehash the evidence on this issue. But one wonders: If the screening process isn't catching the deviants, is the process "designed" to weed them out or merely to prune the orthodox men from the vocations vine?

■ ■ ■

The psychological evaluation that is mandatory for each seminarian is equally remarkable. A psychologist, who may not be Catholic or even Christian, probes the sexual and emotional history of a young man, often getting into a line of questioning that seems a tad perverted from the average man's perspective. (Anything goes, it seems, when psychology is involved.) It is not uncommon for the psychologist to inquire about the applicant's beliefs on issues of homosexuality. Whereas one might understand this line of questioning if it is undertaken with an eye to root out those inclined to homosexuality or those who are involved in the "gay lifestyle," the intent is more often to discover if the applicant is able to accept the practice of homosexuality in today's society or, more to the point, in his study and work environment. If the psychologist isn't looking for an approbation of immoral acts, he at least would like to discover that the applicant is "open-minded" in this regard.

And what if he's not? The orthodox applicant may well state Church teaching on homosexuality—e.g., "love the sinner, hate the sin," or "homosexual acts are intrinsically disordered and contrary to the natural law." But when he does, the psychologist is liable to report that the applicant has an "unhealthy sexuality," is "sexually immature," or has "sexual hang-ups." Yet the applicant who is "open-minded" is deemed healthy and mature with an "integrated sexuality."

Thomas Beresford remembers making an application to an Illinois diocese. "There is no way my parish priest could have been more supportive of my vocation," recalled Beresford. When his application was routinely received by the diocese, he was joyfully anxious until he traveled three hours from his home to take a psychological exam comprised "a battery of tests that included 1,900 fill-in-the-circle questions."

"Many of these questions were devised in such a way," he explained, "that to answer them meant there was no way around committing a sin." One such question he remembered was: "What would you rather do: masturbate or read pornography?"

When Beresford refused to answer such questions, explaining that he chose to do neither, the psychologist told him he was "required" to make a choice. "The diocese found great problems with me leaving these irrelevant and unintelligible sex-related questions unanswered," said Beresford.

On another day, as part of his evaluation, he visited a psychiatrist in St. Louis for one hour. "I eventually started to feel unsafe in his office when his line of questioning came to asking such things as 'Have you ever had sexual relations with your father or grandfather?'"

Joseph Aarons also remembers his 1999 interview with the psychologist as a part of his application to a midwestern diocese. Aside from what Aarons considered to be an overemphasis on sexual issues, the psychologist, he said, "displayed a genuine ignorance of Catholic belief and practice." When the evaluation arrived a few weeks later, the psychologist had written that Aarons tended to be "inflexible and to have strict ideas about right and wrong." Further, in response to his statement that it is essential for a priest "to maintain a celibate lifestyle in order to serve God with an undivided heart," she wrote, "It is unclear how realistic your views are concerning management of, and commitment to, a celibate lifestyle."

The psychological evaluation came just days after his interview with the vocations director. "During this interview," recalled Aarons, "I openly expressed many of my beliefs, for example, as articulated by the Apostles Creed. When asked why I wished to be ordained to the priesthood, I responded that my desire was to bring souls to Christ and I felt this could best be accomplished by teaching orthodox Catholic doctrine and administering the sacraments to those who would be placed in my care by God." In response to this, the vocations director, said Aarons, suggested his approach to the priesthood was not "pastoral," and that consequently he was not suited for the diocesan priesthood.

Aarons was formally rejected by a letter from the vocations office that stated as much: "After reviewing the contents of your application, the committee members came to the judgment that your gifts and talents are not indicative of one called to be a diocesan priest."

Rick Birch was in a similar rejected-before-he's-ever-given-a-chance situation. After meeting with Father Gerald L. Reinersman, vocations director for the Diocese of Covington, Kentucky, Birch was sent to the Behavioral Science Center in Cincinnati for his psychological evaluation. Known as a conservative teacher of religion at one of the diocese's parochial schools, Birch related that Reinersman was reluctant even to begin his application process, but finally relented. Birch still believes the vocations director's reluctance was due to Birch's reputation as an orthodox instructor of the Catholic faith, although Reinersman never admitted to Birch to having any information about him prior to the aspiring priest's arrival at the Covington vocations office.

At the Behavioral Science Center, Birch was evaluated by Dr. Joseph Wicker. After attempting to reach Reinersman for two months about the results of his psychological evaluation, Birch was finally given the news. After suggesting that Birch withdraw as a candidate, Reinersman read him Wicker's report: "Though [Rick] is an intelligent person and scored high on the mental ability tests, he is deficient in emotional and personality areas that would not make him a suitable candidate for ordained ministry. He is a man of deep anger, somewhat socially maladjusted, and is sexually immature. He cannot deal with his inner feelings. I suspect he is only using the ordained ministry to keep from dealing with his inner feelings. He is not sincere in seeking the ordained ministry and I cannot recommend him.... However, if [Rick] would be willing to undergo a year of therapy, I might be able to consider him at some future time."

Birch was not just surprised. He was stunned, not because he thought he was "psychologically screwed up," but because he knew he was not. Birch had given away all his possessions, moved in with his mother, was taking theology courses at Cincinnati's seminary at his own expense, only to be told by a psychologist that he was "insincere" about wanting to be a priest.

Despite what Reinersman called excellent recommendations written on Birch's behalf, including one from his pastor, he was rejected by the admissions committee based on the psychological evaluation.

Not long after Birch's rejection, *The Wanderer*, a nationally distributed lay Catholic newspaper, published an article about how Wicker was rejecting more candidates for the priesthood than he was recommending. Closer to home, on May 8, 1991, the *Mt. Washington Press*, a weekly community newspaper in Cincinnati, published an article about Wicker's elevation to the head of a local Masonic order. "Men who wish to become Catholic priests in the Archdiocese of Cincinnati," the article began, "are first assessed by the Worshipful Master of Mt. Washington Masonic Lodge 642."[6] Written by Gregory Flannery, a former seminarian himself, the article ("Masonic Master Screens City's Catholic Priests") pointed out that Wicker was a fallen-away Catholic and that participation in Masonic sects is condemned by the Catholic Church.

"The principles of Masonry," wrote Flannery, "have always been considered irreconcilable with the Church's teaching." But for Wicker, who said he no longer considers himself a Catholic, that is no matter. "I go to church once in a while, but I'm not really a practicing Catholic," he was quoted as saying. "One of the things I found I didn't like about religions is they tend to be narrow-minded and exclusivistic. Masonry doesn't exclude anybody," he added, although Masonry, unlike any mainstream religion, excludes all women.[7]

Wicker also admitted to being a member of the Rosicrucians, a sect that has been condemned by the Catholic Church as being destructive to the principles of Christianity, Flannery reported. Wicker's professional specialties include practices such as "past-life therapy" and "transpersonal psychology," which is reflective of Rosicrucian beliefs such as reincarnation. "I have memories of a previous life," Wicker told Flannery, and added, "Whether they're true memories, I'm not sure. I don't wholeheartedly accept the Christian system of one life, then purgatory and heaven."[8]

When Catholics addressed their concerns about Wicker's suitability to screen seminary applicants to the archbishop of Cincinnati, Daniel E. Pilarczyk denied that there was any conflict of interest. In a letter to Dr. Joseph Strada in 1994, Pilarczyk defended the archdiocese's use of Dr. Wicker in the screening process: "He earned his Masters Degree in Theology at the University of Dayton, and has completed course work for a doctoral degree in theology at Fordham University. His background both in the realities and expectations of seminary formation and in Catholic theology is thus extremely strong."

After reading the *Mt. Washington Press* article, without even being aware of the denial on Pilarczyk's part, Birch felt somewhat vindicated. He had never understood how Wicker arrived at the conclusions of his evaluation based on the brief meeting they had, in which he asked stock questions about homosexuality, fornication, and other areas of sexual morality. But Wicker's outright denial of the basics of the Christian faith and his prejudice against religions being "narrowminded" gives a fair indication that he was not being completely objective in his evaluations.

Despite the fact that Birch now felt vindicated, his psychological evaluation proved to be the death of his vocation. After informing friends and family that the Diocese of Covington had rejected him as a candidate for the priesthood, he spent a week with the Glenmary Fathers in central Kentucky. During his interview with their

"discernment committee," they informed Birch that he would be required to take a psychological evaluation from the same Dr. Wicker
at the Behavioral Science Center, seventy-five miles away in Cincinnati. When he told the fathers that Wicker had already given him a
negative evaluation, they thanked him for visiting but told Birch he
had no vocation to the Glenmary Fathers.

To make personal matters worse for Birch, a week later he received a call from Catholic Social Services in Covington. A counselor
asked him when he could come in for therapy. "Therapy!" Birch ex-
claimed. "I didn't call anyone for therapy. Who told you I need
therapy?" The counselor informed him that the Glenmary Fathers
took the liberty of informing them.

Coincidentally, Birch had already made arrangements to get a
second opinion from Dr. Frank Miller of Catholic Social Services in
nearby Cincinnati. Miller, according to Birch, agreed to test and interview Birch over a five-week period during the summer of 1988.
At the end of the evaluation, Miller concluded that he could not find
anything seriously wrong with him. Miller also told Birch that this
wasn't the first time men have had trouble in their diocese with some
form of discrimination or other, "and it may be so in your case, I
don't know. But you have talents and maybe God wants you to fight
harder to reach the goal that you want, or maybe He wants." Miller
suggested that Birch try applying to another diocese.

Thus, following his suggestion, Birch applied to the Diocese of
Lexington, which has always had a severe shortage of priests. The
vocations office there requested copies of both Wicker's and Miller's
psychological evaluations of Birch, and he was again turned down,
based on the negative evaluation from the Behavioral Science
Center, written by a fallen-away Catholic who believes that all religions are "narrow-minded and exclusivistic."

Since the time Birch was rejected by the Diocese of Covington in
1988, several young priests of the diocese have left the priesthood
and at least one other is on requested leave. Another Covington
priest, Father Earl Bierman, pleaded guilty to molestation charges
involving six adolescent boys and was imprisoned in a state peniten-

tiary. One victim sued the diocese, and the jury, in awarding the victim $750,000, said that the diocese was more responsible for the abuse than was Bierman himself.[9] Meanwhile, Birch went on to teach in a private Catholic academy in Cincinnati, where his coworkers and students speak very highly of him. The diocese continues to suffer a severe shortage of priests and seminarians.

To reiterate, the issue of taking sexual matters into consideration during psychological evaluations is understandable considering that, especially after many multimillion-dollar lawsuits, dioceses must be careful to screen out those who demonstrate tendencies toward sexual perversion. The evidence, however, shows that many of the psychologists hired to carry out the screening for dioceses refuse to recommend men who hold to Church teaching on sexual matters, especially regarding celibacy in the priesthood and homosexuality. These applicants are labeled "sexually immature" or "sexually dysfunctional." Thus, those who embrace priestly celibacy as it is properly understood by the Church and give evidence that they do not accept homosexual relations as normal and acceptable modes of behavior are treated as the ones who show signs of sexual perversion.

Dr. William Coulson, director of the Research Council on Ethnopsychology, explained that many psychologists "screen out the most worthy candidates, because if they admitted that these were the right people to bring into the seminaries, they would have to admit that their whole program is wrong.

"If you look at the data on the religious beliefs of licensed psychologists, you find that to a much higher degree than in the general population they are non-believers. I should say, they're not non-believers; they believe in something totally different from what most people believe in."[10]

The problem can be distilled down to this: Many psychologists who are contracted by dioceses and religious orders hold beliefs that differ, sometimes markedly, from the beliefs of Catholics (even if sometimes these screeners are nominal Catholics themselves). As such they often fail to be objective in their evaluation of an applicant, using their own belief system as the standard by which to judge an applicant's suitability for the priesthood. This seems especially true regarding matters of sexual morality.

Dr. David J. Brown, a clinical psychologist who screens candidates for the Diocese of Altoona-Johnstown, Pennsylvania, is a case in point if only because he has never been shy about broadcasting his opinions and beliefs. Brown, in his statements at local school board meetings in State College, Pennsylvania, and in local papers, has gone out of his way to make the case that homosexuality is "perfectly normal." Brown has argued publicly in many instances that "the sin of Sodom was inhospitality," that St. Thomas Aquinas in his *Summa Theologica* challenged natural law arguments, and that "homosexuality is natural, not unnatural" and "homosexuality among animals is natural, not unnatural."[11]

Testifying before the public school board in State College, he argued on spiritual grounds for legitimizing homosexuality as an alternative lifestyle in the public schools there. Brown told the board that he was "appalled" that the school district had excluded known militant homosexual speakers from Penn State University from making presentations to teachers at in-service day workshops. Brown was referring to speakers who are on record as promoting homosexuality as an "alternative lifestyle" and who are either homosexuals themselves or homosexual advocates. He stated that he was a Christian and that "hate" was not a Christian message, implying that hate was the motive behind those who refused to invite the prohomosexual activists—a typical "homophobia" straw-man argument. Brown then went on to claim that Jesus Christ himself would be "appalled" if the promotion of homosexuality were not included on the teacher in-service venue.

The fact that someone would pose such an argument is not news itself. But when such a man, whose views are publicly known, is contracted to screen applicants for the seminary, what is remarkable is the obvious incompatibility.

■ ■ ■

In 1999, the Catholic Medical Association issued a position statement on psychological evaluation of candidates for the priesthood.

This paper was drafted by a task force of eight physicians (four of whom are psychiatrists), a consulting psychologist, and a moral theologian. "There are numerous reports that mental health professionals who do not support the teachings of the Catholic Church on sexuality," the statement began, "have been chosen to evaluate candidates for the priesthood and reject candidates who do accept the Church's teaching on grounds that they are 'rigid.' There are also reports that some mental health professionals do not report homosexual attractions and conflicts in candidates for priesthood to diocesan officials or religious superiors."[12]

The statement further explained that "the choice of mental health professionals for the evaluation of candidates for the seminary who do not accept Church teaching on sexuality may be based on the belief that such persons would be more 'objective.' There is, however, growing recognition that in the mental health field an objective or neutral approach to the evaluation of a person's mental health is probably not possible nor advantageous.

"Everyone brings cultural bias to his work: therefore, the growing trend which recognizes the value of matching the therapist to the client. Shared background and culture can be extremely helpful in evaluating mental health. For example, behavior [that] in one culture might be viewed as pathological, such as the excessive expression of anger, in another, is viewed as expected and normal."[13]

In addressing this issue, the Catholic Medical Association offered the following recommendations:

> Mental health professionals chosen to evaluate candidates for the priesthood should as far as possible share the cultural background of the devout, faithful, mature candidates they are to evaluate. The professionals should be Catholics in good standing, who support the Church's teaching on sexuality, life, contraception, homosexuality, celibacy of the priesthood, the ordination of only men, and the hierarchical structure of the Church. The CMA will be happy to assist bishops and religious superiors in

this activity by preparing a list of qualified mental health professionals who meet this criteria. Non-Catholics and Catholics who do not support the teachings of the Church should not be employed in this task.[14]

■ ■ ■

Other interviews with members of vocations teams, including the vocations director or one of his associates, also play a major role in the applicant's evaluation process. One of two results too often emerges. First, the applicant himself is sometimes turned off so badly by those with whom he is required to meet that he of his own volition decides to abandon the discernment process, as was discussed in the previous chapter. Second, interviews with the vocations director or admissions committee lead to a dismissal of the applicant for ideological reasons.

A few years ago Timothy O'Keefe inquired into entering an East Coast religious order. After he filled out the requisite paperwork and had several phone conversations with the vocations director, an interview was arranged. O'Keefe met the vocations director for his first serious step toward entering the centuries-old order.

O'Keefe recalled that the interview was most comparable to a secular job interview, answering questions such as, "Are you responsible? How long have you had your present job? Do you like people?"

O'Keefe was disappointed. He had expected to be asked what he deemed more relevant questions regarding his suitability. For example, "How's your prayer life? Are you afraid of celibacy? Do you accept all the Church's teachings? Do you go to Mass and confession regularly?" There were no such questions, O'Keefe explained. "I do remember, however, making the point that I was deeply interested in the faith—especially in Holy Scripture and theology." The only theology-related question asked of him, however, was regarding the ordination of women to the priesthood, to which O'Keefe answered that he would follow Church teaching on the subject.

"At the end of the interview he truly shocked me," O'Keefe recalled. "The vocations director said, 'Tim, if you don't believe in the ordination of women, then you don't belong in our order.' " These words still ring through his head, he lamented. "I left depressed. I wanted to live in Gospel poverty; I wanted to forsake wife and children to preach the teachings of Christ; I wanted to feed the poor with bread and eternal Truth. Yet all this vocations director cared about was the acceptance of their redundant political agenda."

Father Randall Goedlers* was ordained a priest for an orthodox midwestern diocese in 1999, yet he did not begin his vocations inquiry there. He first approached the vocations director of his home diocese in 1991. "After working through all the 'why nots' of a twenty-one-year-old trying to do what God wanted," he recalled, "I never expected to hit a wall with a vocations program."

When Goedlers expressed hopes of attending one of the seminaries he knew to be reliable and orthodox, he was presented with a list of "where we send our men," a litany of institutions he had been warned about. He knew former students who had experienced discrimination at these seminaries because of their orthodox views of Catholicism.

The second "blow" delivered by the vocations director was when he informed the young Goedlers that "conditional to further consideration for acceptance" to that diocese "there would be a two-year period of 'observation' while working in a parish." In other words, he would have had to undergo a two-year waiting period before he was even considered further for acceptance into what he understood to be one of several heterodox seminary programs.

"I felt kind of smashed," he remembered. "Who knew it would be so hard to give your life away in service to Christ?" he asked himself repeatedly.

In the late 1980s George Lomax approached the vocations director for the Archdiocese of San Antonio, Texas, expressing an interest in a vocation to the priesthood. Lomax still remembers his interview. "I was very excited about the possibility of serving God as a priest," he said. "The director asked me why I had an interest in becoming a priest, and then began probing into the most personal area of my life, my sexual history."

The director ended the interview by telling Lomax that if he was interested in pursuing the priesthood any further he could attend monthly meetings sponsored by the archdiocese designed for men discerning a vocation. Lomax attended the meetings for one year.

"What surprised me the most about the interview was that I always thought a vocations director would be very excited when anyone began to investigate the priesthood or religious life," said Lomax. "What I experienced was exactly the opposite. I was definitely not encouraged, and I left feeling 'brushed off.' "

Lomax said that he didn't understand the vocations director's response until a few years later when he discovered that other men had met with the same lack of enthusiasm from the archdiocese when they inquired about the possibility of serving the Church as priests. Each man, he said, had approached the vocations director with what he calls "orthodox zeal" to lead souls to Christ by following the teachings of the Church. "I would never have guessed at the time that I was not wanted because I was too 'conservative,' " he explained. "I thought I was not welcomed because I was not worthy."

John Horton once applied to his native archdiocese of Oklahoma City. "All the good intentions in the world will not get you into the seminary if the vocations director perceives you as too loyal to the pope or too 'obsessed' about Church teachings," he commented when thinking back on his application process.

"I had been a daily Mass server in my local parish throughout junior high, high school, and college. Once I received my master's degree I applied to be a seminarian for Oklahoma City," he explained. Horton said he received a very positive recommendation from his pastor and attended all the meetings with the vocations board of five priests, logging over 1,500 miles for individual meetings with every priest in the western half of Oklahoma.

"The decision of the vocations director and the board was that, first, I was simply looking for something to do until something better came along; and, second, that I was simply interested in the externalities of religion," Horton lamented. "That was the kind of response I got after serving daily Mass for ten years and working on any number of other activities at the parish during the same time."

Horton had made it clear to each of the priests on the vocations board that he followed the teachings of the Church, especially on the ordained priesthood, and that he looked to the pope for spiritual guidance and practical direction. Yet he too was turned down for being "too rigid" and "too dogmatic."

Li Chang Yen* also considers himself an orthodox Catholic, accepting all the teachings and disciplines of the Catholic Church. When he approached his diocese he was careful to be discreet about his orthodox view of Catholicism, yet even that didn't prevent his receiving the same sort of discrimination others before him had experienced. Yen, a parishioner at a parish that has a "conservative" reputation, explained that his "stumbling block" was one purely of association. In meeting with the two different vocations directors for his diocese—the diocese changed directors at the end of 1999 as a result of a change of bishops—both asked Yen to switch parishes. Apparently the diocese considered Yen's parish to be too "traditional," or, in the exact words of one of the directors, "not a typical parish."

"I asked the second director to clarify this point," said Yen. "He responded in writing that he would not accept people with preferences like those of my fellow parishioners," he explained, due to the traditional focus of the parish, which includes daily Eucharistic adoration, traditional devotions, processions, and a Gregorian chant choir.

Yen then made his biggest "mistake" by being honest. He communicated to the vocations director that his policy seemed inconsistent with the often repeated desire for "diversity" within the diocese. He confided to the director that it might be difficult for him to work with someone who was "more concerned about me being from the right parish than whether I wanted to serve God."

The vocations director turned Yen's words against him, informing him that he was "accusatory, antagonistic, and obstinate," adding that he expected Yen would be that way considering the parish he was from. The final judgment from the vocations office was that Yen's "gifts would not be of benefit to the diocese."

In the late 1980s, Stephen Carrigee was active in an organization at Louisiana State University called Catholicism on Campus when he felt called to pursue a vocation to the priesthood with the Archdiocese of New Orleans. "A number of the more experienced members warned me that I should purposely act effeminate and talk with a lisp if I really wanted to be sponsored by New Orleans," said Carrigee. "At first I thought they were being funny, but they were dead serious because they knew from personal experience."

Carrigee routinely met with each member of the vocations evaluation board for his formal interviews, "trusting them as representatives of the Church," he said, "to have my best interests at heart."

He was then required to attend a week-long retreat, at which he mentally noted some of the "peculiar practices": Prayers began "In the name of the Creator, the Redeemer, and the Sanctifier," in order that they not have to make any masculine references to God. He also remembered one long talk about how Catholics need to grow in the understanding of God as Mother, and leave behind the old "patriarchal baggage."

The next step in the admissions process was the psychological evaluation. Carrigee was sent to an independent psychological clinic, where he spent two days taking tests and "being interviewed by a stone-faced stoic who wore a Masonic ring."

"Some of the lines of questioning were intrusive," he recalled, "and proper only to the confessional. But I answered them honestly, fully trusting in the archdiocese's good will and the good will of the clinical professional who stood before me."

Carrigee admits that he did not take some of the psychological tests with grave seriousness. The first test he was administered was a 375-question true-or-false test asking questions such as: "Are you afraid of your penis?"; "Do you feel like there is a soft spot in the top of your head?"; "When you are asleep in your room at night does your soul leave your body and float around the room?"; and "Do you feel like people are following you wherever you go?"

Several weeks later Carrigee returned to the clinic to hear the doctor's report on his psychological health. "I sat down," he explained, "while he read from an eight-page report that indicated in no uncertain terms that I had serious psychological problems— grandiose, narcissistic, trouble distinguishing between reality and fantasy." Listening to the litany of neuroses from which he allegedly suffered was unsettling enough for Carrigee, but when the doctor recommended that he enter into therapy, he was shocked.

"I requested a copy of the report, which the doctor was very reluctant to release to me, but I insisted," he recalled. "I took it home that night and pored over it. I was literally distraught that I might be seriously ill in the head. That is, until I read through the explanations the doctor gave for the conclusions he reached."

Carrigee cited as an example that the doctor reported that "Mr. Carrigee believes that his relationship with God is based on fear." He explained, however, that during the course of his interviews, he was asked what he fears in life. "I answered that we should only fear offending God, but that I was also afraid of heights." Looking back on the experience, Carrigee believes the doctor deliberately took his statement out of context and "twisted a new meaning into it."

The next morning, said Carrigee, he met with his vocations director, concerned about where he stood now in light of his "mental illnesses." It didn't take long into this meeting, he recalled, before he was told that he was "not what the archdiocese is looking for."

"I was told that I was 'too rigid' and 'too focused' to be a priest," he said. "But I innocently pursued the issue. I wanted to know exactly what my problem was. After a lengthy pursuit, I was then told that 'too rigid' meant that I took the pope too seriously, and 'too focused' referred to my devotion to the Blessed Mother and my practice of St. Louis de Monfort's Marian spirituality.

"I took the rejection as a personal rejection of my person. For a long time I struggled with the numbing and castrating belief that there was something very wrong with me. The Archdiocese of New Orleans said so. My family was ashamed of me because even in a time of a severe shortage of priests I was rejected as being mentally unfit for the priesthood. They could not understand what was wrong with me. My reputation was lost because they believed that 'the Catholic Church' had rejected me. I cannot emphasize enough that this time in my life was a very serious crisis of faith for me, that if it wasn't for extraordinary amounts of grace, I could have very well lost my faith altogether."

For some time after, Carrigee continued to appeal to the archdiocese to reconsider him. When he said he was willing to "fix the problem," he was sent to a priest-psychologist for regular psychiatric help. Carrigee was told that if this psychologist "gave the go-ahead," he could reapply to the archdiocese. Carrigee met with this priest for several months of counseling, but left when the priest-psychologist started leading him in guided meditations in which he was to imagine he was God.

Carrigee eventually transferred from Louisiana State to Franciscan University of Steubenville in Ohio. When he graduated he made one final inquiry into the priesthood with the Archdiocese of New Orleans, but this time he was told that because he had left counseling, the archdiocese would never again consider his application, saying they didn't need any "disobedient priests."

■ ■ ■

Such discrimination against orthodox men is also evidenced in the case of those applying to a diocese's deacon training program. Glenn Jividen, a retired air force colonel and dentist from Dayton, Ohio, is a case in point. With his family reared and his periodontal practice maturing with the addition of his eldest son, Jividen felt he had the time and calling to better serve the Church. Having viewed firsthand how helpful a deacon could be in assisting a parish, especially one served by only one, frequently overworked, elderly priest, his pastor suggested he consider the Lay Pastoral Ministry Program run by the Archdiocese of Cincinnati. This is the program that would prepare him for the permanent diaconate.

"The process began with an interview in Dayton with a friendly nun who seemed genuinely interested in me as a candidate," he recalled. She explained to Jividen that the archdiocese's lay ministry program meant a two-year study commitment, including a special project carried out under the direction of a counselor.

"Oddly," he remembered, "Sister asked me several times if I understood that the Church was changing, and if I thought I was able to be 'flexible enough to accept a pluralistic Church.' "

He replied that "change was an inescapable fact of life," and then asked her if she believed that some truths never change. She seemed tolerant of his question, he thought, but continued on without answering. She informed him that all candidates were expected to take the Myers-Briggs personality test, which would be given in Cincinnati by a priest-psychologist. That initial interview, he said, ended on a friendly note.

During the next part of the application process, Jividen was asked to write an autobiography of a thousand words or so. In this essay he included what he thought were important highlights of his devotion to the Church. First, he noted, he was involved in pro-life activities where he met "many wonderful spirit-filled people who greatly impressed me with their love and devotion to our Church, the Blessed Mother, and the Holy Father." Second, he joined Catholics United for the Faith (CUF), a group of lay Catholics formed in 1968 to defend the Church's teaching on *Humanae Vitae* and many other Church teachings and disciplines, such as the male, celibate priesthood. "I was motivated to strengthen my own knowledge of our Universal Church," he wrote of his involvement with CUF.

There were about a dozen candidates taking the psychological tests for evaluation purposes along with him. The priest-psychologist gave an introductory briefing in which he explained the tests would help the committee decide which type of ministry they were best suited for, and, recalled Jividen, "to remember that, above all, there is some place for everyone to serve."

When he arrived a week later to discuss the test results, the priest-psychologist received him in a friendly manner, yet the conversation soon turned to his participation in CUF. According to Jividen, "the psychologist stated that he had heard that those [CUF] people were very rigid and unwilling to change their position on anything." Jividen politely asked what were the matters which were the subject of their inflexible attitudes, but the psychologist changed the subject and asked him to explain what God meant to him.

"I answered that I was not a theologian, but that I thought the Apostles Creed well reflected my beliefs and those of the Catholic

Church," he remembered. "I also commented that we in CUF fully support the Vicar of Christ and the magisterium." The priest-psychologist, however, was quick to reply that the pope only rarely speaks *ex cathedra*[15] and Catholics should use their own God-given intellects to decide most issues.

"I asked if we Catholics should follow the various encyclicals the popes have issued, and he said that encyclicals mean 'different things in different countries of the world,' " Jividen recalled.

The conversation then turned to some of Jividen's previous activities, including a CUF chapter protest of Charles Curran at the University of Dayton; the psychologist commented, he said, that he had read Curran's books and "really didn't see much wrong with them."

The priest-psychologist then began a thorough review of the Myers-Briggs test, which suggested that Jividen was basically a "well-adjusted introvert."

"Father told me I function best on a one-to-one basis, and that I was ideally suited for dentistry. After thirty-seven years in the field, I was happy to hear I had chosen the right profession. The interview ended on a friendly note, but I was gently reminded that I would probably 'feel uncomfortable with my CUF friends after entering the Lay Pastoral Ministry Program.' "

There was to be a two-day "assessment weekend" as part of the next step in the application process, but Jividen did not make the cut. A letter signed by two laywomen and two sisters informed him that "after prayer and consultation with the priest-psychologist," it "would be in your best interest to postpone consideration of the LPMP." They also suggested that he take some approved courses to "update" his theology, as well as contact a spiritual director to help him develop a "personal spirituality." They enclosed a list of twenty-five recommended spiritual directors, twenty-two of whom were women.

■ ■ ■

Rejection for a candidate interested in serving the Church as an ordained deacon ends straightaway if he is turned away by his home diocese, but pursuing a priestly vocation is a bit different. Rejection of a potential seminarian by a diocese has ramifications for the applicant well beyond the borders of his diocese. Once rejected by one diocese, an applicant often finds himself "blackballed" in other dioceses, many of which are careful not to consider a man rejected by another diocese or religious order.

In the mid-1990s, Gerald St. Maur* was thirty-six years old when he received a damaging psychological evaluation from the psychologist who screens candidates for the Archdiocese of Detroit. He was summed up as "inflexible" and "rigid" for his expressed adherence to orthodox Catholicism and for outlining his prayer life as consisting of Eucharistic adoration, the rosary, and weekly fasting. Subsequently he was rejected by the Detroit archdiocese for admission into Sacred Heart Seminary.

He then made several inquiries into other dioceses hoping to be considered there. He found out quickly that his rejection by Detroit was an impediment for them to even consider his application. In September of 1999, St. Maur wrote a letter to the vocations office in the neighboring diocese of Lansing: "I explained that I had been turned down by the Archdiocese of Detroit and asked if they would be willing to form their own opinion about my suitability for the priesthood."

Two months later he received a letter from a priest in Lansing saying that after speaking with the vocations evaluation board in Detroit, he was not willing to consider St. Maur as a candidate for the priesthood. The letter, signed by Father J. Thomas Munley, concluded, "It is my hope that you are able to continue your discernment and find the place where God is calling you."

Once he received that letter, St. Maur understood that it was going to be quite difficult to get another chance. He tried a different approach next. He knew that at some seminaries laymen could enroll in philosophy courses that are prerequisites for the study of theology. He could do so without being formally attached to a diocese or religious order. Thinking this might be the best way to begin his studies and at the same time make himself a more acceptable candidate for the priesthood, he decided to contact the rector of one of these seminaries.

When asked by the rector why he thought that Detroit had rejected his application, St. Maur replied that he had received a bad psychological evaluation that essentially "indicted him as too or-thodox." Subsequently, the rector asked St. Maur to present a copy of the evaluation so that he and his staff could review it.

After six weeks passed without hearing back from the rector, St. Maur called the rector with a proposal. Understanding that he was being judged again on the Detroit evaluation, which he thought was spurious, he asked the rector to choose a psychologist anywhere in the United States whose judgment he trusted. He added that he was willing to travel to meet with the psychologist at his own expense, as well as to pay for the evaluation out of his own pocket. Then, he sug-gested, this report could be compared with the Detroit report.

The rector suggested instead that St. Maur find a Catholic psy-chologist of his own choosing to whom he could talk over a period of several weeks. If this psychologist could say that there was no merit to what was written in the Detroit evaluation, then he would seriously be considered for admission.

St. Maur was able to locate a well-respected psychologist who was a former seminarian himself. "Here was someone who knew about the Catholic faith and the priesthood, so I had some confidence that I would get an honest evaluation," he said.

Following the second interview with the Catholic psychologist, St. Maur asked him if he would be willing to phone the rector, he ex-plained, "to make sure we were all on the same page in terms of what we were trying to accomplish." The psychologist said he would and also said that he would phone the vocations office at the Archdiocese of Detroit to see what information he could get from them.

When St. Maur arrived for the third interview a week later, the psychologist told him there was a "problem." In his conversation with an official of the archdiocese, he was able to confirm that the archdiocese found St. Maur too "orthodox" in his beliefs and that he had been denied admission to Sacred Heart primarily for this reason. He also stated that after his conversation with the rector of the second seminary, he discovered that the seminary had no intention of accepting him unless he "changed." According to the rector, the formation staff wanted the psychologist to put St. Maur through some sort of therapy that would result in him no longer being so "conservative." The psychologist told the rector that St. Maur was psychologically healthy and that he considered any such therapy to be unnecessary and even unethical. He also told the rector that if the pope were administered the same psychological exam in Detroit, he too would likely be labeled "rigid" and "intolerant."

St. Maur believes to this day that the rector of the seminary must have been in close contact with the Archdiocese of Detroit to have adopted such a firm stance against him. St. Maur had only talked briefly with the rector on two occasions.

Considering that seminary rectors and vocations directors across the country maintain close communications, St. Maur is likely correct in his assumption. This "network" seems to have prevented many orthodox men from applying to, or being accepted by, dioceses or religious orders after being rejected, however unjustly, by one diocese.

This issue of "blackballing," as many seminarians and aspiring seminarians call it, is a serious one. It is more prevalent—and more serious—among seminarians who have been dismissed, or "non-endorsed" as they say in seminary parlance, from a seminary after investing a year or more of their life studying for the priesthood. Many, as stated before, are dismissed for legitimate reasons. But too many seminarians have either political or personal clashes, unrelated to their suitability as a candidate for ordination, that lead to dismissal and subsequent blackballing. The actions of the seminary formation staff or its representatives is often not only unfair but unethical and, in moral terms, constitutes outright calumny.

That's exactly the opinion of Father John Lewandowski of the Fargo diocese. After protesting the use of what he considered a "pornographic" textbook in a mandatory class on Human Sexuality at Mount Angel Seminary in Oregon, then rector Father Patrick Brennan issued an evaluation that Lewandowski said amounts to calumny.

"I hate to use the word 'calumny,' but I can find no other word to express what Father Brennan had done to me at Mount Angel Seminary," he said. In Brennan's response to a requested evaluation of Lewandowski to Holy Apostles Seminary in Connecticut, Brennan "did a good job of what today is called 'character assassination,' " explained Lewandowski.

Holy Apostles shared the Mount Angel evaluation with Lewandowski, and both he and his soon-to-be new seminary came to the same conclusion: not one word of it was true. Their conclusion, said Lewandowski, was based on the fact that Brennan changed "his story" on the pornographic textbook scandal. Lewandowski elaborated: "I sat in Father Brennan's office for two hours while he enumerated the many reasons why I should not 'make any waves' over the use of a pornographic textbook that in no way presented the Church's moral teaching to seminarians. The seminary professors and staff, he assured me, were qualified to make proper judgments in the choice of teaching aids. I was told I should just take the course, and none of this need to be reported on my evaluation."

Lewandowski was not intimidated by the possibility of a "bad evaluation." In any case, despite his previous positive evaluation, that's just what he received. In the new evaluation Brennan stated that Lewandowski had "sexual hang-ups" manifested by the fact that he could not get himself to look at the pictures in the book—e.g., graphic illustrations showing men performing oral sex on one another—without being disturbed. In fact, to make matters worse, said Lewandowski, Brennan recommended that he submit himself to Dr. Torres, the faculty member who used the textbook in his Human Sexuality course, for psychological counseling.

"I would like to think that his evaluation of me was just one big misunderstanding, but Father Brennan told me personally 'that there was nothing wrong with the book, and that it was necessary to the curriculum,' " Lewandowski explained, adding that "at one point he told me that he had not read the book, and at another he told me that he had only reviewed it."

On the subject of his evaluation he commented: "If I am indeed the kind of person that Father Brennan evaluated me to be, then I should certainly not have been ordained a priest. But if I have an authentic call from Christ to be a priest, and someone is deliberately trying to hinder me from attaining that goal, then that someone has much to answer for, especially if that someone is a priest himself."

In order to demonstrate to Holy Apostles Seminary that Brennan's evaluation of him was an anomaly, Lewandowski obtained many letters of support from people both on the seminary grounds and in the Mount Angel area who vouched for his character. These letters are in gross contradiction to Brennan's assessment.

He also obtained positive letters of recommendation from people on the seminary board in the Diocese of Gallup, New Mexico, some of whom are priests. "I even had a letter from the retired bishop of Gallup," he said, "with whom I lived and was in daily contact for over a year. All of these good people gave me their full support; they all encouraged me to go on with the pursuit of my priestly vocation."

Lewandowski also showed Holy Apostles a copy of the previous year's evaluation from Mount Angel, also signed by Brennan, which makes none of the accusations of his later evaluation.

"It seems that what Father Brennan was attempting to do in his false evaluation of me was to make *me* the issue. In fact, the real issue was Father Brennan, Dr. Torres, the pornographic textbook, and Mount Angel Seminary. What I did is to protest against a shameless book and staff who were willing to use a book that encouraged the practice of sexually immoral and deviant activity. The book in question, with its advocacy of homosexuality, oral and anal intercourse, masturbation, and even bestiality, had the potential to do untold damage to the salvation of souls. It is precisely because these people were intending to use it in a Catholic seminary that I made my protest. Seminaries are institutions brought into existence for the purpose of training and preparing men in holiness, who train both spiritually and academically for the special work of saving souls.

"Father Brennan had agreed that he would not expel me, since there could be no good reason for him to do so. I could then go on with my studies if I could find a seminary to accept me. But, in effect, he did expel me by giving me an evaluation that any expelled seminarian would rate." While many believed that Lewandowski got

along with virtually everyone at Mount Angel, as his numerous recommendations attest, Brennan wrote that he did not get along with
either his student peers or the seminary staff. Brennan also claimed
that Lewandowski was "disruptive" in class because he challenged
several professors for asserting opinions that were contrary to the
Church's teaching. He did so, Lewandowski defended, "in a manner
proper to academic etiquette and formality."

"I do not consider myself a criminal for insisting on proper moral
teaching in a Catholic seminary," he concluded. The evidence, when
weighed against Brennan's evaluation, was so overwhelming that
Lewandowski was accepted into the seminary program at Holy
Apostles and later ordained for the Diocese of Fargo, North Dakota.

■ ■ ■

Seminary officials don't always succeed in keeping a man from ordination, as in the case with Father Lewandowski, but too often they
do. Then, in the words of Father Andrew Walter, who survived fourteen years of blackballing, "the seminarian walks away from his vocation with his tail between his legs," often so stunned that he is
unable even to explain to friends and family why he was rejected, and
afraid to discuss what transpired at the seminary.

That is the subject of the forthcoming chapters, each of which
looks at a particular aspect of the political agenda in seminaries that
cannot be questioned without serious repercussions.

CHAPTER 4

The Gay Subculture

How Homosexual Politics Discriminates Against Healthy, Heterosexual Seminarians

The issue was never one of my suitability for ordination. Rather it was that the gay clique had been given veto power over who got ordained.
—Joseph Kellenyi, former seminarian,
Mundelein Seminary, Chicago

If the applicant is accepted into a seminary program, he is liable to encounter homosexual issues many times throughout his seminary career, sometimes in more direct ways than others. "For decades we have been hearing stories about priestly training and religious houses that would have made Boccaccio blush."[1] These stories effectively deter many Catholic parents from encouraging a priestly vocation for their sons. It has, to be sure, deterred many young men from testing their vocations in certain dioceses.

One popular book acknowledges what the author calls a "gay subculture" in many Catholic seminaries. Written by Father Donald B. Cozzens when he was rector of St. Mary's Seminary in Cleveland, *The Changing Face of the Priesthood* warns of a growing public concern that the priesthood is becoming a "gay profession." He spends considerable time addressing the issue from his perspective *inside* the seminary.

Cozzens states that "straight men in a predominantly or signifi-cantly gay environment commonly experience chronic destabiliza-tion, a common symptom of which is self-doubt."[2] Compounding the challenge of studying, praying, and living alongside gay semi-narians, he adds, "are seminary faculties which include a dispropor-tionate number of homosexually oriented persons."[3] In other words, this "gay subculture," comprised of both students and faculty at cer-tain seminaries, deters the heterosexual man from continuing to study and prepare for the priesthood.

This is to put it mildly. How can any healthy, heterosexual semi-narian expect to be properly formed and prepared for the Catholic priesthood when constantly subjected to that which is so clearly con-trary to Church teaching and discipline? How many heterosexual seminarians, whether orthodox or not, have decided to leave the seminary and abandon their vocations because of the "gay subcul-ture" they were forced to endure, because they had been proposi-tioned, harassed, or even molested? We're not talking here about the presence of a few homosexually oriented men who conduct them-selves with perfect chastity. Rather, there exists an intense and often threatening atmosphere.

According to former seminarians and recently ordained priests, this "gay subculture" is so prominent at certain seminaries that these institutions have earned nicknames such as Notre Flame (for Notre Dame Seminary in New Orleans) and Theological Closet (for Theo-logical College at the Catholic University of America in Wash-ington, D.C.). St. Mary's Seminary in Baltimore has earned the nickname the "Pink Palace."

Father Andrew Walter, ordained for the Diocese of Bridgeport, Connecticut, in 2000, spent several semesters at the Baltimore school as a seminarian for the Diocese of Paterson, New Jersey. The problem was so bad when he was there, he explained, that "some of the students and faculty used to get dressed up in leather to go to 'the block,' Baltimore's equivalent to 42nd Street in Manhattan."

Seminarians, sometimes accompanied by faculty members, would do this regularly, Walter explained. "They would meet in the foyer, and then head for the gay bars." This situation is not new, and the claim is not uncommon. In March of 2000, Father Andrew Greeley, a well-known liberal priest-sociologist from Chicago, testified that seminary professors "tell their students that they're gay and take some of them to gay bars, and gay students sleep with each other."[4]

Walter also remembers a lecture that the vice rector at St. Mary's delivered in front of at least 150 people, wherein he stated that "yes, we accept openly gay seminarians; that's our policy," an acknowledgment that merely confirmed what was already commonly known at the seminary.

Walter said he tried to explain to his bishop, Frank Rodimer, what the atmosphere of the school was with such an open acceptance, and sometimes encouragement, of the gay subculture: "My constant theme to the bishop was that this is not just about homosexuality; this is about an agenda in a celibate seminary. It's something directly in conflict with the teaching of the Church. These people are promoting this conflict."

Father John Trigilio of the Harrisburg, Pennsylvania, diocese remembers visiting St. Mary's in Baltimore when he was a seminarian in Pennsylvania. "There was no discretion at all," he said of the gay subculture there. "The few times I was there, some of the seminarians would literally dress like gays from the Village. They would even go so far as to wear pink silk; it was like going to see *La Cage aux Folles*."[5]

"In my day at St. Mary's," said Father John Despard,* now a religious order priest from the Southeast, "down the hall there would be two guys together in the shower and everybody knew it."

Ada Mason,* a philosophy professor at a prominent Catholic university, once served on the board of a seminary in the upper Midwest. In that position she was shocked to discover a gay subculture extremely active there. "Open homosexual behavior was more than tolerated," she admitted. "I was even told by one of the seminary faculty that every Friday a van took priesthood students to a nearby large city to cruise the gay bars."

"When my associates at the university heard that I was on the board," Mason continued, "they began to confide in me. A graduate student in theology, for example, told me that his mother, who was a cleaning lady at the seminary, had at first been shocked at the male pornography she saw in the students' rooms, rooms that she assumed were those of women students. Her shock was deepened, however, when she learned that those were the rooms of seminarians who were studying for the priesthood. I found these and other reports credible at a subsequent meeting of the board, when the rector boasted to us, 'We don't ask our candidates about their sexual orientation or their sexual histories. It would be a violation of a man's civil rights to deny him ordination on those grounds.' "

According to several priests and many former seminarians who attended Detroit's Sacred Heart Seminary and St. John's Provincial Seminary in Plymouth, Michigan, both schools were "veritable hothouses" for homosexuals in the 1970s and 1980s (and, with Sacred Heart, into the early 1990s).

Father Justice Wargrave,* who was a seminarian at St. John's in the mid-1980s, recalled that homosexual promiscuity was widespread during his years there. Among the nearly seventy seminarians (from all the dioceses of Michigan except Grand Rapids), "there was a lot of openly hostile camps, and a certain meanness." Some of the camps, said Wargrave, were of "self-defined gays who formed strong cliques. Everyone there knew what was going on. There were visits at night as gay seminarians cruised from room to room." Little effort was made to hide either the sexual orientation or the homosexual activity of these seminarians at St. John's, he added; and "it was not uncommon to see seminarians acting out sexually in a fairly public setting."

Wargrave recited a long list of active homosexuals who were ordained: Some of the priests are active in the local Dignity chapter, and others later left the priesthood to take up a full-time gay lifestyle in the San Francisco Bay Area. At least two are known to have died from AIDS.

St. John's was closed in the mid-1980s, the word among many priests being that the closing was due to Vatican intervention because of its moral decadence. Its programs were taken over by Sacred Heart, with many of the St. John faculty moving to the Detroit seminary.

While rampant homosexuality has reportedly not been present at Sacred Heart since the mid-1990s, according to orthodox seminarians studying there, some Detroit-area priests today are still unwilling to recommend the seminary because many of the staff are holdovers from the "hothouse" days. One former employee of the Detroit archdiocese said he knows of at least a dozen men who are studying for the priesthood in other dioceses specifically because their pastors have recommended they avoid Sacred Heart.

In 1996, a priest of the Archdiocese of Chicago, Father Wayne H. Wurst, publicly charged on a Chicago radio program broadcast on WBEZ-FM that seminarians at St. Mary of the Lake in Mundelein, Illinois (known simply as "Mundelein"), were coerced by upper-class students into having sex with faculty members in the 1970s.

Wurst said in his taped remarks, "Many of the younger students would be placed into situations in which they compromised their sexual integrity. This would be used against them by older students for favors. And these older students actually had faculty members who would request from time to time a friend who would come and visit them because they were lonely. And these students would supply fresh meat. So there were madams, pimps, and prostitutes all in a major seminary system that, from the outside, if you were to walk through, would look very holy."[6]

Wurst added that "a large number of students had been convinced by some liberal teachers that sexual promiscuity with the same sex was not a violation of celibacy," an outrageous distortion of Catholic teaching.[7]

Those who would hope that things may have turned around at Mundelein since Wurst's days will be disappointed. Joseph Kellenyi, a seminarian at the Chicago-area seminary during the 1998–99 school year, confirmed that Wurst's portrait of the sexual immorality and shenanigans remains unchanged at the dawn of the twenty-first century. "I won't go so far as to say that some of the members of the formation team at Mundelein were literally 'pimps,' but one or two in particular certainly facilitated Chicago priests meeting the 'cute' seminarians." Kellenyi wondered why these priests would be interested in being introduced to certain seminarians who were favorites—and therefore "recommended" by openly gay faculty members.

"One hall in the seminary dorm," related Kellenyi, "is nick-named the 'Catwalk,' known as the residence of the more fashionable gays." "Catwalk," he explained, was a reference to the runways of fashion models, but also reflected the campy, feline-like personalities of those who lived in this area of the seminary. One member of the formation faculty in particular, he said, was known to take seminarians to high-profile gay events such as a popular gay production in Chicago's Lincoln Park.

According to Kellenyi and several other seminarians who attended Mundelein during the 1990s, one of the big events at the seminary was whenever a seminarian would "come out" as being a homosexually oriented person. The openly gay seminarian-to-be would do so by telling one or two of his closest friends, and, sure enough, the word of another "orientation proclamation," they said, would travel quickly throughout the halls of the seminary, especially to the formation faculty members. Oddly enough, attested Kellenyi, once a seminarian "came out," he would be wined and dined—literally—by certain faculty priests. "In my opinion," he said, "it's highly inappropriate to wine and dine any favorite students, orientation aside." But the special status given to openly gay seminarians, he said, is beyond the pale.

The gay subculture, said former Mundelein seminarians, was the dominant culture at Mundelein. "One of the faculty priests," related seminarian John Edmundson,* "has even been known to pinch and touch seminarians while joking. Others have seen this, but nothing is ever done. Some of the other faculty members, those who clearly don't go along with a lot of the program, feel they are powerless when faced by the Chicago machine of priest structure."

The problem, charged former seminarians from Mundelein, is mainly with the formation faculty rather than with the academic faculty, which seems to be more under the direct control of Francis Cardinal George, who, Chicago insiders have suggested, has been trying, but with great difficulty, to reform the many perceived ills at Mundelein.

Nonetheless, said seminarians, there does exist an "underground network" of orthodox seminarians at Mundelein, but they keep their prayer life and spiritual direction with orthodox priests in strict confidence. According to Gregory Banks,* "students who are loyal to Church teaching and oppose the gay stranglehold on the seminary trade notes, conference tapes, and spiritual reading. It's not a great system, but without it, very few of us would survive. Second, there are some 'closet-orthodox' members of the faculty who try to offer the truth, although they must often do so surreptitiously."

When Stephen Brady, president of the Springfield, Illinois–based Roman Catholic Faithful, faxed Father Bart Winters a list of complaints that seminarians and recently ordained priests had made against Mundelein seminary, Winters replied in an August 4, 1999, letter denying any problems: "I appreciate your concern about the seminary," he wrote to Brady, "and I am disturbed by the allegations made by the priests and seminarians who have written you. My only response is to say that the kinds of behaviors you have described are not tolerated at the seminary, and I am not aware of anything of the nature you describe taking place here."

In stark contrast to Winters's denial, Father Michael Shane,* a 1999 graduate of Mundelein, had addressed his concerns about the seminary's moral decadence directly to rector Father John Canary in a letter dated April 20, 1999:

> Upon my arrival at Mundelein, I assumed there would be "some" gay students. I also assumed that I could handle that. I am a straight man, not a homophobic monster. Still, nothing could prepare me for the

"underculture" of homosexuality that has been supported by the formation staff....

It's pretty offensive to a straight guy, because if I ever
brought women in, played dance music rather than
show tunes, and told jokes about which classmates were
coupling with whom, I'd be booted out in a minute....
It's common knowledge that there are "gay couples" [at
Mundelein] (and I mean "couples," not friends).

The other problem at Mundelein is that if a straight
student complains about this, he gets blackballed as a
"conservative." There are several of us who are trying
to be chaste. It's difficult, but to have to live among this
gay culture is too much. To be at events where guys
seem to have their Cam priest's blessing to be "out,
proud, and open" about their love life really bothers
me. And I am not alone.

It has shocked me for the years I've been at Mundelein. It's got to stop, even if it takes getting a new formation program.... Something must change. My
vocation director has told me that my bishop wishes to
hear what I have to relate about Mundelein. I will be
telling him this, not to hurt Mundelein, but to help
other possible candidates know what they are getting
into. It's not about gay vs. straight. It is about appropriate behavior and role modeling. At Mundelein, it was
sorely lacking, unless you were among the "in" crowd,
and at your seminary, the "in" crowd happens to be gay!

Two years earlier, in 1997, Canary in his rector's address of November 6 told the student body that he "doesn't want to hear any
more complaints." Another seminarian mocked Canary with this notice posted on the student bulletin board (ellipses appear in original):

Come on boys...Don't Grumble...Even When...
Your rector has no vision...

Your formation has no substance...

And you have no priestly identity...

What your seminary does have is:

Lots of homosexual priests on the formation team...

Lots of students, up through their 4th year discerning
their vocation...

A student body that does not know how to act at a
Catholic liturgy...

A general sense of apathy...

A strong resistance to outside intervention by a fearful
administration...

If you can't take the heat Canary...Resign...We'll
pack you up!

For those seeking more evidence of the gay subculture in seminaries across the United States, journalist Jason Berry, in his 1992
bestseller *Lead Us Not into Temptation*, provides similar examples:

> Seminaries should be centers of scholarship, where
> moral teaching is strengthened....Located on [Wash-
> ington, D.C.'s] Catholic University campus, TC
> [Theological College] was once considered a premier
> American seminary....The most impressive TC stu-
> dent I met was in his final year and has since been or-
> dained....Said he [of seminary life], "I was aloof in
> some ways because I did not want to be sexually at-
> tractive....Some do hit the gay bars. Some abstain
> and see the vow through, others are acting out in ways
> not characteristic of priestly life....I have thought,
> What's going on here? Where is the faculty? Every-
> body can see this."[8]

Berry vividly chronicled the case of Mark Brooks, who in 1984
sued San Diego's bishop, Leo T. Maher, and the diocese over his expulsion from St. Francis Seminary in southern California. Brooks

claimed he had been sexually assaulted by one priest on the seminary faculty and harassed by other faculty priests. (The lawsuit was settled out of court in April 1985 for approximately $23,000.)

"It gradually dawned on Brooks," wrote Berry, "that at least a third of the seventy-five seminarians were homosexual."[9] Brooks related that seminarians were full of "coming out stories" and spoke of being "wounded" by homophobia. Furthermore, reported Berry, seminarians were instructed not to report homosexual relationships, and that they were "growth experiences." Brooks said that with that sort of atmosphere, homosexual activity proliferated.

He recounted how the vice rector, Father Stephen Dunn, propositioned him a dozen times over a period of two years and how Father Nicholas Reveles, who taught music, was having sexual relations with at least four seminarians and tried to convince Brooks of the "goodness of homosexuality":

> Brooks grew miserable. In line for communion he saw students grabbing buttocks. Affairs blossomed. A seminarian in his late thirties took a sixteen-year-old boy to live with him. The boy eventually left, and in time so did the man. Brooks complained to [the vice rector] Steve Dunn about the climate of promiscuity.[10]

Yet Dunn, Berry reported, at the behest of six seminarians said to be part of a "gay clique" with whom Brooks had repeatedly clashed, ordered him to undergo alcoholism rehabilitation and was hospitalized. Dunn threatened that if any seminarian were to visit Brooks in the hospital, they would be expelled. Brooks was released three weeks later. Doctors diagnosed Brooks not with alcoholism, but with post-traumatic stress syndrome.[11]

■ ■ ■

As the Brooks case evidences, seminary life can be made difficult for the "dissenting" seminarian, he who does not condone deviancy of this sort. I have heard many accounts of seminarians being propositioned or harassed by fellow students and of faculty members who do not take this issue seriously.

In 1999, for instance, one man studying for the priesthood at St. John's Seminary in Boston was forced to procure a restraining order against a fellow student after the administration summarily dismissed his complaints of being sexually harassed by an "out-of-the-closet" gay classmate. He finally left that seminary, while his fellow seminarian advanced in good standing.

Paul Sinsigalli (whose following account is corroborated by a former official of the Boston archdiocese, who said he would "stand by Sinsigalli in court" if he had to) was not the seminarian who was harassed, but he played a significant part in this particular affair at St. John's. When he arrived there for his first year of studies his first impression of the seminary was a positive one. He thought he was "in the right place," he said, that he was "studying with men who wanted to be good and holy priests, men who were trying to live the Christian ideal while learning more about the Church and how to serve her people."

By the second semester, however, this façade of ideal seminary life crumbled as Sinsigalli began to sense that something was very wrong. It soon became apparent that many of the students and faculty did not have a view of the Church that was consistent with the Church's teaching, particularly on sexual morality. This became increasingly upsetting for Sinsigalli; he had entered the seminary fully expecting to study with men who shared his faith and love for the Church. Some faculty members, he said, were just as much a problem as the liberal seminarians. Church teaching was always questioned in an underhanded sort of way; "in our classes, rarely outright," he said, but outside of class "it was clear that we had to line up on one side of the fence or another."

Many of the problem areas, he said, pertained to the Church's teaching on human sexuality. "I was shocked to find out that two big topics that were discussed, not just in the college but throughout the whole seminary, were homosexuality and masturbation," Sinsigalli lamented. "Everyone was always talking about these things. It was a constant litmus test to determine what side you're on and how you're going to show yourself."

Sinsigalli estimated that during his four years there, 30 percent of the student body considered themselves "gay," and in the graduate school of theology it was an even higher percentage.

His own problems started one night with an evening trip back from the refectory, where several seminarians had gone for a cup of hot chocolate. On the walk back to their dormitory several of Sinsigalli's classmates were poking fun at two of their fellow seminarians, who were not present that night. The discussion centered around their homosexuality and that they had been heard in the act.

"They were ruthlessly making fun of these guys," Sinsigalli recalled. "It was vulgar, and I didn't say anything," he explained, "because it wasn't my style to make fun of this sort of thing, but they kept going on and on about it.

"I finally said, 'You know, guys, it's not so nice to be talking like this behind their backs. If you really think this stuff is going on at least give them the chance to defend themselves.' "

Although Sinsigalli was actually defending the rights of the accused, Terrence O'Rourke,* one seminarian who had been joking about them, became confrontational if not illogical. "So you're saying you would go up to them and accuse these guys?" he asked Sinsigalli.

Sinsigalli responded by explaining himself, telling O'Rourke that he wasn't accusing them of anything, but if they thought these seminarians were involved in a homosexual relationship, then they ought to "ask them to their faces and be men instead of hens gossiping behind their backs."

Deliberately distorting Sinsigalli's meaning, O'Rourke approached the two the next day and told them that Sinsigalli was accusing them of being gay lovers and that he was going to confront them about it soon.

"Then he went to the dean of students," Sinsigalli said of O'Rourke, "and later told virtually every member of the faculty the same lie about me: that I was publicly accusing two seminarians of being active homosexuals."

Soon thereafter Sinsigalli was called into the dean's office. The dean, a psychologist, sat with his legs crossed and said, "Paul, I hear you have some concerns about some of the students here." Sinsigalli, an ex-cop and a straightforward type, didn't care for the dean's line of questioning.

"I told him the truth, that no, I didn't have any problem with anyone at St. John's," he explained. The dean then "flipped out," said Sinsigalli. "He said, 'You know damn well what I'm talking about. I spent hours trying to figure out the right way to say this. Just tell me what's going on!' " So Sinsigalli then explained the situation, but he didn't think the dean believed him, and the dean almost said as much.

The dean then organized a mediation meeting between O'Rourke and Sinsigalli. "Whenever O'Rourke said something that was contrary to the facts, I stopped him immediately," he explained. "I told him, 'You know this is not right; it's not what I said; not the way it happened.' And then I'd go on to explain what really happened. I proved my case."

Sinsigalli, who in addition to being a former police officer came to the seminary with a military background, was used to being around men "who acted like men," he said, "but guys at St. John's like O'Rourke never acted like men. They acted like children, like little girls. They don't handle things like men do. I never once would have thought of going to a faculty member and saying, this is what so-and-so said."

The mediation session with the dean was inconclusive. Sinsigalli left feeling that the dean still didn't believe him, and later felt that he had erroneously been branded a "homophobe," the worst of political offenses at St. John's.

A year later O'Rourke "came out" to his classmates. To the faculty, said Sinsigalli, O'Rourke said he was "struggling with homosexuality," but at the same time, "he was prancing up and down the halls proudly proclaiming how gay he is."

While an outpouring of compassion flowed from most members of the faculty, O'Rourke fully expected that everyone should not only tolerate but embrace his self-professed sexual orientation.

"He expected me to literally embrace him and become his best friend," explained Sinsigalli, "and when I didn't, others started to read that as 'Gee, Paul must hate gays'; but the fact is I don't hate homosexuals. This guy was a jerk, plain and simple. I didn't care what his orientation was. After he lied about what I had said, and got me into trouble, I didn't want anything to do with him. He made my life hell at the seminary every chance he got, and I was expected to give him a big hug every time I saw him? He played the homophobe card. The ironic thing is that before I went into seminary, I heard things about homosexuals in the news, but I never really gave it any thought. I know I'm not a homosexual. I never had any doubts about my sexuality, and I feel bad for those who do struggle with sexual issues. I was just never involved in any of the homosexual agenda— never gave it any thought one way or another. And when I got to the seminary, all of a sudden it was in my face, and I was expected to say, 'It's okay if you commit sodomy in your room in the seminary and explore your sexuality that way.' "

What kind of priests are these men going to make? Sinsigalli wondered, pointing out the overwhelming public scandal of sexual abuse of children and teens by priests in Boston, where the *Boston Globe* revealed that the Archdiocese of Boston settled child-molestation claims against *at least* seventy Boston-area priests in the previous decade.[12]

"The priesthood of Jesus Christ demands men of high integrity and character and strength. It is not an easy vocation, so if these guys are like this in seminary, I can't imagine what they are going to be like in parishes."

A few months after O'Rourke began wearing his orientation on his sleeve, he became sexually obsessed with Charles Kent,* a first-year theology seminarian, a man Sinsigalli described as a "healthy heterosexual."

Kent worked at the seminary library one night each week, and sometimes the library was nearly empty in the evenings, explained Sinsigalli.

"On one occasion O'Rourke visited the library," he explained, "and piled up books about homosexuality in front of Kent, saying,

'Read this and you'll get the message.' Another time, O'Rourke came back and started screaming in Kent's face because he was rejecting his sexual advances.

"This O'Rourke had a campaign of harassment against Kent to the point where he was scared. He didn't know what O'Rourke would do next. He went to the rector and to his advisors and the dean of students, but nobody did a thing. Nobody would help him. Since they were all so full of compassion about O'Rourke and his 'struggle' with homosexuality, it seemed O'Rourke could get away with virtually anything.

"O'Rourke was getting more and more violent and agitated. So Kent asked me for some advice because I have a law enforcement background. I told him he had two options after the faculty did nothing. The first was to simply leave the seminary, and the second was to get a restraining order[13] from the Brighton District Court to keep O'Rourke away from him. And that's what he did. I went with him to the courthouse, and he got it without a problem. The next day a cop showed up at the seminary to serve the restraining order.

"Then the s—t really hit the fan. Charles Kent was called into one of the dean's offices and the dean started screaming at him, saying that he was embarrassing the seminary. He had no concern for what Kent was going through or for his safety. It was always concern for the homosexual. That was what counted—the only thing that counted."

At the end of that year, neither Kent nor Sinsigalli was approved to advance in the seminary. Effectively, both were booted. Yet O'Rourke continued on with impunity. "It never ceased to amaze me that O'Rourke could do anything he wanted to because he was homosexual." And, added Sinsigalli, O'Rourke was not "out of the ordinary" at St. John's.

Bill Eversleigh* attended St. John's for four years of graduate theology studies. "He was touted as a superstar," recalled Sinsigalli. "The faculty loved him. They thought he was great and smart and was going to make an exemplary priest one day."

Many at the seminary quickly concluded that Eversleigh was an active homosexual. "Word got around that he was 'dating' guys at

St. John's and when he went to work in a Boston-area parish he was 'dating' a guy there too."

After Eversleigh was ordained to the transitional diaconate, the final step before becoming a priest (when the man must promise to lead a celibate life), he was assigned to a parish in the Archdiocese of Boston. "He met this guy," explained Sinsigalli, summing up the "buzz" at the seminary, "and they started 'dating.' At the end of his assignment he returned to his home diocese. He wasn't there two weeks before he decided that he was hopelessly in love with this guy. He just packed up in the middle of the night and left. Then he moved in with his lover, even though he was already ordained a transitional deacon."

An unidentified priest from the Archdiocese of Boston told the *Boston Herald* that he and many others also experienced harassment by the gay clique during his seminary years. "The problem is," said the priest, "there's a subculture of gay priests and everyone knows it. I went through seminary with a lot of them and got hit on. And when I reported it, I was harassed to a point where, emotionally, it was very difficult to get ordained. I'm not the only one who had to fight to get through it; I know guys who left because of it.

"It was clear there was a cabal tacitly saying, 'Don't bother reporting this stuff.' You wouldn't believe the self-justifications, like, 'Well, celibacy only applies to not getting married, so since we're not getting married, we can do whatever we want.' It was horrible, with a lot of intimidation, but I stayed because I felt this was what God was calling me to do; besides, if I'd walked, they'd have won."[14]

Seminarians who accept the Church's teaching on sexual morality have not only been dismissed from seminary as "troublemakers," they have also been threatened by classmates and faculty, especially in religious houses, that if they did not submit to homosexuality—to espouse and defend homosexual acts, if not take part in them—their priestly careers would be in jeopardy.

In his mid-thirties, James Thesiger* attended a midwestern seminary. From the time he first arrived there, he found that his orthodox views of the Church were not wanted. He was even accused many times of leading the younger seminarians away from what the formation staff was trying to instill in them.

During the second year of his seminary studies, he was visited late one night by three of these younger seminarians, who looked up to Thesiger as somewhat of an older brother and role model. Taken off guard, Thesiger was frightened by what they had to relate. "They began to describe how the college director had been forcing them into sexual situations and how they had begun to wish they were dead," he recalled.

Having a background in social work, Thesiger took the side of the seminarians and spoke to them as any counselor would, he said, about empowerment of rape victims. "My main instruction to them was they had a right to say, 'no.' " He also advised that none of them inform the director that they had spoken to him about the sexual abuse because it would mean "vocational death" to them all.

Eventually, however, one of the young seminarians let the information slip. "From that time on, my life became a living hell at the seminary," he recalled. Thesiger soon asked his diocese if he could transfer to another seminary. At first they seemed happy enough to accommodate. However, when Thesiger received his final evaluation it was "terrible."

"I had always received glowing evaluations in my prior reports," he explained. Thesiger figured that since the college director knew of Thesiger's knowledge of his sexual abuse of several seminarians, he had decided to sabotage Thesiger's vocation. The "vocational death" he had predicted some months before came to pass, at least for him. Once his diocese reviewed the seminary's evaluation of Thesiger, written by the college director, they decided they could no longer endorse him as a seminarian. "I received a two-paragraph letter stating this decision," he lamented.

Although Thesiger still feels called to the priesthood, now when he begins to think about applying to another diocese, he gets "panic attacks," wondering if he'll have to endure all this again.

Joseph Kellenyi was thirty-nine years old when he left behind a $300,000 annual salary as a corporate executive with Paine Webber in London, England, to enter Mundelein Seminary near Chicago in the fall of 1998. During his pretheology year there, he earned a 4.0 grade point average and was well liked by his fellow students and most of the faculty. He was, however, disturbed by what he calls "some blatant homosexual behavior among the formation faculty."

"I gradually became aware of a gay subculture in the seminary," he explained. "I noticed some things there that I only later came to understand. First, there was the very close allegiance between the more militant gay priests on the faculty and the nuns who wanted to be priests. Second, I noticed the formation faculty was overwhelmingly gay, while the academic faculty was predominantly heterosexual."

Although Kellenyi was never accused of being a "homophobe," nor does he consider himself one, he admitted that he avoided "the most militant 'in-your-face' gays on the faculty." He also noticed that one nun, whom he describes as "feminist," gave him a hard time about his masculinity. Kellenyi, a former football coach and competitive rugby player, was told by one of the formation faculty priests that the nun and some of the gay priests were "a bit afraid" of him. In short, he was seen as too masculine to be walking around a Catholic seminary. He was then advised that these faculty members had considerable power and that he should accommodate them at all costs.

By the end of the year he knew he did not want to be a priest in Chicago: "I admit that I had no desire to be a priest in a place where I would always be on the 'outside,' and never be appreciated, simply because I was not gay."

In the summer of 1999, Kellenyi became a seminarian for the Diocese of Venice, Florida, and was cosponsored by the military archdiocese. He had been in the military earlier in his adulthood and was interested in serving as a chaplain in the armed services. In a meeting with Kellenyi, Mundelein's rector, Father John Canary, told him that, although he was leaving the Archdiocese of Chicago, he was welcome to return to Mundelein in the fall, though he was warned that some of the faculty did not find him "transparent" enough, and if they were not accommodated, they could prevent him from being ordained. Kellenyi needed their "votes" in order to be approved to continue studies at Mundelein and later to be recommended for ordination.

Kellenyi told his rector the basic problem was that these faculty members were part of the " 'alternative lifestyle clique' and that people like them don't like being around people like me," that is, decidedly straight men. Ambivalence about sexual orientation is okay, said Kellenyi, but he who was certain of his heterosexuality and considered it healthy was unacceptable at Mundelein.

In fact, he estimated that while he was there, upwards of 60 percent of the school's seminarians were overtly homosexual, which caused serious tensions, especially between the "gay" and "nongay" Hispanic students.

"The issue was never one of my suitability for ordination," Kellenyi explained. "Rather it was that the gay clique had been given veto power over who got ordained in Chicago. Furthermore, the faculty members in question were not willing to settle for tolerance from me, which I could give. What they wanted was affirmation and my respect, which I could not give. It must be noted too that at no time had it ever been suggested that I had a problem dealing with gay men, or was 'homophobic.' The issue was that they had a problem dealing with me. And the rector even admitted again that gay men don't like people like me. This of course raises the question of 'heterophobia.' I have heard time and again that the sexual orientation of priests and seminarians does not matter, as long as they are celibate. Yet when gays come into positions of authority they knowingly and consistently appoint gay men to important key positions."

As fate would have it, Kellenyi did not return to Mundelein the next fall, which he said he would have preferred since he had made some good friends there. Instead, his new bishop wanted him to study and continue his priestly formation at the Catholic University of Louvain in Belgium, at which the American College seminary operated by the U.S. bishops is located. It was there that he would come into closer contact with the homosexual clique that dominates many seminaries.

At Louvain, Kellenyi's best estimate was that half of the theology seminarians were homosexual, based on their behavior, self-description, or "obvious flamboyance."

"The gay seminarians tended to hang out as a group, and made no effort to make me feel welcome at the school when I arrived," he recalled. But that was the least of the "arrogant display of homosexuality and power" he experienced at the school, he said. At the time of this writing, Kellenyi was in the United States seeking legal counsel about suing the seminary for sexual harassment in a case that promised to be similar to John Bollard's suit against the California Jesuits.

Kellenyi, who retained dozens of pages of documentary evidence, was expelled from the American College at Louvain after refusing to submit to an "intimate relationship" that was demanded by a senior seminarian. After he declined the gay seminarian's offer in no uncertain terms, he was labeled "homophobic" and denounced for not being "open to embracing gay and lesbian issues." Thus began months of a "gay rage" by the senior seminarian, he explained, who oddly was put in charge—although unofficially—of Kellenyi's priestly formation by then rector Father David Windsor. "My remaining time there at the American College seminary," said Kellenyi, "was a living nightmare."

"The way it worked," he explained, "I was expected to become this seminarian's best friend, hang out with him, socialize with him, spend my free time with him, and so forth. I was supposed to open myself up to him, discussing all my personal and formation issues with him as if he were my spiritual director. He would then report back to the rector. In other words, a big part of my theological, spiritual, and academic training was to consist of my learning from a homosexual who was obsessed with me. But also, he was to observe me, then 'intervene' and correct me in my personal formation. The relationship I was expected to have with him entailed him being my best friend, mentor, formation advisor, academic advisor, and quasi-spiritual director, all rolled into one. An obvious issue here is why any rector would think some seminarian is so wonderful that he should be given such a role."

Later in the semester, after Kellenyi had tried his best to keep his distance from this man, the senior seminarian informed him that if he was not willing to enter into a "relationship" with him, he and Father Windsor would make him want to leave the seminary. By that time, Kellenyi was aware that the gay seminarian who was placed in charge of his formation had become "obsessed" with him, and others noticed this as well. "I had been receiving unwanted attention from him for months," said Kellenyi. "He told me I had no idea how serious it was that I was avoiding him."

When Kellenyi raised the issue of this unwanted attention to a faculty member, Kellenyi was asked if he thought it was about sex. Kellenyi explained that it was not sex, but sexual harassment. "That is much more serious," he said. "There is a big difference. Sexual harassment very seldom involves an explicit demand for sex—most people are not that stupid. Sexual harassment involves both sex and power."

Kellenyi described the seminarian's interest in him not as a "crush," but as an "obsession, which goes way beyond mere sexual attraction. It was a brutal demand for close contact and that I completely submit to him."

Kellenyi explained that the obsession was manifest in several ways. First, he said, the seminarian told him that he thought of him all the time. "This was weird," Kellenyi commented, "because he said it while demanding that I be his 'friend.' Second, after he told me he thinks of me all the time, he went into great detail about how my body, my body language and my physical presence, affected him. It was obvious that he was staring at and watching me all the time. He told me one time that the way I was sitting in my chair made him want to fly across the room and grab me. This guy wanted me to alter my body language so it would not affect him so much. He went on and on about this in front of the rector. I had to explain to him why it was not normal for him to be so aware of, and upset by, my body language. Lastly, his written words on his peer evaluation of me clearly showed the nature of his obsession. They are very damaging. They reflect what he demanded of me verbally—he wanted to be involved in and control every aspect of my life. His words show his being hurt by my rejection of him, his sexual jealousy of my casual friendship with other seminarians. His obsession was a sort of 'fatal attraction.' He wanted absolute control and constant companionship."

In his rambling and often incoherent peer evaluation of Kellenyi, which Windsor assigned him to write, the seminarian wrote:

> I do not see any connection with his spirituality and his education. He is very critical of any of the concerns that are part of the Church today. Women's issues, gay issues, marginalized—all these are absolutely not important to Joseph.... He does not seem interested in learning from his peers. They are not engaged and [are] totally dismissed if they disagree with him. He has dismissed my input on many occasions with, "Well, we all know you are a liberal."...I do not see that he can interact with all groups in the community so I have to question that ability in general. He hangs out with the youngest members of the community and has no interest in close contact with the more senior members even after advances were made.... He shows no interest in learning what he needs to participate in the community.... Those people that he likes he spends time with, but he avoids those that will challenge and help him to grow. He does not want to change....Joseph is not at all open to other points of view. We have talked on more than one occasion so I think he will take time if asked but [he] does not initiate any conversations on his own with me.... I think Joseph may have many strengths but they are hidden. I think if he was only open to others that would be a huge step in the right direction.[15]

In general, the senior seminarian's evaluation of Kellenyi did nothing more than express his frustration and jealousy that Kellenyi was able to form friendships with others inside and outside of the seminary, while personally rejecting his own "advances." This evaluation stands in stark contrast to others that Kellenyi received, which described Kellenyi as "a brilliant thinker...outspoken proponent of the Church's principles and social teaching...dedicated to living out the lifestyle appropriate to a first year seminarian with genuine hopes of one day soon becoming a priest." Another seminarian wrote:

> I have concluded that Joe [Kellenyi] has a deep and very thoughtful concern, not only for the sanctity of the liturgy and communal prayer, but also for the mission of the Church as a whole in the world....Joe commands an impressive knowledge of secular and sacred history....His academic humility is the perfect complement to his academic prowess....He is friendly, knowledgeable and engaging, and shows some positive leadership tendencies....I experience Joe to be a fun, positive, life-giving person with which to live. Joe also tends to be fairly understanding of people and circumstances.[16]

Kellenyi explained the sexual harassment situation in a letter to the formation faculty at the American College. He used the term "sexual harassment," he said, because if the faculty failed to act it would create a legal liability for the seminary. The crux of the matter was that a senior seminarian who was obsessed with Kellenyi was placed in control, even if "unofficially," of his priestly formation by the rector. Repeated written complaints to Windsor and the formation faculty met with no palpable response. The student was able to continue to harass Kellenyi to the point of threatening that he would have Kellenyi thrown out of Louvain.

This threat subsequently came to pass, he said, in that the highly critical peer evaluation was given undue weight in determining Kellenyi's future as a Louvain seminarian. Although his formation advisor, Father Kevin Codd, wrote in his final evaluation of Kellenyi that "Joe is a person who seems to understand himself well, has a great deal of self-confidence and is committed to his pursuit of his academic and theological development. I support him as he continues on the path towards ministry in the Church,"[17] Kellenyi was not approved to continue his studies at Louvain. He was expelled.

Judging from Kellenyi's "Theology I Evaluation," assembled by the rector and dated April 25, 2000, one can conclude that the major issue of concern that led to his dismissal was his refusal to engage the senior seminarian in a close relationship. Repeating nearly verbatim from the highly critical peer evaluation, Windsor wrote: "My observation is that Joseph does not actively engage with his peers but rather connects better with those in the community who are twenty and twenty-one years of age. While one seminary student rightly observes that this is Joe's 'entry group,' and they were all outsiders together, it is worth addressing the cross-generational issue."

On August 25, 2000, Windsor wrote to Kellenyi informing him that the reason he was dismissed from the American College was for "calumny against The College and its personnel" and a "pattern of deception and abuse." The rector also informed Kellenyi, "In my opinion, you are in serious need of psychological help before you cause yourself and others untold damage."[18]

While Kellenyi was being expelled, the other seminarian was approved for ordination to the priesthood and is now a priest working in a U.S. parish.

Two years later, Kellenyi explained that it had been difficult to come forward with accusations of sexual harassment, especially since he knew he was placing his vocation in jeopardy by doing so. As a seminarian aspiring to the priesthood, "there is tremendous pressure to stay silent," he admitted, "but if I would have stayed silent I would have been complicit in the cover-up of a great moral evil."

■ ■ ■

Dr. Angela Sutcliffe,* a professor who taught for more than a decade at an East Coast seminary, said her experience confirms this (Sutcliffe insisted on remaining anonymous because she feared she would be physically harmed were she and her seminary named). The atmosphere concerning homosexuality she described as "borderline militant." Several of her students, members of one religious order in particular, she explained, "confided that they had been threatened repeatedly by other seminarians *and faculty* that if they did not submit to homosexuality they would be severely physically beaten and their 'careers' in that order would be in jeopardy."

They told Sutcliffe they had tried to seek help and advice from other superiors in their order, but they apparently received no help. Sutcliffe said she was careful to assure them that this was not what the Church or their order taught or condoned, and then sent them on to other priests who were more experienced and trained to help them deal with this abuse.

Not only were her philosophy seminarians being pressured by these superiors to espouse, defend, and take part in homosexual acts, but they were also pressured to confront Sutcliffe about her qualifications as a teacher because she openly held to the Church's position on homosexuality and other issues of sexual morality. While some seminarians were clearly unwilling to take up a posture against Sutcliffe, the self-proclaimed homosexual seminarians seemed to delight in doing so. They would aggressively confront her, she related, at the beginning of her courses about her "position" regarding homosexuality, and whether she agreed with what they scornfully called "Church authorities."

"If I attempted to gloss over the challenge and return to teaching philosophy, these students would interrupt me and demand that I 'take a stand,' " she explained. "Of course, gently and compassionately I did take a stand, and tried to explain why the Church teaches what she does concerning homosexuality." But this only served as an excuse for them to counter her and the Church's arguments in front of the other students during the class. One student even told Sutcliffe during class that he would "just simply refuse to learn anything" in her course. For the rest of the semester he took his place at a desk seat in the first row directly in front of her, folded his arms, took no notes, and glared at Sutcliffe. "I tried setting up meetings with him," she said, "but he refused any efforts at communication." Accordingly, he flunked all of his exams, after which he came to Sutcliffe and angrily threatened her. He apparently had expected that she would give him a passing grade in light of his own avowed homosexual orientation, despite having done none of the required work for the course and intimidating the professor on top of that.

One year, said Sutcliffe, she was advised by several of her students that "exhaustive methods" were being used by students and faculty members of this same religious order to spread untrue rumors to other faculty and students that she did not really hold a Ph.D., that she had flunked her comprehensives and was academically unqualified to teach anywhere, that the rector intensely disliked her, that she flunked any student who did not like St. Thomas, and "several other such baseless and silly rumors."

The homosexual clique at this seminary was very disturbing, she said. "There were some of the faculty members, particularly the younger ones, who were definitely homosexual. A number of the older faculty members were also. They would give sweetheart looks to one another, touching and flirting. They also tended to form alliances on the intellectual level on the faculty when needed."

The atmosphere was intensely hostile to anyone who did not subscribe to their militantly homosexual agenda, she said. Sutcliffe described the actions of some of the gay faculty members during faculty meetings as "hostile, immature, and childish, huddling together across the table, whispering and sending notes to each other, refusing to speak to me, or countering my every word."

For instance, Sutcliffe quoted Thomas Aquinas (who presented a convincing argument that homosexuality was an offense against the natural law) in one faculty meeting. Suddenly one of the faculty priests, whom she knew to be homosexual, leaped up out of his chair, almost climbed atop the table, and spit in her face. He told her, "We are sick and tired around here of hearing about Thomas Aquinas. I don't want to hear his name again." It took faculty members on either side of him to pull him away and restrain him.

Sutcliffe also recounted the story of Jonathan Whalley,* one particularly notable case of sexual harassment. Whalley came to her seminary from a small religious house of formation.[19] He took academic classes at the seminary and received his formation at the religious house. When he got into seminary, she said, he was constantly accosted by homosexual superiors. Although a homosexual himself, Whalley wanted to be chaste.

One night around 2:00 A.M. Sutcliffe received a call from Whalley. He was in the recovery room of a nearby hospital, and he had phoned to ask her for help. He had had emergency surgery, and the hospital chaplain wouldn't leave him alone, he complained. The chaplain was trying to molest him while he was in the recovery room.

So Sutcliffe drove over to the hospital and went up to Whalley's room to find the chaplain sitting on his bed and Whalley helpless and almost hysterical. "As I walked into the room the chaplain turned to me and looked as if he was going to bite my head off," she recounted. "He came stomping at me, and we were chest to chest, nose to nose, eyeball to eyeball. He was threatening me and I looked at him and said, 'You get out of this room and don't ever come near this seminarian again.' Then he finally did leave."

The gay priest chaplain was harassing him, she believed, because he knew Whalley was a seminarian and because Whalley was obviously in a vulnerable position.

A few weeks later Whalley placed a second late-night phone call. Again, he pleaded for her help. He told her he had just been kicked out of his religious house because he refused to submit to his superior's sexual advances. He told her that all of his belongings and clothes were out on the lawn.

He told her he had no place to go and that he'd called other seminaries but they refused to take him in. "So I got in my car and drove down to his neighborhood and found this seminarian sitting on the lawn of his religious house with all of his belongings. He was in tears," she explained.

The religious superiors began to see Sutcliffe as "a real troublemaker" because their seminarians now had someone to go to if their own superiors would not respond to their fears and anger and cries about being sexually harassed and assaulted by their superiors.

"I have been appalled at what I have seen," said Sutcliffe, whose position was eventually cut from the seminary because, seminary officials claim, they could not attract enough students.

Sutcliffe's years of experience were mainly with religious order priests and seminarians. From my own research, it appears that, although there is a very serious problem among seminaries that cater primarily to those training for the diocesan priesthood, the homosexual problem is deeper and more pervasive among the religious orders.

Although Sutcliffe was not referring to the Jesuits, the problems she related about her experience on the East Coast bear a striking resemblance to John Bollard's experience, which, as mentioned in Chapter 2, was made public by his May 1999 appearance on CBS's *60 Minutes*. At that time Bollard, a Jesuit scholastic (i.e., seminarian) from California, claimed he was subjected to unwanted sexual advances over a period of five years. He was seeking $1 million in damages:

> [Bollard's] idealistic image of the priesthood was shattered, he said, when he began receiving cards from Jesuit superiors depicting sexually aroused men— images he considered "shocking," he said. Bollard also told interviewers on "60 Minutes" that during his seven years as a Jesuit, at least 12 priests made unwelcome sexual advances and invited him to cruise gay bars. At first, he refrained from reporting the advances, he said, out of fear that he would jeopardize his future with the order. When Bollard did take his complaints to the Jesuit provincial in California, Father John Privett, they were brushed off, he said. He said Privett gave him a coffee cup that bore the words "no whining" and asked him to sign a paper releasing the Jesuits from legal liability. Bollard refused to sign. In his suit Bollard contended that he left the Jesuits because his life in the religious order had become intolerable.[20]

Typically those seminarians who are studying to be religious priests will receive their formation (which is much longer and more extensive than the formation for diocesan priests) at a "religious house," where they live in community with other members of their order. By the very nature of living in community, the effects of homosexual cliques at religious houses can provide even greater challenges and distress for the young man who accepts the teachings of the Church and rejects the militant homosexual agenda.

Once homosexuals come into positions of authority in their orders and in their religious houses of formation, it is difficult to attract even one heterosexual man to the order. Consequently, the impression given in some religious houses is that they are "gay houses," that is, made up of either all or a strong majority of homosexual priests and brothers. Those who remain and dissent from the dominant homosexual agenda are often ruthlessly persecuted.

Charles Enderby,* a former businessman from Ohio, was in his thirties when he began his novitiate for an East Coast religious order in the early 1990s. He was immediately struck by the outwardly "homosexual mannerisms" of some of the other novices. One of them, Joseph Mercado,* had worked as a massage artist before entering religious life. "He actually brought his massage table to novitiate," Enderby recalled.

While Mercado was only mildly open about his homosexuality, Franz Ascher* was "militant." Enderby described Ascher as a little man in his early forties who had a highly inflected voice. "He had a sense of humor," said Enderby, "but consistently mocked Church teaching on celibacy and particularly liked to mock Mother Angelica.[21] One day he even said he wanted to make sundresses out of the altar linens."

According to Enderby, Ascher began almost immediately to harass Geoffrey Raymond,* whom Enderby regarded as the only novice other than himself who was definitely not a part of the dominant gay subculture. Feeling threatened, Raymond confided in Enderby. He told him that Ascher first was trying to convince him that he, Raymond, was a "latent homosexual" who just needed to accept being gay. Ascher said it in a way that reminded Raymond of fundamentalists who claim that we just need to accept Jesus as our "personal Lord and Savior" in order to be saved. Ascher also claimed to know that

St. John the Evangelist was gay, and told Raymond that "St. Paul should have his balls cut off and shoved down his throat."

With Enderby's assistance, Raymond, who was in his early twenties, brought a complaint of sexual harassment to their novice master, Father Sixtus.* Although he acted concerned and sympathetic, said Enderby, the novice master took no action.

Ascher's harassing behavior continued, and a second complaint was made to Father Sixtus. This time the novice master appeared less sympathetic. "He literally threw up his arms and asked us," related Enderby, "what he was supposed to do if the vocations office keeps sending him gays."

"When Raymond and I complained the third time," said Enderby, "Father Sixtus threatened to kick us out. He was very angry with us, and we realized then that our novice master would do nothing to solve the problem of homosexual harassment."

A few months later, on a cold night in March of 1994, Enderby recounted, Raymond and Ascher were watching television in the community room, and each had been drinking wine. After Raymond retired to bed that night, Ascher entered Raymond's room uninvited—the doors had no locks—and sexually molested him. The next morning Raymond, angry and dejected, told Enderby what had happened and then informed him that he was leaving religious life. After a few brief words with Father Sixtus, Raymond bought train tickets and left, never to return.

Although Ascher later attacked and raped another novice, said Enderby, he emerged again with impunity. "Not only was he not asked to leave, he was promoted to the position of dean of novices, a position that had not even existed before that," said Enderby. "I can understand that homosexuals can sneak into the seminaries and religious life, but if discovered—especially raping two young men— they should be removed immediately."

But Ascher was not the only problem at the novitiate. Brother Thomas,* who taught a spirituality course, was also openly gay, sometimes "in an aggressive way," said Enderby. What was even more disturbing for him was that the vocations director for the province was also openly gay, according to Enderby.

It later became apparent that this vocations director was actively recruiting openly gay men. In October of 1993, twelve men had been recruited into the postulancy program.[22] Fortunately, said Enderby, "a solid priest served as master of postulants that year, and had ejected eleven of the twelve men from the program, allegedly for homosexual problems."

As a consequence of the gay subculture, Enderby's own spiritual life suffered deeply. Not only was grave injustice afoot, scandal was the plague of the day. He eventually left the order, understandably disgusted.

Once back out in the world Enderby contacted Raymond to tell him that he too had left the order. "It took him months before he could even set foot in a church again," said Enderby.

A final example comes from an author-priest. Father Norman Weslin began his studies for the priesthood in 1982, after his wife died. A former career U.S. Army officer, Weslin was ordained at the age of fifty-six. In his autobiography, *The Gathering of the Lambs*, published in 2000, he explained the homosexual atmosphere of Sacred Heart Seminary in Hales Corner, Wisconsin, a seminary that is suited especially for "late vocations."

In Weslin's estimation, "Forty percent of the seminarians at Sacred Heart were 'practicing homosexuals.' "[23] Explaining the extent of the problem there at that time, he wrote, "The rector, at one point, wrote a letter to all seminarians stating that those who were frequenting the homosexual bars in Milwaukee were causing the police to investigate complaints and that prudence was necessary to avoid scandal."[24] He also explained that classes were conducted to orient the seminarians toward accepting homosexuals and their homosexuality as a viable lifestyle. "Those heterosexuals who objected were singled out for psychiatric evaluation," he wrote.

"The homosexuals were well organized," he continued, "and since they had the support of the seminary authorities, they openly intimidated us heterosexuals. I was told to attend a psychiatric course because I openly resisted their intimidation and their effort to have homosexuality accepted in the seminary."[25]

■ ■ ■

The orthodox seminarian is presented with another predicament in this regard: If there is anything deviant or immoral going on at the seminary and he brings it to the attention of his superiors, he is likely risking expulsion. Many members of seminary faculties do not appreciate those who go to superiors with complaints, especially about sexual foibles. Reflecting on his experience at Mount Angel Seminary in Oregon, Father John Lewandowski remarked, "Many of my fellow students reminded me of the three monkeys: one with his hands over his eyes; one with his hands over his ears; and the other with his hands over his mouth." The maxim "See no evil, hear no evil, speak no evil" seems to be a standard survival tactic in seminaries. Yet that type of formation doesn't exactly prepare a seminarian to be a bold preacher of the Gospel. Nevertheless, that's the environment in which many priests are being formed today.

Countless other seminarians, driven out by the gay subculture, left in virtual silence. John Macarthur,* who attended a seminary in Waterloo, Ontario, that is now closed, was one such student. "I never told my parents nor later my wife that this was the 'real' reason for my leaving," he said. "They would have been scandalized."

"I still cannot believe that homosexuality was tolerated in the seminary," he added. "At one point I even questioned my own sexuality, wondering if I was the nut case because I wasn't 'gay' like many of the others."

Macarthur's comment raises another question—one that may be unanswerable right now—about seminaries that accommodate the gay subculture: Do some of the seminarians who attend such institutions "convert" to homosexuality while there?

In *The Changing Face of the Priesthood*, Father Cozzens concludes that not only has there been a "heterosexual exodus from the priesthood" due in part to the unrestrained gay subcultures in some seminaries, but also the resulting "overwhelmingly gay clergy culture will have an effect on how the laity views the priesthood and it will have an effect on incoming vocations. Potential candidates for the priesthood who are heterosexual will be intimidated from joining an institution where the ethos is primarily that of gay culture."[26]

Chapter 5

The Heterodoxy Downer

How False Teaching Demoralizes and Discourages the Aspiring Priest

When we were asked a question like "What is Original Sin," we couldn't answer what we thought the Church taught about Original Sin; we had to answer what the professor was claiming it to be. I had to do this the entire four years, which meant that I didn't come away from there completely unscathed—the system left a scar on everyone.
—Father Eduard Perrone, former seminarian,
St. John's Seminary, Plymouth, Michigan

Beyond issues of grave sexual immorality, the seminary environment presents a number of other deterrents to the orthodox seminarian. The most obvious and perhaps the most insidious is heterodoxy, open or subtle dissent from the official teachings of the Church. Many faculty members are averse to teaching what the Church teaches, and some find it onerous even to hide their disdain for Catholicism. The seminarian who arrives on campus expecting to find faculty and staff that love the Catholic faith and teach what the Church teaches can be sadly disappointed.

All too often seminary faculty members use textbooks written by noted dissenters from Catholic teaching—for example, theologians Richard McBrien, Edward Schillebeeckx, Hans Küng, and Charles Curran—and they parrot the dogmas of Catholic dissent: that the Bible is not to be taken seriously because it is "culture bound"; one religion is as good as the next; the pope is not infallible; the magisterium is authoritatively abusive; the Real Presence of Christ in the Eucharist is just an old pre–Vatican II myth; Christ was not really divine; God is feminine; Mass is simply a meal in which we should eat bread that "looks like real bread"; women should be ordained priests in the name of equality; homosexuality is normal; and contraception is morally acceptable.

This has been standard fare in many courses taught to future priests over the past thirty-odd years. Anthony Gonzales, a former seminarian at St. Patrick Seminary in Menlo Park, California, remarked on the content of the courses offered at his seminary: "The faculty followed everything from *Pascendi Dominici Gregis* down to the last detail." He was referring to Pope Pius X's encyclical which catalogued the errors of Modernism.

Yet many of the ideas being taught in seminaries today go way beyond the scope of even these "mainstream" errors of Modernist doctrine. Aggressive feminist theories often put forth by religious sisters devoted to liberation theology and various incarnations of Jungian psychology make it clear that some faculty members who are entrusted with the formation of future priests do not support the Catholic priesthood as the Church defines it. In fact, they do not support the Church, her hierarchy, her Eucharist, or her liturgy.

For seventeen years Sister Barbara Fiand, a sister of Notre Dame de Namur, taught at the Athenaeum of Ohio's seminary in Cincinnati before her teachings and attitude toward her seminarians were called into question publicly and she was subsequently dismissed. Her seven books betray a deep-seated animosity toward the Catholic Church, and the male, celibate priesthood in particular.

One of her courses was taught primarily from one text, her 1993 book *Embraced by Compassion*, which is in and of itself confirmation of seminarians' many complaints about her. In the book she denigrates orthodox Catholic theology as being obsessed with statements of the Creed (e.g., "I believe in God, the Father Almighty"), and proposes to replace this "misguided" and "boring" conceptual framework with one of her own, based on psychological conjecture.

Fiand also regards the Church's seven sacraments as superfluous because she believes salvation is attainable within oneself. "To be changed," she writes, "I need to see the self that I hate as other, as a man abandoned on the cross. That is my sacrament. That is my baptism. That is my bread and wine. That is my love."

Fiand's writings are an obvious target of criticism, considering that she was hired to teach and form young men into Catholic priests. Drawing upon the philosophies espoused by anti-Church personalities such as psychotherapist C. G. Jung, Fiand arrives at a theology that claims an "androgynous creator God." Since, as she claims forthrightly, she cannot accept the "Father" as the first person of the Blessed Trinity, she refers to God with the androgynous "Him/Her" throughout her books.

Fiand has also resolutely positioned herself as a critic of the Church and an enemy of sacred tradition. In her book *Releasement*, she is forthright about her support for the ordination of women to the priesthood. Fiand believes that the "stubborn resistance to the ordination of women, which uses nothing less than Scripture and tradition (misinterpreted though they may be) to justify itself, is probably the clearest example of the repressed feminine now turned sour." Elsewhere in the same book she writes, "When women in our churches... will be allowed to do what men have been doing for centuries, justice will have been served, without a doubt."

She also consciously places herself outside the Catholic Church, judging the Church's interpretation of Scripture to be erroneous. She proposes to supplant the authority of the Church with the "personal embrace of one's inner core," which she calls "releasement" in her 1987 book of the same name.

Father William H. Hinds, ordained for the Diocese of Covington in 1987, confirmed that Fiand never gave the impression in her seminary courses that she supported the Catholic priesthood as it is understood by the teaching authority of the Church. "She used to yell at me in the hallways," he said of his time at the Cincinnati seminary, "because she thought I was a pig-headed male." He added, however, that not only did Fiand disapprove of the orthodox seminarians—the few there were—but "she didn't even support the liberal, homosexual seminarians who went along with her program. She gave the impression that she wanted no man to be ordained a priest."

Richard Knighton,* a seminarian at the Athenaeum in 1985, was so disgusted with Fiand's attitude, and that of two other professors there, that he left the seminary even though to this day he still feels called to the priesthood. "I wasn't going to play that sort of game," he said of Fiand's teaching, which, he added, was not at all identifiable as Catholic, but served only to advance her own personal agenda.

Several other seminarians studying at Cincinnati's seminary a few years later agreed that she obviously disliked the idea of an all-male, celibate priesthood. In fact, they felt she was out to raze vocations to the priesthood.

Dr. Aaron Milavec, a former Marianist brother and professor of Church history and historical theology, taught at Cincinnati's Athenaeum for twelve years, until leaving in 1996 after an expelled student threatened to sue the seminary for falsely claiming to be imparting Catholic theology.

In 1995, Thomas J. Ruwe enrolled in Professor Milavec's course on "Medieval Christendom and the Reformations: 600–1600 C.E." The fact that the title of the course used the secular nomenclature of "C.E.," or "common era," rather than the Christian equivalent "A.D." (*anno Domini*, in the year of our Lord), was cause enough for pause. But the class, for Ruwe, would prove far worse.

Before Milavec's course began in September of 1995, Ruwe, who had enrolled through the school's Special Studies division, purchased the textbook at the Athenaeum bookstore in order to prepare for the first class. Reading through Milavec's *Exploring Scriptural Sources*, published by Sheed and Ward in 1994, Ruwe discovered that much of what the professor had written did not square

with the mind of the Church on biblical interpretation and fundamental Catholic doctrine.

Milavec advertised his book as a "case-study methodology that encourages students to reach their own conclusions." Before classes
even opened for the semester Ruwe wrote to Milavec with his observations of the textbook. He objected that the book "adopts the
Protestant approach to determining Christian truth, namely, if a
person, place, thing or event is not reported in the pages of the New
Testament, that person, place, thing, or event did not occur." In just
the first five pages of the book, Milavec ridicules everything from the
Church Fathers to the *Baltimore Catechism*, denies the Catholic doctrine of Original Sin, and disparages the tradition of the fallen angels. He begins by mocking the way he was trained in religion class
as a boy by the Ursuline sisters in Euclid, Ohio:

> When I was a young child, the story of salvation which
> I heard from the Ursuline nuns was so simple, so com-
> pelling, and so wonderful. Adam sinned and we inher-
> ited the consequences: the gates of heaven were sealed
> shut. For thousands of years people were dying, but no
> one was able to get into heaven. Everyone was waiting
> for God to send a redeemer. Then, Jesus finally ap-
> peared and died for our sins on the cross. And, as my
> *Baltimore Catechism* so clearly demonstrates, at the mo-
> ment that Jesus died on the cross, there, way up in the
> clouds, the gates of heaven were being opened. Finally
> the souls of all the good people who had died could
> enter heaven and be with God for all eternity.[1]

Milavec goes on to say that he was thirty years old before he "discovered" that what the Ursuline nuns had taught him was not a universal truth. To explain, he focuses his crosshairs on the Church
Fathers, especially St. Augustine, who, he claims, invented the concept of Original Sin. For the Church Fathers, he writes, "the Jewish
narratives surrounding the Garden of Eden took on an importance

they never had previously. For one thing, the 'serpent' was no longer
to be understood as the ancient Canaanite symbol of wisdom but as
an angel in disguise." Milavec reasons that because Genesis makes
no mention of "the fall" of the angels, it therefore did not occur. He
continues by claiming that St. Augustine invented the doctrine of
Original Sin in order to justify the baptism of infants, a contention
that is clearly at odds with the teaching of the Church. In contrast,
the *Catechism of the Catholic Church* teaches that "the account of the
fall in Genesis 3 uses figurative language, but affirms a primeval
event, a deed that took place *at the beginning of the history of man*.
Revelation gives us the certainty of faith that the whole of human
history is marked by the original fault freely committed by our first
parents."[2] The *Catechism* too devotes a whole section (nos. 391–395)
to "the Fall of the Angels."

Ruwe recognized that Milavec's required reading made no mention of the teaching authority of the Church on these issues or
others, such as whether penance and holy orders are presented as
sacraments in Scripture. That the Church has linked those sacraments to Scripture is "defined teaching, infallibly protected by God
the Holy Spirit," said Ruwe.

During the next class, according to Ruwe, Milavec stated that
"Jesus' death was not a sacrifice; the only thing that was on Jesus'
mind on Holy Thursday was the Passover, and not the institution of
the Eucharist."

"I asked Dr. Milavec," Ruwe told the *Hamilton Journal-News*, "if
Jesus did not ordain the Apostles, then who changed the bread and
wine into the body and blood of Christ? His answer: No one."[3]
Thus did Milavec, a professor hired to teach a generation of fu-
ture priests, deny two essential and fundamental doctrines of the
Catholic faith: the ministerial priesthood and the Real Presence of
Jesus in the Eucharist.

Ruwe then wrote to seminary rector Father Robert J. Mooney
(who soon thereafter left the priesthood to marry) and Cincinnati's
archbishop, Daniel Pilarczyk, advising them of Milavec's deficient

teaching. He also requested an investigation of Milavec's book and threatened to sue the seminary for consumer fraud in misrepresenting itself as teaching what the Catholic Church teaches.

Thomas Lustenberger, another of Milavec's students during the 1995–96 academic year, remembered his professor as a good-natured man with quite a sense of humor, but he too was surprised by what he called Milavec's "blatant heresy."

Milavec, recalled Lustenberger, explained that no Masses were ever said in the Roman catacombs during the first centuries of Christianity, which he repeatedly referred to as the "common era." He added that veneration of relics is not biblical and concluded that relics cannot be part of the authentic Christian tradition but rather are mere superstition conjured up in later centuries. Once he got those statements past his students with little objection, he escalated his attack.

Lustenberger, who taped Milavec's classes (and this writer has listened to the tapes), explained that he was not too impressed with the other students in the course: They were "docile, dull-witted, and as St. Paul says, 'itching for strange teachings.' "

"Most of them accepted everything hook, line, and sinker. No one except me ever questioned him on his teachings. His word was Gospel," he explained. Everything Milavec said in class, every move he made, was designed to undermine the Catholic faith, "and this man was teaching required courses to seminarians for twelve years," he added.

Two incidents stood out vividly for Lustenberger, who said on occasion he would challenge Milavec's conjectures and misstatements. During one class, Milavec explained that the source for the thinking that Christ's death on the cross was an atoning sacrifice was not the Christians of the early Church but rather St. Anselm in the twelfth century. Anselm, he explained, wrote a theological treatise on how he viewed Christ's death on the cross, and therefore Anselm "invented" the idea that Christ died to atone for our sins. The reason Milavec put forth such a theory was clear to Lustenberger: He

wanted people to think that Christ's sacrifice was simply an idea from
the Middle Ages, thus eliminating the sacrificial nature of Christ's
death and invalidating both the Mass and the Catholic priesthood.

"I thought that if I challenged him on this point," Lustenberger
explained, "he would just shoot me down. So here's what I did: I
raised my hand and quoted a verse from St. Paul (Col. 1:19–20), in
which he states the very same thing that Milavec attributed solely to
St. Anselm. I asked him if St. Anselm, with his medieval ideas, would
say something like this: 'For in Christ all the fullness of God was
pleased to dwell, and through him to reconcile to himself all things,
whether on earth or in heaven, making peace by the blood of his
cross. And you, who were once estranged and hostile in mind, doing
evil deeds, he has now reconciled in his body of flesh by his death, in
order to present you holy and blameless and irreproachable before
him, provided that you continue in faith.' And Milavec emphatically
replied yes, that's what St. Anselm would say. That's his kind of medieval thinking. And then I told him that I just quoted St. Paul from
Colossians. The thinking that Christ's death on the cross was not a
product of the twelfth century but really was there from the beginning, right there in the New Testament. St. Anselm was merely ex-
tending the metaphor that already existed in the early Church. After
I said that, there was dead silence in the room, but Milavec was quick
to recover. He told us that, of course, 'St. Anselm did not work in a
vacuum.' But it should have been clear to all at that point that the
necessity of the crucifixion was already known in the early Church,
despite the fact that Milavec wanted us to think that it was a false
idea that was invented 1,200 years later."[4]

Another incident revolved around the primacy of Peter, which
Milavec assailed from many angles. Lustenberger recalled how
during the course of one class Milavec taught that when Christ
changed Simon's name to Peter (Cephas) He was simply giving
Simon a nickname, like we might call someone Rocky. "His conclusion was that Peter was never made a pope. 'Peter' was just a nickname given to one of the apostles. So I objected to that too. 'This is

a moment of meaning, import, and drama and you're trivializing it down to Rocky?' " Milavec pressed on, he said, by saying that since St. Matthew's Gospel was the only one to record the incident it was nothing more than an "obscure passage." Lustenberger responded by saying that the wedding at Cana was only mentioned in John's Gospel, but that doesn't mean that it didn't happen.

With regard to seminary professors such as Fiand and Milavec, one may naively ask: Why don't they become Protestant theologians and Protestant seminary professors? In order to answer this question one must realize that the essence of their academic careers doesn't seem to be to teach their idiosyncratic theology, although that is a perquisite. It is to change the structure and mission of the Catholic Church. They appear to be teaching at Catholic seminaries primarily to train seminarians *not to be* priests.

Father Eduard Perrone of Detroit remembers his days at St. John's Seminary in Plymouth, Michigan, during the late 1970s. Much of the teaching he received there was similar to the theological and spiritual diet that seminarians received at the Athenaeum under the tutelage of professors such as Fiand and Milavec. "My experience was bad," he said. "We were fed very questionable theology. In fact, we read as much Protestant theology as Catholic material, and the professors were avowedly liberal in their outlook."

Many seminarians lost their faith there, he lamented. "One guy I remember in particular," he recounted. "He lost his faith because of a Christology course we were all required to take." In that course, Perrone explained, the seminarians were taught the German Protestant biblical exegesis popularized by German Lutheran Rudolf Bultmann,[5] and the first book they read was Albert Schweitzer's *Quest for the Historical Jesus*, which Perrone called "a very damaging book" that dismissed all of the Church's teachings as unreliable myths. "And we had similar books in the same vein."

Even worse, Perrone added, was watching some of his fellow classmates begin to accept the misleading teachings of Bultmann and like-minded scholars. "They were being formed, so to speak; there was a pressure to conform," he said. The few, like himself, who did not buy into what they were being taught only survived the program by writing on the tests and answering in class what the professors wanted to hear: "When we were asked a question like 'What is Original Sin,' we couldn't answer what we thought the Church taught about Original Sin; we had to answer what the professor was claiming it to be," Perrone said. "I had to do this for the entire four years, which meant that I didn't come away from there completely unscathed—the system left a scar on everyone. Even though some of us knew what they were teaching us was false, we never fully discovered what the truth was. When someone gives you a contrary opinion, you sharpen your wits a bit, but all that time we could have been learning a lot of good stuff in those classes."

Many other seminarians who refused to regurgitate what they were learning were dismissed for being "rigid" and "narrow-minded," while a few other students left almost immediately. "They were the ones," said Perrone, "who sensed straightaway that something was seriously wrong."

Scott Ballor ran into similar circumstances during his two years as a seminarian at the Oblate School of Theology in San Antonio, Texas. Ballor left the seminary after two years, he said, precisely because the school was not teaching the Catholic faith. First, he recounted, the primary textbook used in his Basic Theology course was *Catholicism* by noted dissenter Father Richard McBrien. His textbook is one of the few that have received a censure by the National Conference of Catholic Bishops, meaning that the text, due to its errors and omissions, should not be used in the education of future priests.[6] "Other required texts," he added, "were written by other noted dissenters such as Hans Küng and Charles Curran."

Ballor, who was studying to be a priest for the Diocese of Phoenix, set down his seminary memories in two articles he published in *Catholic Sense*, a newsletter that circulated among orthodox Catholics mainly in the Southwest. At that time, in the mid-1990s, many people were absolutely shocked by his claims, figuring that the teaching couldn't be as bad as he made it out to be. Yet Ballor's account reflects nothing that has not been recounted by dozens of other seminarians and priests across the U.S. and beyond.

The Catholic faith was undermined from many directions. For example, in a Church History class, said Ballor, the instructor claimed that Jesus did not intend to found a hierarchical Church, and that there was no authority structure in the early Church. He was also astonished at claims made in his Fundamentals of Moral Theology course. In the first week of school, he recalled, "the instructor led the class in a session of joking about and ridiculing the moral theology manuals that predated Vatican II. It was a shameful display of mocking and lambasting the Church."

Worse than the actual teaching at the school, however, was the atmosphere there, said Ballor. "There were three terms that were frequently used at Oblate School of Theology: 'openness,' 'tolerance,' and 'pastoral.' Although never formally defined, it seemed to me," he said, "as though they were used as follows: 'Openness' meant we must be open to other perspectives including heretical ones. 'Tolerance' meant we must tolerate deviations from our moral and doctrinal beliefs to the point of abandoning our beliefs. 'Pastoral' meant anything goes; don't deny anything to anyone except those who accept the traditional teachings of the Church."

Amid these chants for "openness" and "tolerance," Ballor pointed out, the Oblate school was conspicuously "close-minded and intolerant" when it came to considering traditional Catholic viewpoints, those for example that can be found in the *Catechism of the Catholic Church*. His Christology professor, he said, even defined tradition as the "living faith of the dead" and traditionalism as the "dead faith of the living."

"The theological relativism, false ecumenism, and the loss of the missionary imperative that I experienced there was very upsetting and heartbreaking. I feel sorry for any seminarian who is sent to this school," Ballor concluded, summing up his reasons for leaving the Oblate seminary.

Often the heterodox teaching being presented to seminarians involves the hot-button issues of sexual morality. What has come to be known as the "Sex Text" scandal at Mount Angel Seminary in St. Benedict, Oregon, illustrates well the magnitude of the deviance from Catholic teaching proffered to aspiring priests.

In 1991, Dr. Robert Torres, the staff psychologist who had been providing psychological evaluations and counseling to seminarians for years there, taught a human sexuality class mandated for pretheology and first-year theology students using the textbook *Our Sexuality*, by Robert Crooks and Karla Baur.

When Torres began his course in September, according to Father John Lewandowski, a Mount Angel seminarian at the time, he held up the book and explicitly stated twice that *Our Sexuality* was written by two "good Catholic authors" and that "there is nothing in the book that is opposed to Catholic teaching today."

Yet early in the book, which the publisher claims is the most widely used textbook in college sexuality courses in the U.S., the authors candidly admit to "some biases" they have against two themes of human sexuality that "are of longstanding in our culture." The first, they say, is that sex is for reproduction:

> Many people have learned to view [foreplay] activities and other practices—such as masturbation, sexual fantasy, and anal intercourse—with suspicion. The same is true of sexual activity between members of the same sex, which certainly does not fit into the model of intercourse for reproduction. All these noncoital sexual behaviors have been defined at some time as immoral, sinful, perverted, or illegal. We will present them in the text as viable sexual options for those who choose them.

The other theme the authors admitted opposing is the "rigid distinction between male and female roles." Crooks and Baur believe that "rigid gender-role conditioning limits each person's full range of human potential and produces a negative impact on our sexuality."

"The idea of sex for reproduction," they explain, "is associated with Judeo-Christian tradition. Childbearing was tremendously important to the ancient Hebrews. Their history of being subjected to slavery and persecution made the Hebrews take action to preserve their people—to 'be fruitful and multiply, and replenish the earth' (Gen. 1:28)."

In the course of explaining their bias, Crooks and Baur assail Thomas Aquinas's teaching on human sexuality. St. Thomas, they write, "maintained that human sexual organs were designed for procreation and that any other use—as in homosexual acts, oral-genital sex, anal intercourse, or sex with animals—was against God's will and therefore heretical. Aquinas's teachings were so influential that from then on homosexuals were to find neither refuge nor tolerance anywhere in the Western World."

Thus their bias against believing that human sexuality is primarily designed for sexual reproduction belies their advocacy of homosexuality, oral sex, male-to-female anal intercourse, and even bestiality, each of which is an obvious contradiction of Church teaching. Indeed, the rest of the textbook, lavishly illustrated with drawings of different positions for sexual intercourse, close-up photographs of women's breasts and pubic areas to show how all are different, photographs of men and women who have had sex-change operations, photos of various contraceptives and sex devices, supports the advocacy of these sexual variants and explains and illustrates them in graphic detail.

"A lot of the seminarians were just struck dumb by this book," explained Lewandowski. "They were confused. They didn't know what to say. You expect to see this stuff out in the world, but in the seminary it's shocking."

The following are direct quotations from the text that illustrate the lengths that the authors went in order to render their overtly un-Catholic view of human sexuality (EXPLICIT DESCRIPTIONS FOLLOW):

- "Sexual fantasies may also help overcome anxiety and facilitate sexual functioning or compensate for a somewhat negative sexual situation. For example, a woman who is bored with her marital relationship states the following: 'When having intercourse with my husband of 17 years, I often fantasize that I am taking a young virgin male to bed for the first time. I show him what I want done to me just the way I like it, while at the same time giving this poor young boy an experience he will long remember.' " (An oriental block print shows a young woman fantasizing about having intercourse with her lover while she masturbates.)

- "A woman's masturbation fantasy: I fantasize about being seduced by another woman. Although I've never had an affair with another woman, it makes me sexually excited to think of oral sex as being performed on me or vice versa. A man's masturbation fantasy reflects one study's findings that one in three men have same-sex fantasies."

- "Masturbation has been a source of social concern and censure throughout Judeo-Christian history. The state of affairs has resulted in both misinformation and considerable personal shame and fear. Many of the negative attitudes toward masturbation are rooted in the early Judeo-Christian view that procreation was the only legitimate purpose of sexual behavior." (Explicit sketches of men and women masturbating accompany text.)

- "You may wish to experiment with using body lotion, oil, or powder. After the gentle stroking try firmer massaging pressures, paying extra attention to areas that are tense.... Specific techniques for masturbation vary. Males commonly grasp only the penile shaft with one hand, as shown in figure 9.1. Up and down motions of differing pressures and tempos provide stimulation."

- "If you want to use a vibrator for sexual pleasure, experimentation is in order." (Accompanying sketch illustrates female masturbation.)

- "...masturbation can be considered a normal part of each partner's sexual repertoire."

- "Readers who would like to experiment with some or all of the steps are invited to do so.... Try to clear your mind of thoughts related to the 'rightness' or 'wrongness' of self-pleasuring and allow yourself to concentrate instead on the positive physical sensations that can come from self-stimulation." (Accompanying photos depict four types of vibrators.)

An entire chapter is then dedicated to "masturbation exercises," followed by another chapter devoted to: "Specific Suggestions for Women Becoming Orgasmic." One sketch accompanying that chapter shows mutual oral-genital stimulation. Yet the sketch appears to be of two *men* performing oral sex on each other. Then Crooks and Baur devote themselves to a section on "anal stimulation," which provides step-by-step instructions on how best to have anal intercourse.

In their chapter on homosexuality, in addition to providing detailed information and illustrations on oral and anal sex, the authors discuss the option of having an "open coupled" relationship, having one primary sex partner along with many auxiliary partners; and a gay couple is shown in a photo being married by a minister of the Metropolitan Community Church in Honolulu.

A chapter on contraception, entitled "Burden of Fertility," is equally biased against Church teaching and the natural law. The authors describe the Catholic view of contraception this way: "Many contemporary religions favor the use of birth control. Furthermore, there is great diversity of views among leaders of the Catholic Church. For example, a study commissioned by the Catholic Theological Society of America states that 'the mere fact that a couple is using artificial means of birth control cannot provide sufficient basis to make a judgment about the morality or the immorality of their married life and sexual expression.' "

Back in the Human Sexuality class, the professor's own biases seemed to mimic those of the authors, and Dr. Torres proved that he could be equally bizarre in his teaching. According to a 1991 handout to his students, he asked the following questions of his seminarians:

- "Are you comfortable using sexual words? Thinking about your own sexual story? What is your level of body awareness?"

- "Are there any ways in which you have been sexually abused as an adult? Sexually embarrassed? Sexually shamed? Abused others?"

- "What is the content of your sexual fantasy life today? Are there any evidences of violence toward others? Manipulation? Self-depreciation? Note: A healthy sexual fantasy involves picturing yourself in situations which are pleasuring, mutual, age appropriate, and in no way violating of another."

- "How do you deal with your sexual feelings? What are your experiences of self-pleasuring? Do they seem balanced and healthy to you? With whom can you talk about your sexual feelings? Sexuality?"

- "If you were to talk with your genitals, what would you like to say to them? What would they like to say to you?"

"Torres," related Lewandowski, "openly told seminarians that it was important for them to feel comfortable with their sexual orientation, 'whatever it may be.' " His view of life, in the opinion of Tom Hartigan,* another former Mount Angel seminarian, is that "every problem in life is a sexual problem, based largely on sexual repression, and the solution is sexual liberation."

"There were many young men who were obliged to take Professor Torres's class," said Lewandowski, in his forties at the time, "who were confused by what was being taught. Because they were lacking in knowledge of their faith—perhaps through no fault of their own—and proper moral teaching, some appeared to embrace these gross errors; others were just shocked. I really feel that I would have incurred some guilt were I to have let this go unchallenged. I cannot stand by and watch my brother's faith and morals be destroyed."

Consequently, Lewandowski took up the issue with his formation director, the academic dean, and finally with the rector—all to no avail. "I asked the rector that I be released from this course," he said, "on grounds that it was against my conscience to participate in a course of study that took a blatant and directly immoral stand against Church teaching. My hope was that, at the very least, he would permit me to fulfill my academic requirements with another course or independent study, or at best in suspending use of *Our Sexuality* at Mount Angel Seminary."

Lewandowski was informed by the rector, Father Patrick Brennan, that it was a required course and that he could not be dispensed from it without permission from his bishop. At that point he informed the local bishop of the matter. In a letter dated September 13, 1991, he wrote:

> I am absolutely appalled by the content of the textbook being used for the Human Sexuality (required) course, *Our Sexuality* by Robert Crooks and Karla Baur. I think you would agree that the pictures go far beyond any useful instruction or healthy "need to know" regarding human sexuality. Needless to say, they are in several cases, perverse and pornographic . . . I am especially concerned with the open invitation the authors give the reader, "to experiment in the various methods of masturbation," with the instruction to suspend any thoughts of the "rightness" or "wrongness" of masturbation. In other words, we are to deny that faculty which is essential to the formation of a "good" conscience. We should deny ourselves the formation of conscience, which is absolutely essential to be in accord with the Church's moral and ethical teachings for good actions.
>
> The authors do not just present the so-called facts of life. They implicitly and explicitly espouse what the Catholic Church has always taught as objectively sinful activity. The authors deliberately encourage the reader to "experiment" with masturbation, "self-loving," and "self-pleasuring" techniques, with ample pictures of

both male and female in the act of masturbation. Male and female, and male and male partners are shown in the act of mutual oral stimulation of the genital area.

We as seminarians should not have to wade through a sea of trash to redeem a smidgen of truth; indeed no good Christian should have to. Today's modern psychologists would have us believe that we must see, feel, and touch, and even experience every kind of deviant activity. That we must know all the sordid details "experientially" of the fallen "human condition," in order to understand them. This is false!

Lewandowski photocopied many of the pages of the book and sent them along with his letter, as evidence to Portland's archbishop, William J. Levada.[7] But it was only after the "Sex Text" scandal was made public in the pages of *The Wanderer* that the seminary took any action. In fact, when *The Wanderer* first contacted Father Brennan about the use of the textbook in one of Mount Angel's required courses, he acknowledged the text was used but denied that there were any problems with the book.

"Father Brennan felt this material was really needed," said one seminarian. "His point of view is that this is what is out in the world, and we should know it so that we can counsel people. He's concerned that there's a lot of pedophilia among the clergy and the bishops are concerned about it, and the seminary's response to the bishop's concerns is more sex education.' "[8]

In an editorial in *The Wanderer*, Al Matt Jr. asked the obvious:

> Why did such a foul text find acceptance in a Catholic seminary in the first place? What of the competency and integrity of Prof. Torres, who selected the book? What about the judgment of the rector, Father Brennan, who not only allowed the text to be continued in use after complaints were made, but who entrusts Torres with psychological assessment of seminarians—

a role that likely determines which men are admitted and which are not? And what does one say about the pastoral vigilance of Archbishop Levada and his supervision of the key institution in his diocese? ...

In the case of this scandal involving *Our Sexuality*, both Father Brennan and Archbishop Levada warned the editor of the potential for scandal if *The Wanderer* were to publish the details of this sordid situation. Father Brennan even went so far as to suggest such a report could "destroy the seminary." ... However, all of the evidence suggests that those in authority did not intend to summarily remove the text from the course nor remove the offending Prof. Torres. ...

One would hope that this tragic instance of corrupting the minds and morals of future priests within the very precincts of a seminary is an isolated case. Reports as well as conversations we have had with hundreds of laity and priests over the past few years suggest it is not.[9]

Only after Mount Angel received such negative publicity did Archbishop Levada order that use of *Our Sexuality* be discontinued.

Joseph Trevelyan,* who is now a prominent Catholic layman (who still aspires to the priesthood), began his seminary studies at Mount Angel the year after the "Sex Text" scandal. "I went there from the pretheologate at Franciscan University in Steubenville, so it was like going from the mountaintop to the Garden of Gethsemani," he explained. "I was apprised of what was going on there but I didn't know it would be quite as bad as it turned out to be."

One of the problems he encountered during his year there was the deference paid to nonseminarian students, who took classes alongside seminarians and, in some cases, non-Catholic seminarian students. The most vivid example Trevelyan recalled was Frodo Okulam, a professed "witch" and lesbian activist who was studying to be an ordained minister for the Metropolitan Community Church, which caters exclusively to gay, lesbian, bisexual, and transsexual persons.

"She had her own study carrel in the library," he said, "and she had pro-gay symbols like the pink triangle all over her cubicle and on her clothes. She drove around with witch bumper stickers on her car, and she shoved her ideas 'in your face.' " And when she wore her black leather suits with "witch hats" on campus, he added, "if the seminarians were to object to her, they would be persecuted."

Trevelyan recalled that the "witch" hung out with one of the nuns who was studying at Mount Angel. "This nun had a bumper sticker on her car that said, 'Magic is alive and the goddess is afoot!' "

"In the Church History class we were walked through William Jurgens's text on the Faith of the Early Fathers," said Trevelyan. "I remember we were coming up to this section on sexual morality, about what the Fathers of the Church said. We were reading along one day and all of the sudden the professor, a priest, skipped over a bunch of hard sayings on sexual morality because this lesbian witch was sitting right there in class. I guess he didn't want to offend any professed lesbian seminarians. He clearly wanted to give the impression that we Catholics are open and embracing, and that we can believe whatever we want."

Although Trevelyan left after just a year of study at Mount Angel—he dropped out for fear of being unfairly expelled and therefore blacklisted from other seminaries—Frodo Okulam[10] graduated from the Catholic seminary on Mother's Day in 1995. Okulam, who calls herself "priestess of the goddess," went on to serve as coordinator of SisterSpirit, an organization formed in 1985 in Portland, designed to "birth a women's spiritual community." SisterSpirit promises a "safe space" to reclaim spiritual traditions from "patriarchal guilt and fear."[11] On graduation day, Okulam attended the ceremonies at Mount Angel, where she posed for several pictures with rector Father Brennan and her friends. Portland's *Catholic Sentinel* wrote up the graduating news, reporting that after she received her master's degree, she would "continue [her] work in Portland."

"The worst part about the matter of having a witch attend your seminary," said Trevelyan, "is the persecution you get by faculty when you object to the witch's presence and her attitude toward the Church. This was very demoralizing for many of the men there."

Dr. Louise Leidner,* who taught students from the Washington Theological Union (WTU) in Washington, D.C., for several years during the 1990s (although she did not teach *at* WTU but another Washington-area seminary), complained about the education her students were receiving at this Catholic seminary, which educates mainly seminarians from a number of religious orders that consider themselves progressive in Church matters. She said her Catholic seminarian students had been educated over the years with arguments as to why divorce, premarital sex, homosexuality, adultery, abortion, euthanasia, and in vitro fertilization were morally acceptable.

"If other students in the class objected, they were mocked," she said. "Yet these same students are not prepared academically to address these issues from any scholarly familiarity with the Bible itself or with any Church history, natural law theory, encyclicals, instructions, declarations, or other Church documents."

Some seminarians from WTU expressed their concerns to her that in their formation programs they were required to use very strange Gnostic and New Age methods, e.g., enneagrams, crystals, paraliturgies, tarot cards, ouija boards, and so on.

"Unfortunately these old heretical, pagan, pantheistic Gnostic ideas and theories, which historically can be traced as far back as 2000 B.C., are definitely back in style," she explained, "and are rapidly having a serious impact. What is amazing to me is that almost no one in the Church—especially in the seminaries—seems to be aware of it, to be able to identify Gnosticism when they see it, or understand that it is the larger umbrella under which many of the above concerns fall. Gnosticism is quite clever, and approaches especially religious people and institutions in terms of 'gentleness,' 'love,' 'peace,' 'caring,' 'forgiveness,' and 'spirituality.' As a teacher, it is abundantly clear to me, as it is to any teacher, that you can't teach what you don't have. If the teachers at WTU don't know the teachings of the Church, or despise them, then what they teach will not be the truths of the Catholic Church but their own 'truths' and a hatred of the Church."

Leidner related that her experience over the years consisted of "a constant stream of their seminarians coming to me out of desperation to express their concerns about being discriminated against if they contradict the popular view." Plurality of opinions seems to be acceptable only if those opinions confirm and agree with the dominant dissident theories at WTU, she added. "I have even had their students come to me concerned about not trusting their superiors to keep their solemn confidences in confession or in formation matters. Some students have confided to me that it was necessary to go to 'outside' confessors in order to find confidentiality, spiritual help, and guidance, which often takes the form of advising the students not to 'rock the boat' and to get out of WTU and into different religious orders that are loyal to the Church.

"Often my orthodox students are publicly mocked by their WTU peers and by WTU faculty and superiors for taking positions consonant with the Church's teaching. Accordingly, these students are isolated, left out of programs, meetings, and activities, and made to feel that they were 'weird.' My students also complain of their phone calls and mail being unduly monitored by superiors suspicious of them and antagonistic towards them."

Several of her students, Leidner related, were actually kicked out of their religious houses because they expressed orthodox opinions that were "dangerous and harmful to other people." She recalled one incident in which two of her students at WTU were suddenly informed by their superiors that they had twenty-four hours to pack their bags and get out of the WTU in midsemester because their orthodox ideas, those you would find in the *Catechism*, would "negatively infect and unduly influence and contaminate" the other students.

These two students came to her the next day distressed, she recalled, trying to explain why they could not finish their course with her. "They both angrily packed their bags that afternoon and immediately left Washington altogether, probably having lost their vocations as well as their faith in the process. These boys were kind, gentle, very bright and talented students," Leidner lamented.

■ ■ ■

Being exposed to dissenting opinions in a Catholic seminary seems to have demoralizing effects on seminarians. It is not only academic struggles that seminarians must endure, but formation struggles as well. At the typical American seminary each student will be assigned to a "formation team," a group of priests, nuns, and laypeople who are charged with the spiritual formation of those in their care. One person in the formation group usually serves as a spiritual advisor and confessor. The formation team almost always recommends to the rector whether a student will pass on to the next stage of formation, including ordination, or be discarded as unsuitable for the Catholic priesthood.

Lawrence Redding,* a seminarian at Sacred Heart School of Theology in Hales Corner, Wisconsin, considers himself orthodox in the Catholic faith. He said he cannot say as much for his seminary, where any attempt to embrace what the Church teaches is viewed as being "ultraconservative, rigid, and unwilling to learn."

"My formation class is headed by two people," Redding explained, "a discontented priest and a liberal nun who both support homosexuality and abortion issues, along with stem cell research." During the weekly "formation class," he said, "we start with a liberal interpretation of a Gospel, and then receive a photocopied handout from the *Program of Priestly Formation*. We then skim through the document, never discussing it thoroughly, and move quickly on to the 'spirituality' portion of the class."

According to Redding, this often involves handouts "bashing the Church from disreputable authors such as Charles Curran" and "the liberal writings of Archbishop Rembert G. Weakland."

"We discuss these articles in depth and the formation team carries on about how insightful and wonderful these people are. We are then subjected to watching Anthony DeMello[12] videos for a half hour. To conclude the session, the nun goes into a fifteen-minute

'Consciousness Examen' while we all sit there and endure this tor-
ture." Redding's formation team, he added, views any ideas or opinions that are taught by the Church, expressed by seminarians, as
"disruptive and nonproductive."

In some schools seminarians are so upset about the formation
they're receiving they "go outside" the seminary—though they
cannot do so openly—for proper spiritual direction.

Mark Gaskell,* who attended St. Ambrose University for one
year as a seminarian for the Diocese of Davenport, Iowa, remembers that the spiritual formation director for seminarians, Father
Edmund Dunn, was an outspoken critic of the Church, not
someone Gaskell thought was a logical choice to form young men
who aspire to the priesthood. Indicative of his viewpoint, in 2000,
Dunn told *Quad City Online*'s "Progress 2000" that the challenges
facing the Catholic clergy—most notably, a shortage of priests—will
continue into the next century "until the ordained ministry opens
up more. And married and female clergy could likely become com-
monplace in the next century."[13]

Gaskell said that Dunn's pessimistic outlook on the ordained
ministry had an "extremely negative effect" on some of the seminarians. "He seemed to enjoy being a provocateur, and attacked
Church teaching at every opportunity," he said of Dunn, who, he
added, was a spokesman for the dissenting Catholic group Call to
Action of Iowa.

As a result, seminarians received spiritual formation that was
equal to the type of teaching they received at St. Ambrose. Gaskell
said he recalls being equally shocked at what he was being taught.
In one course, Father Drake Shafer, whom Gaskell remembers as
always dressing in a necktie and suit, promoted Matthew Fox's
"creation spirituality."

"Fox, of course, was a former Catholic priest," he explained, "who
left the Catholic Church to become a collaborator with the self-
professed witch who calls herself Starhawk."[14] Maverick theologian
Fox's book *Original Blessing: A Primer in Creation Spirituality Presented in Four Paths, Twenty-Six Themes, and Two Questions*,[15] which

presents an "alternative" to the Catholic Church's teaching on Original Sin, was used as the textbook for the course.

A similar perspective was given seminarians who took philosophy courses from Father William Dawson, said Gaskell. "We began each class period with a Buddhist meditation and studied the 'Gaia principle'—worship of Mother Earth," he recalled. "We also studied Joseph Fletcher's 'situation ethics.' It was an environment in which there were very clear taboos against expressing orthodox views."

"I found these 'open and enlightened' professors at St. Ambrose to be very cowardly," Gaskell reflected. "They were prepared to attack Church teaching, but they were not prepared to defend their own views. One professor, a graduate of the Biblicum in Rome, told the chairman of the theology department that he would never have me in another class, because I challenged his particular take on the historical-critical method."

Father Edward Corrigan,* ordained for a midwestern diocese in the mid-1990s, studied at St. Paul Seminary in Minnesota, where, he recalls, there were "deep-seated problems." The final straw there for Corrigan was a classroom incident in which a nun instructor encouraged all of the seminarians to get on their hands and knees on the floor and pretend they were cats—rubbing their "whiskers" up against each other. Corrigan was fortunately transferred to a more conservative seminary where he was able to receive a proper formation and education.

Two years after Father Antony Marsdon* was ordained for a Texas diocese, he joked that he was "still overjoyed and enthusiastic about the priesthood." He said this in jest not because he is anything but overjoyed and enthusiastic, but "because most every priest-professor I had in seminary seemed unfulfilled, angry, and altogether hostile to the Church and her teachings. Of all the professors I studied under, only one was faithful to the magisterium and he was a lay convert."

He added: "It didn't take long to realize that my particular seminary had an agenda, and it wasn't, shall we say, that of Holy Mother Church. One professor, a priest, who supposedly taught Patristics, was no more interested in what the illustrious Fathers had to say than Hollywood is interested in sound morals and integrity. All one needed to do was bash the Church, point out how chauvinistic and anti-Semitic she was, and you got an A. What I learned, sadly, about the Church Fathers, I learned on my own. By the way, I never saw a priest in his clerics unless there was a bishop coming to ordain someone or visit his seminarians. Then all of a sudden, as if by magic, *voila*, they looked like priests. The litany of abuses and erroneous teaching goes on and on, from hostile nuns with axes to grind, to the formation teams wanting to be 'sensitive to the plight of homosexuals.' On one occasion, at Mass, one of the nuns got up for the homily and asked everyone to stand. Then she asked all the men to sit down. When we had done so she remarked, 'How does it feel to be excluded?' "

Marsdon, a "late vocation," admits that he only survived because his theology was well formed long before he entered the seminary. He saw that, for himself at least, there was no need to object to the conflicting teachings he received while a seminarian. "My theology was chiseled in stone," said Marsdon. He felt that he knew his faith, was comfortable with what the Church taught, and saw no need to change his viewpoint.

But for most younger seminarians who are not buoyed by such confidence, the seminary experience can be frustrating if not confusing. When the orthodox seminarian objects to false teachings, he is often mocked and ridiculed for his "old-fashioned" views (even though these are the views that are enunciated in the contemporary *Catechism* published in 1992), called immature or infantile, and singled out for particularly harsh treatment. Again, "plurality of opinions," a much-espoused doctrine in seminaries, is only respected if the seminarian's opinions confirm and agree with the dominant dissident theories at the seminary. Psychological abuse and manipulation in this regard is terribly damaging to the orthodox seminarian. It also leads to loss of faith—and worse.

Dr. Angela Sutcliffe,* who taught in seminary for twelve years, not only corroborates this conclusion—she has witnessed many such cases of lost faith—she adds that "seminarians are not the only ones vulnerable to losing their faith; so too are the good and loyal faculty members who struggle to teach the Church's teachings—clergy and lay."

As for the majority of professors who make up the faculties of American seminaries, Wisconsin priest Father Charles Fiore, another person intimate with the situation, asked:

> If an engineer working for the Space Program were discovered to have deliberately and in knowing violation of procedures used faulty parts, is it likely that he would be retained by that program?
>
> Then why are men and women who clearly do not understand and apparently do not believe the teachings of the Church allowed to educate, form, and train seminarians who will be entrusted with the souls of the faithful? Whatever can rectors and bishops who permit the use of alien texts and alienated professors be thinking? No wonder good and faithful pastors are discouraged from sending young men to study for the priesthood, when all too often [the seminarians] are subverted in their faith and perverted in their morals!
>
> If the bishops and rectors don't know that this kind of rot is eating away at the innards of the Church, at its future vitality, that's misfeasance. If they do know but do nothing to stop it, that's malfeasance! And the faithful should demand top-to-bottom house cleanings where such situations exist! Certainly they are not morally obliged to financially support this ecclesiastical incompetence.[16]

Overt heterodox teachings and attitudes—what Fiore calls "rot"—on the part of seminary faculty members and others charged with the formation of future priests not only result in the "miseducation" of the clergy, who transfer their teachers' attitudes to Catholics in their care, they also contribute significantly to the decline of orthodox vocations. Many good men who are aspiring priests either are driven out of the seminary system for refusing to embrace the political agenda of the day or walk away from their vocation disgusted with the seminary and disenchanted with the Catholic Church. Others, sadly, also suffer a great loss of faith.

CHAPTER 6

Pooh-Poohing Piety

How Traditional Expressions of the Faith
Often Disqualify the Orthodox Seminarian

There were psychological screws under which we seminarians were constantly pressed. The fact was, we had to hide devotion to Mary and to the Eucharist, or any other pious exercise of faith which was not on the list of acceptable activities.

**—Father John Lewandowski, former seminarian,
Mount Angel Seminary, St. Benedict, Oregon**

Liturgical piety is used as another reason for discrimination against the orthodox seminarian. The powers that be in many seminaries have been perplexed over the past few years by the increasing demand by students for traditional devotions such as Eucharistic adoration, benediction of the Blessed Sacrament, public rosary, and novenas.

In response to this, the orthodox seminarian is too often denied the opportunity for Eucharistic adoration and forbidden to pray the rosary anyplace but in his own room. During Mass, it is not uncommon for the priest celebrants, especially those who teach liturgy, to take great liberties with the liturgical rubrics. It is common too for seminarians to be forbidden, against their better judgment and intuition, to kneel at the proper parts of the Mass, such as during the Eucharistic prayer.

One priest said of his seminary days: "It seems like they wanted to break us of any 'romantic notions' we may have had of how Mass ought to be celebrated." And, he observed, this continues after ordination when, it seems, young orthodox priests are placed in parishes with liberal pastors who still fancy 1970s-style liturgical experimentation.

But liturgical abuses—experimentation with inclusive language, seminarians reading parts of the Eucharistic prayer, celebrants with no vestments, standing through the Eucharistic consecration, coffee-table Masses in priests' suites, illicit matter used for Eucharistic bread, and so on—seem to have deleterious effects far beyond offending the seminarian's sensibilities. They speak to the heart of the orthodox man studying for the priesthood. They speak of a crisis of authority and obedience, which all too often leads the seminarian to frustration and even contempt for his superiors. Unfortunately, this gets expressed in ways that are seen as "rigid" and "uncharitable." Again, more black marks for our beleaguered young man.

According to Father John Lewandowski, at Mount Angel Seminary "there were psychological screws under which we seminarians were constantly pressed. The fact was, we had to hide devotion to Mary and to the Eucharist, or any other pious exercise of faith which was not on the list of acceptable activities."

Carl von Deinim* was accepted as a seminarian by a diocese in Wisconsin and sent to Mundelein Seminary in Chicago. During his first week there, he was told by a faculty member that he was prohibited from kneeling at the Consecration or receiving Communion on the tongue. It was said that if he could not follow these instructions, he would be asked to leave.

"I left on my own the next day," von Deinim said, acknowledging that he was unwilling to play the "obedience/disobedience game" in Chicago.

Peter Carmody,* also a seminarian at Mundelein in Chicago, reiterated Joseph Kellenyi's observation that there are some "serious problems" with members of the formation staff, some of whom, he said, don't even bother to attend daily Mass. "Others don't vest for Mass," he explained, "because these 'all-male celebrations' are said to help in the oppression of women."

"Another sad part of the formation staff," he said, "is their constant scrutiny of how we pray. If a student bows before Communion, it is filed against him as 'an obsession with the Real Presence.' Since we don't kneel at the consecration, anyone who chooses to kneel after Communion is observed and remembered. Outward acts of piety are usually challenged. Often, the formation faculty equates piety with rigidity, always followed by an analysis of repressed sexual problems. Then when a bishop comes for a visit, or if a rich donor arrives, we play up our 'Catholic face.' This is sometimes laughable, because the seminarians can't fake knowing how to act, dress, or even serve a bishop's Mass. Consequently, we have seminarians bumping into each other or kneeling at the wrong time! But I don't blame the students; I blame the administration."

This lack of attention to proper liturgical catechesis and formation is clearly at odds with the Church's expectations for seminaries. In *Pastores Dabo Vobis*, Pope John Paul II emphasizes that the summit of Christian prayer for the seminarian is the daily celebration of the Holy Eucharist. Thus "a totally necessary aspect" of the formation of every priest is his liturgical formation:

> To be utterly frank and clear, I would like to say once again: It is fitting that seminarians take part every day in the Eucharistic celebration, in such a way that afterward they will take up as a rule of their priestly life this daily celebration. They should, moreover, be trained to consider the Eucharistic celebration as the essential moment of their day, in which they will take an active part and at which they will never be satisfied with a merely habitual attendance. Finally, candidates to the priesthood will be trained to share in the intimate dispositions which the Eucharist fosters: gratitude for

heavenly benefits received, because the Eucharist is
thanksgiving; an attitude of self-offering, which will
impel them to unite the offering of themselves to the
Eucharistic offering of Christ's charity nourished by a
sacrament which is a sign of unity and sharing; the
yearning to contemplate and bow in adoration before
Christ, who is really present under the Eucharistic
species.[1]

The fact that the pope expects seminarians not only to attend but
to participate fully in the Mass each day emphasizes the importance
of the public liturgy in the life of the seminarian (and, later, in his
priestly life). A perversion of the liturgy can be understandably seen
as a perversion of a seminarian's formation.

Unfortunately, professional liturgists are often very influential in
the seminary, especially, as might be expected, in the celebration of
the Mass. Evidence over the past thirty-some years bears out the in-
disputable fact that those with advanced training in liturgy most
often bring their own liturgical agendas to the local Church at the
expense of the liturgy as the universal Church defines it. Literally,
the liturgy is a battlefield in the seminary, a battle between the orthodox, who believe that they are entitled to properly receive the
sacraments, especially the Eucharist, and those progressive churchmen and women who believe that personality and showmanship take
precedence over reverence and rubrics.

It is on this very point that a clash of cultures plays out. The
liturgy of the Mass is one of the most obvious outward manifesta-
tions of the Catholic faith for the fledgling seminarian. When the
orthodox student brings to the seminary a correct understanding of
what should happen during the liturgy, and then faces a perversion
of that liturgy, he feels at best compromised. For instance, many
seminarians, such as von Deinim, expressed their discomfort at being
told they are required to receive Communion in the hand as opposed
to "on the tongue." These young men, because they understand that
Communion on the tongue is a legitimate option—the case could

even be made that it is the "preferred" option of the Church[2]—are taken aback. The same is to be said of the seminarian who is instructed that he must *not* kneel. As Carmody mentioned regarding Mundelein, the kneeling seminarian is observed to be "suspicious," and invariably "rigid."

The heart of this suspicion is actually ideological, not liturgical. The seminarian who kneels and receives Communion on the tongue is guilty of three things: respect, reverence, and piety, which are indicators that the seminarian has an "outdated" understanding of the Real Presence of Christ in the Eucharist. Accordingly, the liturgist is offended that the seminarian does not share his progressive view of the Real Presence—one that, it must be said, is at odds with what the Church teaches. Again, this is another issue that is politicized inside the seminary and now in the wider Church.

It must be admitted too that the seminary powers that be sometimes do not see the liturgy as a divisive issue in the seminary, but simply an issue about which the orthodox seminarian is wrong. Sister Katarina Schuth of St. Paul's Seminary in Minnesota explains that "students may accuse faculty of not supporting their devotions or loving the Blessed Sacrament, to which faculty respond that they are simply asking students also to see Christ in others and serve accordingly."[3] Schuth's obvious illogic is well understood by seminarians across the United States and will be treated in more depth in a later chapter, but suffice it to say for now that the orthodox seminarian is puzzled when told that his devotion to the Blessed Sacrament somehow prevents his ability to "see Christ in others and serve accordingly," when he understands that such devotion, as well as all properly ordered devotion, will *foster* "seeing Christ in others and serving accordingly." Father Andrew Walter of Bridgeport compared Schuth's illogic to asking Catholics not to pray because it may interfere with their relationship with their neighbors.

"Some seminarians were very reverent and pious toward the Eucharist," Walter explained of his time at St. Mary's Seminary in Baltimore, "and one day at Mass, after Communion had been distributed, a faculty priest blew on the paten when there were fingernail-size

pieces of the Eucharist on it. He did this to make a point to the guys
who were pious, who believed in the teaching of the Church that Jesus
is really present in the Host. He was asking the seminarians, 'Why are
you so rigid?' I'm not going to say this is *verging* on the demonic. That
is demonic," he said of the seminary priest's actions, "and it is connected with so many other things in the life of the Church. It's a sacrilege of the worst kind."

Walter also pointed out that reverence and irreverence in the
Mass accords to belief or lack of belief in one of the fundamental
teachings of the Catholic Church, a teaching which is, in fact,
uniquely Catholic:

> The mode of Christ's presence under the Eucharistic
> species is unique. It raises the Eucharist above all the
> sacraments as "the perfection of the spiritual life and the
> end to which all the sacraments tend." In the most
> blessed sacrament of the Eucharist "the body and blood,
> together with the soul and divinity, of our Lord Jesus
> Christ and, therefore, *the whole Christ is truly, really, and
> substantially* contained." This presence is called "real"—
> by which [it] is not intended to exclude the other types
> of presence as if they could not be "real" too, but be-
> cause it is [a] presence in the fullest sense: that is to say,
> it is a *substantial* presence by which Christ, God and
> man, makes himself wholly and entirely present [em-
> phasis in the original].[4]

Thus, based on the teaching of the Catholic Church it would
seem that Walter's assessment of the priest's action at St. Mary's as
"sacrilege" would be justified. Such mockery of the Mass is invariably detrimental to a young man's vocation, whether he is aware of
it or not. It erodes the orthodox seminarian's confidence in his
seminary. "If they can't get something this basic right, something
that indicates obedience to the Church and belief in one of the fundamental doctrines of the Church, a young guy is naturally going
to become suspicious of other ways he's being 'formed' in [the sem-

inary]," explained Walter, who was sent to psychological counseling for his perceived "rigidness" when he was a seminarian at Baltimore's St. Mary's.

Another effect of liturgical abuse and mockery is driving the seminarian away from proper devotion to the Mass, as the Mass comes to be dreaded—not for what it is but because of how it is abused and mocked.

Father Eduard Perrone recalled the liturgies during his seminary days at Detroit's St. John's in the late 1970s as "awful."

"I remember the day one of the faculty priests came in wearing a pink biretta. It was a mockery. The whole Mass was a mockery that day. [The faculty priests] were so liberal that they didn't care if you came to Mass or not.

"There was a little glass window on the large doors that opened into the chapel. I used to look into the chapel through the peep glass from the vestibule just before Mass and sometimes say, 'Oh no, not today.' I would see something set up like electric guitars or bongo drums, and I'd just skip Mass that day. We had a lot of things wrong with the Mass."

Father Bob Oravetz of Pittsburgh said he received excellent training in the liturgy at Mount St. Mary's Seminary in Emmittsburg, Maryland, but as a board member for the Serra Club, an international vocations-promoting group, he traveled to many different seminaries when he was a student. During his previous career as an international businessman, he made eighty-two flights to China, accruing a great many frequent-flier miles that paid his airfare for these visits.

"Even though my contact with seminarians and faculty at these schools was casual," he explained, "I could get a fairly good understanding for the spiritual life or prayer life there in just a short stay."

Attending the seminaries' Masses, he said, was the most indicative. His most memorable stay, he recalled, was at St. Patrick's in Menlo Park, California. "I looked all around to find the liturgical schedule because I wanted to go to Mass in the morning. I finally found a small notice on one of the bulletin boards indicating that Mass was at 7:30 the next morning. When I went to the main chapel, no one was around and the doors to the chapel were locked. A man dressed in shorts and walking his dog came into the hallway and I asked him about Mass. He said that's where he was going at the moment, and he would show the way. It turned out that Mass was not offered in the main chapel, but in the nun's convent in another building. This was the only Mass offered at the seminary each day. I went in and there were no seminarians at Mass except myself. There were only nuns present. The man who was walking the dog came out vested and celebrated the Mass, with his dog sitting in the corner. After Mass I went to the dining hall for breakfast, and I noted that the seminarians didn't fail to show up there."

Oravetz, who is a priest of the Byzantine rite but also has faculties to celebrate the Latin rite Mass, believes that one of the problems with seminarians seeing liturgical abuses or liturgical mockery in the seminary is that such abuses "will probably not lessen later."

"There are always ways to break the orthodox young man," he explained. "For instance, if he has a spiritual year or a pastoral year serving in a parish, he may well be assigned to a pastor who is very liberal and consequently abuses the Mass's liturgy. Even if he gets ordained, the process continues; he may continue to be assigned only to serve liberal pastors until he has forgotten any liturgical ideals, i.e., legitimate practices, he may have had about liturgy that he may want to follow."

At many seminaries over the past thirty-some years, alternative celebrations, known properly as quasi-liturgies, have been introduced. Many, in the name of "diversity" or "multicultural awareness," introduce popular New Age themes that are blatantly opposed to Christianity. Others, in the name of "gender inclusivism," have incorporated feminist themes.

Father Edward Tressilian* laments the quasi-liturgies he experienced while a seminarian at the Washington Theological Union in D.C., which he attended for a year while he was studying for a missionary religious order. "They were a mockery of the Mass, really," he commented, "all in order to satisfy the feminist nuns' lust for power and domination in the Church."

Father John Rattery* recalled an Indian liturgy he attended while at a West Coast seminary in the early 1990s. The quasi-liturgical rite began: "We greet you, Great Spirit of the Earth. It was from you we came as from a Mother. You nourish us and give us shelter," and included the following prayer:

> All is a circle and a hoop within me.
> If I speak in the language you taught me
> I am all but one.
> Look inside the circle and the hoop,
> You will see your relation and nations.
> Your relation to the four-legged
> And two-legged
> And the winged ones
> And the Mother Earth
> The Grandfather Sun
> The Grandmother Moon
> The Direction and the Sacred Seasons.
> And the Universe
> You will find love for your relation.
> Look further inside the Sacred Circle
> And the Sacred Hoop.
> In the center of the circle and hoop
> You will feel the Spirit of the Great Creator,
> He is the center of everything
> Learn about what you are
> By observing what you are not.
> A circle and a Hoop within me.

The Indian liturgical rite was explained in a handout distributed to the seminarians and others present:

> We begin our worship with the Prayer to the Four Winds, a prayer expressive of Native American spirituality. As we gather, we face the North to proclaim this

prayer and after a brief pause turn and face each new direction.

The symbol of the golden corn is used as we pray toward the North. The gold represents light which is essential of life and protection symbolized by corn. Since light (sunbeams, warmth) is a necessary element of generation, the pollen, a masculine symbol, is the symbol of fructification, vivification, and continuity of life and safety. As we pray toward the East, the fire of the incense, another masculine symbol, represents the rising Sun. The bowl of earth, a feminine symbol, is raised as a symbol of Creation as we pray towards the South. The final prayer is toward the West towards the great waters of the Pacific Ocean. The symbol of water, a feminine symbol, also represents the rains that renew Creation.[5]

In sum, while Indian prayers are suitable for Indian tribal rituals, one must soberly assess the seminarians' situation: who they are; whom they'll serve; how relatively little time they have to learn an incredible amount of uniquely Catholic knowledge and wisdom.

■ ■ ■

Praying the rosary has been another flashpoint of "inappropriate and misdirected piety." Countless seminarians tell the same story: They wanted to pray the rosary, meditating on the mysteries of the life of Christ, yet they were looked upon with a suspicious eye. Sometimes, when public rosary prayer was permitted at the seminary, students who participated regularly in the Marian devotions were given poor evaluations by their formation team, who claimed that praying the rosary somehow showed a deficiency in personality and was an indication that the seminarian may not be suitable for the priesthood. At other times, public rosary prayer was simply disallowed.

"I formed a rosary group, which met daily in my room for evening rosary," explained Father Norm Weslin. "The authorities told me to stop. I asked why. They answered that the floor may cave in. It was a sturdy new building so I seriously doubted their explanation."[6]

Speaking of the attitude toward the rosary at St. Mary Seminary in Baltimore, Father Andrew Walter said the devotion was discouraged. "They said it was divisive. Then they banned the public recitation of the rosary."

When Father Ted Ramsey* attended the Josephinum in Columbus, Ohio, during the early 1990s, a group of seminarians "got together to pray the rosary, and it was noted by the faculty who was doing this," he explained. "There were about eight of us. It became a 'formation issue.' It got brought up in our evaluations. They made it sound like we were trying to be better than the rest of them."

When Andrew McWhirter* first started at Oregon's Mount Angel Seminary, he was careful about being seen publicly praying the rosary. He and a fellow student got together regularly for the devotion. After they noticed another two seminarians were also getting together to pray the rosary, they all gathered together for a group rosary prayer and later began inviting other seminarians to join them each evening. It was finally settled into a routine where they would meet in the chapel after dinner.

"We grew to about thirty guys, which is just about unheard of," explained McWhirter.

> And on special feast days we would put out notices inviting the whole student body. We'd get about fifty guys on those days, sometimes up to two-thirds of the seminarians. But the rector never came even though we invited him not only in writing but verbally, in person.
>
> And then pretty soon we were labeled as "Pharisees," and we were said to be "divisive." Then our numbers just plummeted immediately. These guys were running scared. They said they no longer wanted to be associated with praying the rosary. Pretty soon we were down to ten or twelve guys each night.
>
> We were giving the seminary staff exactly what they wanted: It was "multi-cultural"; we prayed the rosary in five different languages every night—in English, Spanish, Vietnamese, Samoan, and Latin. So we were

"diverse," "tolerant," "embracing," all the stuff that they wanted, but we were praying the rosary, which itself was politically incorrect.

My relationship with my formation director started out okay. I knew I had to play the game and get along and get through. But things started to come up that were "formation issues" or "potential formation issues," like this rosary group. When this subject came up with him one day, he said: "Well, there is one issue that we've got to talk about. This rosary group...."

And I said, "What about it?"

"Well we're hearing things like you guys are doing this and that." He was planting a little seed in my formation report.

In other words, McWhirter's participation in publicly praying the rosary, one of the oldest devotions in the Catholic Church, amounted to black marks for the aspiring priest.

■ ■ ■

Because the public liturgy and public and private devotions are some of the most obvious expressions of the Catholic faith in seminaries, the perversion or prevention of proper and legitimate devotions is one of the leading causes for the orthodox seminarian to leave his seminary. The effects of liturgy on a man are profound: Consistently, improper celebration of the Mass and suspicion cast upon those who practice time-honored devotions (e.g., adoration of the Blessed Sacrament and praying the rosary) naturally have a deleterious effect on a seminarian's spirituality. Owing to these facts, many young men are convinced that they cannot or will not remain in an environment that is so unsupportive of their faith and devotion.

CHAPTER 7

Go See the Shrink!

How Psychological Counseling Is Used to Expel the Good Man from His Seminary

If one or two years of psychological counseling on a fee for service basis is not successful in alienating the man from his faith in the Church, he is given a negative recommendation from the psychologist which usually means another dismissal and another lost vocation.

—Dr. John Fraunces, psychologist and member of the Catholic Medical Association

What happens to the orthodox seminarian when confronted by the host of obstacles discussed thus far—the gay subculture, radical feminism, heterodox professors and spiritual directors, bad liturgy, political correctness, and lack of spirituality? These very "exterior" influences indeed have a profound effect on a young man in a context where he expects himself to grow in holiness and commitment as he makes his way toward ordination. After all, no man is impervious to his environment, especially his spiritual environment. The obstacles take their toll.

Father Amos Perry* of the Diocese of Austin put it this way: "One of the classic dynamics at the seminary was that the young, and hence in some ways immature, orthodox seminarian, hammered from all

129

sides by a system inimical to his faith, his sexuality, and his sense of mature human behavior, would be worn down to the point of 'striking back.' If necessary, this pressure could also be increased by advisors, faculty evaluations, etc., especially when they attempted to rearrange or force the manifestation of a candidate's conscience. Once you 'struck back' you were dead. You were 'insubordinate,' 'had problems with authority figures,' or were 'rigid.' It was sobering at the time to realize how closely the dynamic paralleled the brainwashing strategies of the Communist reeducation camps. Even the connotations of the terms 'rigid,' 'preconciliar,' 'anticommunity,' resonated with Communist terms like 'capitalist,' 'bourgeois,' and 'antidemocratic.' "

Father John Trigilio of the Harrisburg diocese made the same comparison: "The one book that helped me persevere through my twelve years of seminary," he said, "was Aleksandr Solzhenitsyn's *Gulag Archipelago*. His imprisonment and constant surveillance was in many ways identical to my seminary life, in which cultural revolutionaries sought to 'rehabilitate' the orthodox into becoming full-fledged party members of the new dissidence. As in the former USSR, if you opposed the 'party line,' which in the case of the seminary was their particular brand of heterodoxy, then you were labeled as mentally unfit and kept under close scrutiny 'for your own safety.' The mind games, spying, and hidden agenda, as well as the vast bureaucracy of the KGB, were cloned in the seminaries across America. Fellow seminarians spy on one another; blackmail, intimidation, slander, threats, and even violence are employed to protect the status quo. Quote the pope and you are an archconservative, John Birch, KKK, Neo-Nazi; quote Gore Vidal and you are an intellectual Renaissance man."

Sadly, he added, many of his classmates never made it through to ordination in this type of environment. "I actually saw vocations tortured and killed by those who were supposedly there to promote and foster vocations." What Trigilio witnessed, he said, can only be described as "a real persecution and systematic extermination of orthodoxy and manly piety so as to artificially create a climate for married and women clergy."

If an orthodox man gets past the seminary gatekeepers and is later found to be loyal to the papacy and the teachings of the Church, commented former seminarian Charles Enderby, "liberal churchmen will seek to break the orthodox person. They will play with a man's vocation and with his life."

Many of the seminarians, former seminarians, and priests interviewed described what they consistently called "intimidation techniques" to weed them out of the seminary, first by making the orthodox seminarian leave the school of his own volition, and, failing that, getting him to "strike back," as Father Perry described it, so that the administration had a "reason," however illegitimate it might be, to expel him and ultimately destroy his vocation.

The most common of these intimidation techniques is the use of psychological counseling, what seminarians and others commonly call "getting your head shrunk."

"Psychological abuse happens," is the way Jason Dull described his years at Sacred Heart College Seminary in Detroit. "Every orthodox seminarian that I knew while I was at the seminary was sent to a shrink or was going to be sent to a shrink, myself included," he explained. They were sent to ongoing psychological counseling for what Dull calls "rigorism," which he believes was merely a "stoutheartedness in the faith."

"These seminarians had faith; they had humility," he said. "If a seminarian missed one of his counseling sessions, then the seminary would know about it immediately. There was nothing more strictly mandated than going to your counseling sessions. You were to comply, and if you didn't, you were out, no two ways about it."

When the orthodox seminarian is sent to a psychologist, he is not only embarrassed by this turn of events, he begins naturally to wonder, "Am I nuts?" Although the young man likely considered himself perfectly sane without qualification before he arrived on campus, in the seminary he begins to question his sanity, or if he is still perfectly convinced of his sound mind, he is upset and resentful of being a grown man who is made to undergo psychological counseling that he feels is wholly unnecessary.

Greg Hamilton, now an attorney practicing in Iowa, attended seminary at St. Ambrose University in the Diocese of Davenport, Iowa, in the early 1990s. "For all the talk about openness and dialogue," he attested, "too often those who questioned the most—if they had concerns about orthodoxy—were 'answered' through the formation process, rather than in the classroom. There seemed to be a pretty heavy reliance on psychology to bring the troublemakers into line. Such an approach would never have been tolerated in my law school training, for instance, but it seemed pretty routine in seminary. It struck me as an anti-intellectual abuse of power."

Father Lou Ellis,* who was a seminarian at the Pontifical College Josephinum in the early 1990s, was sent to a psychologist on four separate occasions before his vocations director finally stepped in and said "enough."

"If they don't like you and can't find a reason to kick you out of seminary," remarked Ellis, "then they accuse you of being nuts. They always want to send seminarians to a psychologist."

"Most guys aren't willing to talk about this in the open," he explained, noting the embarrassing nature of being sent to a "shrink."

"The problem at the Josephinum at the time was that we had so little substantive contact with the formation team. The college was across the street, and sometimes we had a faculty member from the college who really wouldn't know us. In my experience, they usually did not have any basis for the accusations they leveled against seminarians to send us to psychological counseling. This counseling is designed to do one of two things. You might start to wonder: Do I really have a vocation? Some guys are really just looking for an excuse to say, 'I tried, God. I tested my vocation, but these guys say I don't have a vocation.' It's an easy way out for them because they have a legitimate authority telling them they don't belong. The other reason is that counseling is used as a baseball bat to beat down the orthodox seminarian, to make him submit, or to get rid of him. There's no redeeming value to any of it. I think spiritual direction wins out every time. I don't think psychological evaluations have any place in the Church. With good spiritual direction you won't need a psychologist."

Thomas Royde,* who has taught courses at several Catholic seminaries, confirmed the attitude of which Ellis spoke. According to Royde, the vice rector of a U.S. seminary confided in him that he, the vice rector, was hostile toward the young, orthodox crowd at his seminary. Royde explained that several students at this seminary approached the bishop of their diocese, asking that he encourage the seminary administration to offer them some time each week for Eucharistic adoration. "The vice rector told me that he thinks these seminarians are dysfunctional," he added. "He said we're going to send them away; we're going to force them to do therapy. He considered it 'anomalous and toxic behavior' for these guys to insist upon Eucharistic adoration. He thinks that the young, conservative guys are all part of an evil conspiracy, that they're in touch with some order group or confraternity, and that they're out to sabotage the New Church. He believes their problems stem from repressed sexuality—he scoffs at their belief in celibacy in the priesthood—or that they have some other fundamental emotional or psychological problem. This vice rector is all for psychological therapies. There was one kid, for example, whom he removed from the seminary and sent out to a parish while he was receiving psychological counseling. He said that he hoped the guy would then decide to drop out on his own. Not surprisingly, this was one of the guys who was interested in Eucharistic devotion. The vice rector really doesn't understand why these young guys want to be so prayerful, why they want to dress in clerics, and so forth. To him, they're all nuts."

Paul Sinsigalli from Boston's St. John Seminary College explained the situation in similar terms:

> We'd get these evaluations and they wouldn't make any sense. We had to go to a meeting with the faculty members in order to discuss our evaluations. They would always give us a little positive stuff before coming to the negative. They told me I am "prayerful and punctual and a nice guy but..." and then they would lower the boom. Then they called me "intrusive," "abrasive," and

"rigid." My last evaluation said I lack intellectual ability, emotional maturity, and leadership. For every one of my evaluations I would go in there and say: This is not true. And I can prove it to you. I'd state my case and they would always respond with their catch-all for everything: "It's the consensus of the faculty." And once they say that, forget it. Case closed. And of course it doesn't matter what the evaluation says, if you argue with them then you might as well write "belligerent" on the evaluation too.

They were evaluating us, yet they only see us one or two hours a week. They said, oh, but we observed you at dinnertime. I asked, "Well, what exactly did you observe that brings you to these conclusions?" And they can't come up with anything. It would have been okay if they had. At least I would have known I wasn't being unjustly targeted for elimination.

Sinsigalli also said that he felt some of the seminarians were being "baited" so they would betray their ideological allegiance. "One faculty member," Sinsigalli explained by way of example, "teaches philosophy. At the lunch table I've seen and heard her talking about how there will be women priests before too long, and the Church will finally let priests get married. It's one thing to have those opinions, but she is broadcasting them and daring the seminarians to go against her, to have a different opinion."

Sinsigalli was sent to psychological counseling beginning in his first year at St. John's.

I was in therapy for three years. I was feeling depressed by events at the seminary after I was labeled a "homophobe," and when I told that to my spiritual director he insisted I go see a psychologist.

I thought, "What the heck, it's free and maybe it'll help me." I would talk about things that were going on at the seminary, and many times I felt like he turned it around on me as if I were the problem. I remember one time specifically I said I believe what the Church teaches about homosexuals, and that homosexual acts are wrong and intrinsically evil. I don't think of it as anything personal. It's just objective truth. He was all over me for that. He said, "How can you say that's not personal?"

A lot of the guys went to him and I don't know what he reported to the faculty about me. He said that there was confidentiality, but I wonder about that. I just can't believe that the priests at the seminary didn't get information from the psychologist. It seemed like things were going hand-in-hand. There was a similarity to what I was being told in the seminary which was reiterated again and again by the psychologist in order that I might understand well that I was the one who was out of whack, not my superiors or my liberal peers back at the seminary.

After Sinsigalli was dismissed from St. John's—he graduated from the college but was not approved to continue in the graduate theology program that prepares men for ordination—it took him two months of recuperation, he said, to get back on his feet again, emotionally and physically. "I was in bad shape. Very depressed, confused. I just figured that once I got to theology things would be better, that I wouldn't be under such a microscope. But when I got booted, it just blew me out of the water."

The following year, another Massachusetts diocese agreed to evaluate Sinsigalli's suitability despite the fact that Boston had dismissed him out of hand. "I talked with the vocations director there," he explained, "and found this diocese to be very different from Boston. It seemed orthodox. I told their vocation director I didn't want to get into another problem like I did with the homosexual atmosphere at St. John's, and end up getting sent to counseling for allegedly being a 'rigid homophobe.' He told me his diocese purposefully does *not* send their men to St. John's. They are apparently aware of some of the problems there."

During the summer, however, Sinsigalli began to have misgivings about returning to seminary life, but not because he thought he no longer had a vocation to the priesthood. "As I started to think about it, trying to mentally prepare to go," he explained, "I started having flashbacks. It was crazy. I had anxiety. I had a hard time sleeping because I was so tense. I just knew that if I had gone I would not have done so well because I was so uptight. I still needed time to recover from the trauma of St. John's. The vocations director wanted me to do one more year of undergraduate work at the local Catholic college so he could get to know me. I couldn't get any financial aid because I already had a bachelor's degree. I would have had to go $20,000 into debt. After what I had been through at St. John's I was just scared. I wasn't ready to return to seminary. I was too demoralized."

Instead he was accepted into the graduate theology program at Franciscan University of Steubenville, which he has found both an orthodox and a very positive educational experience, and a place where no one has suggested that he is psychologically ill.

George Mayhew also became depressed once he experienced life as a seminarian in an East Coast religious order. "I was asked to seek personal counseling by a priest-psychologist," he explained, "because they feared I was becoming depressed. I went without much objection *not* because I was clinically depressed, but because they were indeed depressing me. I then had to attend a weekly 'support group' run by an ex-priest, now therapist. It was crap, just emotivism."

Mayhew, who holds a Ph.D. in psychology himself, is a critic of modern psychology. He agrees with William Coulson that it's based too much on subjective humanist theories. Mayhew, who is presently penning a book that critiques human psychology from a Thomistic perspective, believes that the kind of counseling he received was contrary to the Church's teaching on the human person.

"Much of the psychology we get here at the seminary," he said, "is very humanistic. It's all about emotions, and emotions that are not guided by the intellect."

In addition to personal counseling, many seminaries use group therapy techniques like the "support group" meeting mentioned by Mayhew. Many seminarians described similar experiences in such group therapy programs.

"One of the most degrading things the facilitator—they like to be called by this title—attempts to do is to dig up all past sins through group discussion sessions," explained Father Stephen Grant,* who attended a West Coast seminary. "You are expected to reveal all of your past hurts, all the past abuses heaped on you by whomever from any period of your life. The more, the better."

"This may all sound a little cynical," he continued, "but it is very real and potentially damaging psychologically. This kind of probing touches upon the conscience. It enters an area of the human person where no one has a right to go unless invited. This includes the confessor and spiritual director.

"In my experience, this group therapy attempts to batter down the door of conscience. And when resisted, the individual is labeled as a nonconformer or as being uncooperative. This, of course, gets back to his bishop and vocations director by way of an unflattering evaluation. Just to give one example of how deeply people can be affected by this program: I have a good friend who was a doctor in the air force, and he is now a priest in a diocese in the Southwest. He told me that when this program was relatively new, the air force adopted it on an experimental basis. He said that in his group, two men hanged themselves after a number of these group sessions in which they broke down and sobbed out their story, revealing the most intimate details of their lives. In the judgment of this priest, he feels strongly that these men were affected traumatically by the psychological mind-bending of the group sessions."

■ ■ ■

To many priests and seminarians, psychological counseling—"go see the shrink"—appears to be a form of punishment for not towing the politically correct line at seminary. In many cases the poor psychological evaluations are used as an excuse, as previously suggested, to expel the orthodox student from the seminary system.

Father Andrew Walter spent fourteen years making his way through the seminary system. Psychological counseling and evaluation played a significant part in his seminary career. In February of 1995, after having consistently defended Church teaching against faculty at St. Mary's Seminary in Baltimore, Walter was sent to the New Life Center in Middleburg, Virginia, for a two-day psychological evaluation. He was sent there, he said, because of alleged "behavioral problems."

Shortly after the evaluation, Walter was expelled from St. Mary's.

"I wasn't the only one either," he explained. "A good friend of mine at seminary went through the exact same experience. He was accused of having all kinds of psychological problems, sent out to a shrink, and then expelled."

Both Walter and his friend, exiled from St. Mary's and dismissed by their respective bishops, sought out new dioceses to sponsor them. It was then that they made the acquaintance of Dr. John Fraunces, a Philadelphia-area psychologist. A 1997 article in *Catholic World Report* by Leslie Payne relates the story of how Walter, with the help of Fraunces, obtained a copy of his psychological evaluation from the New Life Center. He discovered that he had been diagnosed by therapist Thomas Drummond with "severe sexual dysfunction," "histrionic personality disorder," and "narcissistic personality disorder."

"This evaluation," said Walter, "was based on two written personality tests and a twenty-minute interview. That's how long it took to make that diagnosis."

However, when Fraunces evaluated the test data that Drummond had collected from Walter, it was obvious to him that the tests could not have justified such a diagnosis. That's when Andrew Walter began assembling a lawsuit against Drummond and St. Mary's Seminary. As the evidence was gathered, it became clearer and clearer to Walter that the seminary had sent him to the New Life Center, a place where pedophile priests are sent, in order to receive a phony evaluation that would make it look as if he was a potential sex offender.

Walter said that when he contacted Drummond to get a copy of his evaluation, Drummond refused, saying he doesn't write them for laypeople. But when Fraunces contacted him, Drummond released the evaluation, thinking that Fraunces was evaluating Walter for another diocese. "Drummond thought that when Dr. Fraunces read my report from the New Life Center, he would immediately recommend against me," said Walter.

Fraunces explained to *Catholic World Report* that Drummond's evaluation insinuated that Walter was "homophobic" because he was a "homosexual in denial." Drummond concluded that "Andrew was intolerant of homosexuals, that he experiences his heterosexuality in the negative sense of not being homosexual, and that homosexuality is an aspect of this one personality that Andrew did not have the opportunity to explore growing up."

Fraunces added: "Drummond included on the list of Walter's problems 'a distorted negative reaction to homosexual behavior in others' and complained that 'Andrew believes that his careful distinction between homosexual orientation, which he thinks is fine, and homosexual attitudes and behavior, which he disapproves, should be respected and he cannot understand why others think him homophobic.' He fails Walter for 'his anger at and rejection of values and behaviors with which he does not agree.' In his summary, Drummond cites Walter's 'lack of important intimate relationships among his peers' at the seminary as evidence of developmental delay."[1]

(It is important to recall that St. Mary's Seminary in Baltimore has long been nicknamed the "Pink Palace" for its alleged acceptance and even promotion of the gay subculture in the seminary.)

According to Fraunces, "Drummond stressed that Walter's primary problem was 'tweaking the nose of authority, which prompted the seminary's request for an evaluation.' " But Dr. Fraunces disagreed, saying that Walter's "hostility" to the seminary faculty was prompted by "the authority figure pretending to be Catholic, while in effect violating basic rules of Catholicism—permitting homosexual behavior between faculty and students or adulterous liaisons between faculty members. These people deny the Church's authority, yet demand deference to themselves. Andrew does not have a problem with legitimate authority."[2]

Fraunces subsequently readministered the psychological test that Walter had taken at the New Life Center and found no evidence of personality disorders. He characterized Drummond's report as "a violation of ethics" and said that a report like that would be "the kiss of death for anyone who is a heterosexual and wants to be a priest."[3]

Upon recommendation from Dr. Fraunces, Andrew Walter was accepted as a candidate for the priesthood by the Diocese of Bridgeport, then under the leadership of Bishop Edward Egan, who would later become cardinal archbishop of New York. Walter was sent to St. Joseph Seminary (Dunwoodie) in Yonkers, New York, where he said he received "a decent education." After graduating magna cum laude, he was ordained by Egan in May 2000.

Fraunces also helped Walter's friend Anthony,* who was accepted by a midwestern diocese and ordained in 1999. Six years earlier, during his first year at Baltimore's St. Mary's, Anthony was told by his formation director that he acted like "an old-fashioned monsignor who is stuck in the 1950s. We don't need a s— like you in the Church."[4]

> Anthony complained to his diocese about the seminary, but was warned, "If you want to be ordained for this diocese, you'd better learn how to play the game." Anthony says his second year at St. Mary's was worse than the first. A woman who taught a course on pastoral counseling was very vocal in her dissent from Church teaching on subjects like abortion and homosexuality. She opened her first class with a complaint about women's role in the Church and an admonition that the men were "wasting their time" studying to be priests, when they should become social workers or psychologists instead.
>
> In April of 1995, officials learned that Anthony had looked into switching to another diocese. He was soon sent to the New Life Center for a weekend evaluation because of this "inappropriate behavior."

After an interview with New Life Center Associate Director Sister Carla Przybilla, OSF, and several written tests, Anthony met with Dr. Thomas Drummond, who declared that the tests showed he had "substance-abuse tendencies" and was "homophobic." Drummond predicted, "In five years, you will be an angry drunk who alienates the whole parish council." Anthony says that he replied, "Dr. Drummond, I don't know much about psychology, but I do know that it is common for people who have dysfunctions to project them onto others." Anthony pointed out that he had left a successful career in the business world to enter the seminary; he had earned an MBA degree, become a financial analyst, and was pulling in a $60,000 annual salary. "And then to be treated like an idiot by this guy," he complains.[5]

Both Anthony and Andrew Walter had nearly identical experiences at the New Life Center, and both concluded that they were being discriminated against for going against the political flow at St. Mary's.

When they met up with Dr. Fraunces and Dr. Richard Fitzgibbons, a Philadelphia psychiatrist, they "joined an informal network, small but rapidly growing, of priests and seminarians who say they have been subjected to a Church-run psychiatric gulag, usually operated by theological liberals, often by men who are openly and actively homosexuals," reported the *Catholic World Report*.[6]

Fitzgibbons related that many of his patients, both seminarians and priests, have told him about "clashes with therapists whom they described as openly homosexual, who urged them to 'come out of the closet' and who claimed that opposition to the ordination of women was evidence of a personality disorder. They reported centers where trysts between homosexual patients were permitted or condoned, and where patients who supported Church teaching on sexuality were ridiculed in group-therapy sessions."

Fraunces became so concerned about the abuse of psychology in evaluating seminarians that he penned a compelling article in 1997 for *Homiletic and Pastoral Review*. Based on his experiences with seminarians, he charged that "even in the seminary, the irrational process of eliminating men from ordination continues." He described how orthodox seminarians are routinely sent to psychologists for "growth counseling," in order to reform the man. "But if one or two years of psychological counseling on a fee for service basis is not successful in alienating the man from his faith in the Church, he is given a negative recommendation from the psychologist which usually means another dismissal and another lost vocation."[7]

He added, "For those men who are exclusively heterosexual in orientation and devoutly orthodox in faith, the difficulty of becoming a priest at the present time must be faced in an objective and dispassionate manner."[8]

The numerous questions that have been raised about psychological evaluations and counseling therapy for seminarians led the Catholic Medical Association (CMA) to form a task force composed of eight physicians (four of whom are psychiatrists), a consulting psychologist, and a moral theologian to evaluate the situation. The group's conclusion resulted in a position statement (partially discussed in Chapter 3) that practically begged for corrections on the part of bishops and seminary administration. Its findings are revealing.

The position statement explained that many reports have been made to the CMA that seminarians "who in the course of their studies expressed support for the teaching of the Magisterium, the Catechism, and Sacred Scripture, particularly on issues of sexuality and homosexuality, were told they were rigid and divisive and needed new psychological evaluations."[9] In providing background, the CMA paper explained that many of these orthodox seminarians were sent to Church-related treatment centers for psychological evaluation despite the fact that no more than a few years earlier these same seminarians had passed their psychological testing. Only when retested, after exhibiting signs of orthodoxy, were they diagnosed with having serious psychological problems which led to their dismissal from seminary.

Explaining the standard practice in the profession, the CMA position paper stated that "unless there are signs of a severe mental breakdown, there should be no need to retest a person who has been evaluated within the past five years" because "the basic personality structure does not change."

The CMA recommended that seminary faculty should be clearly informed "that adherence to the teaching of the Church on sexuality and particularly on homosexuality is not a sign of rigidity or mental illness, but of mental health." No seminarian, the recommendation continued, "should be referred for retesting because he supports Catholic teaching. No seminarian should be retested unless he shows clinically significant evidence of a serious mental disorder."

CHAPTER 8

The Vocational Inquisition

How the Orthodox Seminarian Is Identified and Persecuted

I feel that I have been deliberately singled out for such [onerous] treatment because of my traditional, classic concepts in some areas—concepts which are the authoritative teaching of the Church today.
—Father William H. Hinds, in a letter to his vocations director regarding his treatment at Cincinnati's Athenaeum seminary

Although many times psychological "intimidation" comes in the form of personal or group counseling, it often takes other, more comprehensive and insidious forms in the everyday experience of the student at seminary. The case of Father William H. Hinds, a priest of the Diocese of Covington, Kentucky, ordained in 1987, illustrates well what many seminarians and priests call the "vocational inquisition." Fortunately, Hinds had the prescience to save hundreds of pages of documentary evidence from his seminary days. They serve now to document his inquisitorial nightmare.

In the case of William Hinds, his vocation survived the gauntlet of seminary rector, formation team, and vocations office, which hundreds of seminarians—particularly the younger ones—do not survive.

Hinds entered seminary at the Athenaeum of Ohio in Cincinnati during the fall of 1983, at the age of thirty-nine. Although the Athenaeum program is typically a five-year commitment, Hinds was able to complete the program in four. The first two years consisted of academic preparation, the third year was served out in a parish internship, and during the fourth year he completed his coursework, earning two advanced degrees, the standard Master of Divinity (M.Div.) as well as the Master of Arts in Biblical Studies (M.A.B.).

Cincinnati's seminary holds to a pattern of student evaluation in which the seminarian is evaluated by a formation team after the completion of his first year. The second evaluation comes at the end of the second year and is taken as a "standard" of evaluation for the remainder of his time in the program. During the third year the seminarian is evaluated at the parish where he completes his year-long internship. It is not supposed to be an evaluation of the student's theological ideas but rather of his pastoral performance and aptitude. If the seminarian receives a positive recommendation from the parish, he's ready for candidacy, which he'll typically get during his fourth year. A year later, in the fall of his fifth year, he will be ordained a transitional deacon, and ordination to the priesthood normally follows the next spring.

At the end of Hinds's first year of studies at the Athenaeum, he received a largely positive evaluation from the formation team. In part, the evaluation stated that Hinds "is a bright student who spends a great deal of energy on his studies and is very interested in what he can learn by way of inquiry." And although the formation team felt that "he can sometimes intimidate people by the strong positions he takes," it had no problem with recommending Hinds to continue his preparation for the priesthood.

It was at the beginning of the second year of studies that Father Richard Sweeney, head of the formation team, and later dean of the seminary, caught wind of Hinds's orthodox stance on issues of sexual morality. One weekend evening Hinds attended a party in one of the seminary's dormitory halls. The party, thrown by a fellow seminarian, was attended by faculty members such as the rector and the seminary dean. One particular seminarian that night was giving out "big, public, juicy kisses—pretty obvious and lasciviously," to a male friend he had invited up, Hinds remembered.

Hinds approached Sweeney about this, complaining that this kind of sexual kissing was not by any stretch appropriate behavior for a seminarian. Sweeney, however, dismissed the complaint, saying that the seminarian was simply growing into his sexual identity and that he seriously doubted whether the seminarian was truly a homosexually oriented person. Even though Hinds made no more of this, Sweeney watched Hinds closely for other signs of perceived "rigidity" in sexual issues.

Hinds related that homosexuality was looked upon kindly at the Athenaeum. "There was a group of seminarians," he explained by way of example, "who would be sitting around watching the television show *Falcon Crest*, and every time one particular actress came on camera they would whoop and shriek and do all this kind of stuff—acting effeminate, imitating the woman."

Thus, two questions Hinds posed to Sweeney were: "Is it appropriate for a seminarian to act in a gay manner in the seminary or later as a priest?" and "Does a seminarian grow in his sexual identity by 'acting out'?"

Hinds also recalled another incident: He complained about a fellow seminarian hanging a large poster of transvestite pop singer Boy George on the outside of the door to his dormitory room. "Anybody who's walking along the hallway would see this picture of Boy George with the eye shadow and painted face," he explained, "so I brought it up one time in a meeting. How is everyone going to know that is not the door to *my* room? Then, to make my point I said, why don't I take that poster and put it on the rector's door? Would *that* be appropriate, I asked? I got called to the carpet for that."

In February 1984, the seminary made its stance on homosexual seminarians clear in a letter sent out to all students. Entitled "Celibacy and Sexuality: Reflections of the Formation Team," the letter stated that "Among the signs of adequate psychosexual development are the following: An ability to feel comfortable, confident, and competent with one's body and sexuality. Specifically this entails comfort with one's gender identity and a satisfactory awareness and acceptance of one's sexual orientation . . . [and] reverence for the uniqueness and the developmental process of other persons. This reverence will enable one to respect the uniqueness of other persons and refrain from forcing them to undesired self-disclosures or behaviors." The formation team also stated that "the [seminarian's] sexual orientation in and of itself does not determine his suitability for priesthood or capacity for celibate chastity," and further: "One's awareness and understanding of his sexual orientation develops gradually and may shift as one proceeds through various psychosexual stages. Hence [seminarians] are urged to guard against any hasty or rigid foreclosure of their sexual orientation."

Although Hinds took up the positions of the Church with enthusiasm and was prepared to defend them, Sweeney was most distressed not by Hinds's concern about the campy behavior of some seminarians, but by a comment that Hinds soon thereafter made about masturbation. Hinds merely voiced the Church's teaching on masturbation, that it is a "gravely disordered action."[1] Sweeney challenged; masturbation, said the priest, appealing to current opinions put forth by various schools of psychology, can be a "positive good." But Hinds continued to disagree.

"If you can't say with certainty that masturbation is a positive good, then you are not suitable for ordination to the Catholic priesthood," Sweeney finally told Hinds. Thus began an aggressive two-and-a-half-year effort by Sweeney, and later others on the faculty, to block the ordination of William H. Hinds.

■ ■ ■

By way of background, Hinds was a former Jesuit novice who left the order in the 1960s. While drawn very much to the spirituality of St. Ignatius, the founder of the Society of Jesus, he could not reconcile what he experienced in the order with the charism of its founder. He later went on to teach at Catholic secondary schools and to study human developmental psychology.

During the 1970s he continued to contemplate how to properly answer his call to the priesthood. Although Hinds was born and reared across the river in Cincinnati, Hinds had been working for a number of years in northern Kentucky. He decided then to approach Father Roger Kriege, the vocations director in Covington. In April of 1983 he explained where he stood regarding Church teaching. "I will gladly serve this diocese as a priest," he told Kriege, "but I hold orthodox views on sexual matters. If you're not going to back me up on that down the road, tell me now and I won't tell anyone you admitted that, and I won't come back and bother you again. If you accept me as a man and a priest, then you have to accept that I hold positions that are the Church's positions. I can tell you now that I am going to be attacked."

Kriege, himself not known for particularly traditional views, acted like a "prince," judged Hinds; the vocations director consented to back him up on his orthodoxy. Hinds's prediction turned out to be correct. When he would not agree to concede to Sweeney that masturbation was a "positive good," Sweeney launched into what amounted to an inquisitorial campaign to discredit Hinds's suitability for ordination, at least in Hinds's view. The campaign would last over two years.

Hinds had no qualms about expressing the Church's point of view when students and faculty put forth theological opinions to the contrary during classes. But complaints began to trickle in, charging Hinds with an "excessively critical attitude." A few months later Sweeney called Hinds into his office to discuss the matter. He recommended that Hinds temper his criticism and respect the opinions of others, whether or not they agreed with what the Church teaches or even squared with sound reasoning or common sense. Hinds explained that these complaints were often lodged by those who made no effort to understand him, and further, that he was never given the chance to articulate his views fully, which both he and Sweeney recognized as traditional viewpoints carefully defined by the official teaching of the Church.

Responding to his complaint, Sweeney directed that Hinds enroll in a special "Independent Study" course in which he could articulate his theological views and method. He did so under the tutelage of Sweeney and Sister Terry Koernke, another member of the formation team who was employed by the Athenaeum at that time as a professor of liturgy. Koernke, in fact, had been one of Hinds's vocal critics. She considered him to be "rigid" in his theological outlook and, according to Hinds, seemed to view this special course as an opportunity to use his own words against him. Thus began what Hinds believed was a formal campaign to either bring him into line or send him packing.

His first assignment was to compose a term paper on his "anthropological reflections." He completed this first exercise in April of 1985, turning in an eighteen-page explanation that was to help contextualize his responses to the method and content of his seminary education. It was a very personal reflection that revealed incidents from his early childhood, as well as his education and later teaching experiences. He concluded in the reflection that he had "learned to live in the presence of error and deception without getting bent out of shape in unproductive ways."

"I have learned to gauge my responses for effectiveness," he wrote, "rather than simply as responses to evil behavior. It does little good to rant about some awful truth, if people are not going to be changed by such behavior."

His second assignment, completed a month later, was a paper on *Humanae Vitae*, Pope Paul VI's 1968 watershed encyclical on the question of artificial contraception. Hinds outlined the main ideas of the pope's letter, listed some of the frequent objections made concerning the document, and then offered his own response to each of these objections in a systematic fashion.[2] He concluded by offering a summary statement of his own thoughts taken directly from the

Vatican's *Declaration on Sexual Ethics*: "The traditional doctrine must be studied more deeply. It must be handed on in a way capable of properly enlightening the consciences of those confronted with new situations and it must be enriched with a discernment of all the elements which can truthfully and usefully be brought forward about the meaning and value of human sexuality."[3]

When Hinds completed the first term paper on his anthropological reflections, he thought that would satisfy the independent study course requirement, but Sweeney and Koernke asked for an additional paper on *Humanae Vitae*. When Hinds was nearly certain that these two papers would make for satisfactory coursework, they assigned him yet another paper. With only one week left in the semester, Sweeney and Koernke informed him that this one was to be his reflections on the natural law with particular respect to masturbation.

Hinds requested an extension into the summer for completion of this final paper. Besides, requiring this of one particular seminarian who supported the Church's teaching on sexual morality seemed a bit suspicious to him. Hinds believed that Sweeney was looking for a reason to dismiss him from the seminary, if he could not succeed in converting Hinds to his political views.

During the month of June, while attending to his new duties as an intern seminarian, he completed the paper and mailed it in to both Sweeney and Koernke. Later that summer Hinds was surprised to find that Sweeney had mailed him comments on his masturbation paper, hinting that this "inquisitorial process," as Hinds described it, would continue the following year. He even called into question Hinds's appeal to the authority of the Church, writing that this authority "must be analyzed and perhaps critiqued itself." For the most part, Sweeney's comments on this third paper indicated the nature of his criticism, which can best be described as an ideological assessment. In other words, "Does Hinds agree with *me* on the topic at hand?" In some spots, Sweeney commented in his own hand, "agreed!" or "yes," while in others he added his own perspective, for example, writing that masturbation "may at times be 'healthy' when seen within a developmental perspective." Sweeney also notably commented at the end of Hinds's paper that he'd "be interested in hearing" about his own masturbation experiences.

Hinds then appealed to his vocations director. In a letter on September 9, 1985, Hinds wrote to Kriege regarding the masturbation paper:

> In August I received the paper back with comments. Sweeney informs me that he will set up an appointment with Sr. Terry, himself and myself in September. The tone of his comments and the nature of his suggestions that this inquisitorial process might continue seem to me to be onerous treatment. I feel that I have been deliberately singled out for such treatment because of my traditional, classic concepts in some areas—concepts which are the authoritative teaching of the Church today. I resent being repeatedly forced into an extreme revisionist position by means of burdensome questionings, "fishing expeditions," etc. I have copies of the papers from this last course in self-justification and will share them with you if you like. My plans are to ride out the process a bit further, hoping that it winds down under the burden of its own inappropriateness.

Both Koernke and Sweeney had related several complaints about Hinds's papers to his priest supervisor, who was also the dean of students at the time. In a written memo, they lodged four basic concerns about Hinds. The first concern was that he was not open enough to the position that masturbation was sometimes healthy psychologically and psychosexually. Aside from the fact that Hinds had clearly demonstrated an acquaintance with the "experts" in the field of psychology who expressed such a position, he wrote at length on the matter, studied it, and made an informed decision that what the Church teaches on the subject is the truth, especially when considered from the point of view of natural law. Nevertheless, Koernke was concerned that Hinds was using the authority and teaching of the Church as *one* of the sources that formed his belief.

"How can I answer such a complaint?" Hinds asked his priest supervisor when they discussed this. "I don't think I'm blindly and stupidly following questionable Church statements," Hinds said later in a written defense. "I've given the matter my greatest attention and I find the Church presenting a considered, contemporary opinion and asking Catholics for support. I support the position because the Church says it and because it seems logically, philosophically true, and because it seems to me to fit the phenomena. My obedience to the teaching authority of the Church is not, I think, absurd and infantile. I don't understand why this position is being challenged by faculty."

According to the priest supervisor, further concern was expressed that Hinds was "arrogant and unfair" in his masturbation paper when he stated that the other opinions on the subject must be regarded as based in ignorance or not of good will. What Hinds had written, however, was that he believed the Church's position was objectively true and that positions to the contrary could not also be true, a classic illustration of the principle of noncontradiction.

The third concern, expressed mainly by Koernke, was that Hinds's masturbation paper was "hard to follow and understand." She told his priest supervisor that she would have preferred the style of the second paper, the one he prepared on *Humanae Vitae*. In response, Hinds explained that he was assigned the writing project one week before the end of the term. Not only was he rushed, even with the extension he was granted into the month of June, his summer internship duties took up much of his time. Hinds felt that he demonstrated adequately in his first two papers that he could research a topic and present his thoughts and findings coherently. Of Koernke's criticism in this regard, said Hinds, "I felt like the high school kid who reveals himself in an essay and is thoroughly criticized and rebuked for grammatical or format inadequacies."

The last complaint, also lodged by Koernke, was Hinds's use of the word *man* used to mean a human being, either male or female. Koernke said that she was "deeply hurt and offended" by his use of what she considered "sexist and chauvinist" language. Hinds had employed the common and accepted use of the word *man* in the English language as his guide. He had never been told by any faculty member that he was obliged to use "inclusive language" that ran counter to proper English grammar. Hinds emphasized to them that he had intended no slight to women and that he would be happy to follow a school-wide policy in this regard should the seminary issue one.[4]

It was clear to everyone involved at this point that Hinds's prediction to Father Kreige had been fulfilled. Hinds wrote to his priest supervisor, asking for his intervention: "I am sorry that Sister Terry is unconvinced about certain things in my character or belief. I think I have been thoroughly and exhaustively criticized and probed concerning my position on masturbation. I would like the matter to end."

That same summer, the administration at the Athenaeum proceeded with Hinds's vocational inquisition from another direction. Knowing that Hinds held to traditional Church teaching and accepted Church norms, he was assigned to what was commonly considered "the most liberal parish in the diocese."

Despite the liberal atmosphere, Hinds was well liked by most in the parish. In his "Supervisor's Evaluation" of the internship, the pastor spoke of Hinds in glowing terms, describing him as "a prayerful person . . . compassionate . . . a good educator . . . relating well to others . . . generous both with his time and energy . . . faithful . . . happy with ministry," and remarked that "he did an excellent job of teaching. . . . His homilies were generally good, somewhat intellectual and heavy on exegesis." In this overwhelmingly positive review, the only negative comment from the pastor was that Hinds sometimes articulated an opposing view from his at parish meetings. In conclusion, however, the pastor wrote, "I would have no hesitancy recommending him for ordination."[5]

The parish's director of religious education, a nun who also worked closely with Hinds throughout his year internship, also spoke highly of him in her "Pastoral Staff Report" to the seminary. She concluded her evaluation by stating that she believed Hinds was ready to proceed to ordination, and that she "enjoyed working with Bill as a person and as a professional."[6]

Others who evaluated Hinds's performance on his internship, such as the "music minister," the school principal, and the associate pastor, spoke of him in equally positive terms. But the seminary administration was not satisfied. The internship supervisor, a faculty priest, went back to Hinds's pastor after he submitted his evaluation and asked him to tell him more about what was "wrong" with William Hinds, but was unsuccessful in soliciting any ammunition that could be used as grounds for dismissing him from the seminary.

"The papers they made me write didn't work; they tried to get me through my internship, but that didn't work either," said Hinds. Then came the "letter of all letters": On April 23, 1986, Sweeney wrote a memorandum to Father James Walsh, the newly arrived rector, regarding his "personal reflections concerning admission to candidacy of Bill Hinds." In his letter, Sweeney stated: "Through the years by virtue of personal study and life experience, Bill has formed very firm convictions about human personality, theology and Christian faith. Many of these convictions represent what some would consider a more traditional viewpoint." Sweeney recounted that he had required Hinds to articulate his theology in an independent study course, adding that Hinds's most "controversial" positions were those pertaining to sexual morality.

He continued: "Having read the essays that Bill submitted in this independent study course, I can verify that his positions are quite orthodox.... At the same time, Bill's thinking in sexual matters is not representative of what I would consider to be the mainstream of Roman Catholic moral theology today. Nor are they representative of the most recent insights offered in the field of psychology. Obviously, the entire issue of sexual morality remains a controversial theological issue in the Church today. In general, Bill seems to me to be suspicious of much of contemporary moral theology. He is even more suspect of modern psychology."

Sweeney reiterated again that Hinds was "clearly orthodox," but added that he was too adamant in maintaining his beliefs and keeping them in line with the Church's teachings. He also testified that "several times in the last couple of years I have heard a faculty member, a fellow student of Bill's, or a former work associate of his use the term 'bizarre' in referring to some of his ideas and the conviction with which he held them.... In fact, one often gets the sense that Bill feels a need to stand against those who are unwittingly perpetrators of evil." (Hinds recalled that the times his ideas were considered "bizarre" were when he was simply stating authentic Church tradition on issues such as the Virgin Birth.)

The overall intention of the memorandum seemed to be to give some grounds for questioning Hinds's suitability for ordination, even after he had successfully completed three years of coursework with nearly a 4.0 grade point average and a successful year-long internship. Sweeney concluded his critique of Hinds by writing, "I frankly do not believe that people will find him an easy person with whom to work when he occupies a leadership position.... I believe that anyone calling Bill to ordination would need to be aware of all these factors in making an appropriate assessment."

Sweeney's recommendation was that, failing outright dismissal of Hinds, he would do well to "explore some of these issues more at length in an intensive spiritual and psychological counseling relationship with a competent professional."

A copy of Sweeney's memorandum was also sent to Kriege at the Diocese of Covington. Hinds believed that the implication of the memorandum was that he should not be recommended for ordination. "The upshot of the letter," explained Hinds, "is that the rector required me to see a psychologist." From May 29 until August 7, 1986, Hinds went through ten sessions of psychotherapy with Dr. Joseph F. Wicker. (Wicker was the "Worshipful Master" of the local Masonic Lodge, see Chapter 3.)

"Had I been twenty-four years old instead of forty-four, I would have been intimidated by these counseling sessions," admitted Hinds. "I would not have been able to go in there and deal with a psychologist like that. However, at my age, I knew that I wasn't screwed up, and I wasn't intimidated by my failures and shortcomings. This type of intimidation by psychological pressure or by a guy like Sweeney who is a Ph.D. in all this kind of stuff, very few seminarians can survive."

In an August 28 report to Kriege, Wicker wrote that, after ten sessions with Hinds, "I did not discover any serious psychopathology," but that Hinds "seems to have become rather ego-involved with some ideas, values, and moral positions, and may hold to some of them quite tenaciously."[7]

In Hinds's case, he made it through the vocational inquisition to ordination. But, as Hinds noted, most seminarians, especially those in their twenties, would not have the wherewithal to endure such an inquisition. Thus, the result is that many good men are dismissed. In seminaries that see no problem with seminarians kissing other men with their tongues in the dormitory or hanging posters of transvestites on their doors, the orthodox seminarian can be singled out for "vocational inquisition" if only for defending Church teaching, especially in the controversial area of sexual morality.

One interesting aside to the Hinds saga is that after being promoted to dean of Cincinnati's seminary, Father Richard Sweeney left the priesthood to marry.

CHAPTER 9

Confronting
the Obstacles

One Good Man Traces His
Tortuous Route to Ordination

*If you wore a cassock, you were a reactionary "daughter of Trent." If you
wore women's underwear, they'd make you seminarian of the year.*
**—Father John Trigilio, former seminarian, Mary Immaculate
Seminary, Northampton, Pennsylvania**

Some priests have such harrowing tales of a "vocations inquisition" it
seems no less than an act of God that they were ever ordained. Father
John Trigilio, who cohosts *Web of Faith*, a popular apologetics program
on Mother Angelica's EWTN television network, recounted his seminary days as an "overly circuitous route to ordination," spanning three
seminaries, three dioceses, and a host of rejections from others. Because he overtly supported the teachings of the Church, he was targeted as an "orthodox" candidate as early as his high school seminary
years when he was just fourteen years old.

Beginning in the fall of 1976, Trigilio attended St. Mark's High
School Seminary in Erie, Pennsylvania. During his first year approximately one hundred students were enrolled in grades nine through

twelve. By the time he graduated in 1981, fewer than half that number
were enrolled and only eleven students graduated with him in his class.
It was a time of rapid decline, and in fact just a few years later St.
Mark's High School Seminary would close its doors forever.

His first week at St. Mark's set the tone for his experience there.
"I was going into the seminary from a fairly conservative parish in
Erie," Trigilio recalled. "At Blessed Sacrament parish we still had the
communion rail, for example, and the pastor was very Eucharistic
and Marian. So I was entering my first year of seminary quite naïve,
not having any idea what it would be like."

During his first week he was accosted by a faculty priest in the
hallway, a priest that he had not yet met. He startled Trigilio by
saying, "I hear you don't want women priests."

"I was just fourteen years old," explained Trigilio, "so I said,
'Father, what are you talking about?' He said, 'I heard you were
talking about that at the dinner table last night.' And I said, 'Yeah,
some crazy guy was talking about married priests and women
priests.' And then the priest warned me that if I wanted to get ordained, I'd better get those 'old' and 'outmoded' ideas out of my
head. There was a clear ideological threat from week one." Incidentally, Trigilio added, this same priest left the active priesthood
several years after making his threat.

Trigilio's cousin was an elderly priest for the Diocese of Erie, and
when he heard that Trigilio was entering St. Mark's, he gave him a
cassock and a Latin breviary set[1] as a present. Trigilio made the "mistake" of taking the gifts to the seminary with him. Trigilio recalls
that he was the only seminarian in the entire school who owned his
own cassock, which he wore only while serving Mass. When another
faculty priest discovered the cassock hanging in the closet of his
dorm room, Trigilio was chastised and even told that he was "mad in
the head."

"So in my first year," he remembered, "they were telling me there
was something wrong with me because I had my own cassock. I
didn't wear the cassock around school; I just had it hanging in my
closet. Little did I know that the idea about owning cassocks had
gone down the toilet."

His Latin breviary set got him in trouble too.

"Sometimes I'd get a knock on the door of my room late at night, and one of the upperclassmen would slide a copy of *Playboy* under my door. This was the common way to circulate these magazines, but I would slide it right back out. A few days later one of my high school teachers, a priest, asked me why I had a copy of the Latin breviary and the 1917 *Code of Canon Law*[2] in Latin. He asked me how I could read all this if I just started taking Latin this year, and followed that up by instructing me that fourteen-year-old boys shouldn't be praying in Latin and reading the *Code of Canon Law*. He told me that I ought to be 'reading' *Playboy*s like the other guys. I was aghast. Here I was a freshman in high school seminary, and one of my teachers, a priest no less, was advising me to delve into pornography! He actually thought there was something wrong with *me* because I was interested in learning Latin in order to actually read in Latin."

These incidents were indicative of a larger problem, that of the mission of the seminary. One day during his first year Trigilio complained to the vice rector about the military-style hazing the freshmen had to endure for weeks on end. "I told him, 'This is a seminary, so why do I have to worry about waking up at two in the morning to find that someone's trying to set my underwear on fire?' "

The vice rector, said Trigilio, surprised him by his response. "He actually denied that St. Mark's was a seminary. He said it was just a prep school. I had a lot of gumption that day so I told him he should go outside and take down the sign that reads 'St. Mark's Seminary' because it's false advertising. My parents paid money so that I could go there *because* it was a seminary. And this priest was not joking. In their minds, many of the faculty at St. Mark's Minor Seminary thought of it more as a college preparatory school than as a real seminary concerned with the education of future priests."

This attitude had its effects on the students. Trigilio remembers that on a retreat the seminarians were asked how many of them knew they had a vocation to the priesthood. Out of the hundred students, Trigilio was the only one who raised his hand that day. "None of the other guys in the seminary would admit that he definitely wanted to be a priest. It was either 'I don't know' or 'I don't believe in God' or 'I don't even know if the Church is real.' I stood up and looked at them and said, 'Then what are you people doing here? This is a seminary.' "

Trigilio explained that he knew there were indeed others at St. Mark's who were interested in becoming priests and some who were testing vocations. "But those vocations got destroyed," he said, "because of the terrible example given by some of the priests who ran the seminary. Living with them we could see how human they were—yes, and that they made mistakes. That was fine. But some of the priests in that seminary—and they certainly were not representative of the diocesan clergy in Erie at the time—had a lot of problems. They were exclusively there at the seminary and had no parish experience. They were full-time academics, more or less. Maybe one or two would help out at a parish on the weekend, but they were basically at the seminary most of their careers." There were also a few "kind, holy, prayerful, and orthodox" priests on the faculty, Trigilio admitted, but they were in the minority and did not seem to be aware of the scandalous behavior behind the scenes.

Trigilio said that when he tried to tell his parents and his pastor about some of the strange and unorthodox things he was being taught at seminary, they wouldn't believe him, but merely thought that he must be hearing wrong or misinterpreting the facts. During his four years at St. Mark's, Trigilio faced head-on all the obstacles that are commonly placed in the way of an orthodox vocation. Looking back upon his experience now he understands that a serious spiritual battle was taking place around him.

"It became evident that there was a diabolical element at the seminary," Trigilio explained. "There were nights when I couldn't even sleep because I was so scared. I could almost feel the presence of evil in that place. The way the priests had so much disdain for the Eucharist and for Mary, for example, was outright hostility. I remember being humiliated, for instance, because I wanted to pray the rosary."

Even worse than the obvious heresies that were taught, and the overt disdain for students who showed signs of being interested in the priesthood, was the rampant promiscuity. Technically, explained Trigilio, seminarians were not supposed to have girlfriends, "but one or two guys definitely did."

"One of the guys was mixed up intimately with a cheerleader every day there was a basketball game. They got together in the seminary parlor, and every time 'Bunny the cheerleader' came up, everybody knew and looked the other way," he recalled.

But this sort of "girlfriend activity" was insignificant compared to the homosexual activity that went on there. One of the biggest problems, he said, was that the younger students were "preyed upon" by the upperclassmen and especially by the college seminarians. There was even some questionable activity (imprudent at best and scandalous at worst) among a few of the faculty, he said, many of whom obviously had their favorite students. "I think a lot of the younger students were sucked in and brainwashed by the gay subculture there. They most certainly didn't start attending seminary thinking they had homosexual inclinations. I knew some of the guys, and they seemed normal enough. But if they had blonde hair or they were cute or something, then you'd know that Father So-and-so would want them to be one of his little friends. Each priest had his own private quarters, and they'd have their favorite seminarians in there with them until ten or eleven at night—high school kids. Even though most of the time there may not have been anything immoral going on, nevertheless, the appearance of impropriety was there, and it 'just didn't look good' to a prudent person."

None of these priests was ever "called to the mat" for this kind of inappropriate and potentially scandalous behavior, said Trigilio. "At that time nobody would believe you if you told them. In the late 1970s it was a time that even if you had photographs, they would have burned them and not believed you. No one felt he could come forward with that sort of information, because, if you did come forward, it would be used against you, and you could forget about becoming a priest."

The students were actively coached to keep quiet about the seminary's strange goings-on. Trigilio remembered that when two seminarians were expelled for smoking marijuana, "the rector threatened that if we were to go and tell our pastors about this, he would deny it, and we wouldn't be at St. Mark's much longer. We were clearly threatened. We were told that whatever we see and hear at the seminary we are to keep to ourselves. We felt like we were at a POW camp, always being watched. The stuff that was going on there was so bad it was almost an invitation for the devil to pop up at any time. I made the mistake of mentioning this to my spiritual director once, and all he could say was that everything is just fine here at the seminary, and besides, there is no such thing as the devil anyway."

Because Trigilio refused to submit to the decadent moral life there and what he calls "the party line of innovative and dissident theology" promoted by the faculty at St. Mark's, the formation team searched in vain for a legitimate reason to expel him from the program.

"It got so bad that in my last year of high school, I ran for student council president, and one of the priests tried to get the other students to vote against me," Trigilio recalled. "He said to me, 'Don't think that if you become student council president you're going to make this place into a haven for orthodoxy or something.' "

When the faculty failed to find a legitimate reason to expel him from the seminary program, they took a different approach. First, they got some of his classmates to turn on him. "They were spying on me, reading my mail, going through my room. They were looking for anything they could turn me in on," he said. The faculty even tried to set his own parents against him by telling them that their sixteen-year-old son was practicing the black arts. "They said that's why he's into Latin, because he wants to do the Black Mass. They called my parents, who were devastated because they believed whatever any priest told them, no matter what," he said.

Further, because of his public support for Ronald Reagan's campaign for the presidency in 1980, the college formation director tried to convince his parents that he needed serious psychiatric help. "I didn't exactly wear politics on my sleeve, but they made it sound like I was in the John Birch Society. They said I was having 'authority problems' and gravitating too much to the 'Old Church model' ever since John Paul II was elected pope."

The net result of Trigilio's high school seminary education was that he almost lost his vocation because nobody supported him in his orthodox outlook—love of Christ and His Church. Yet Trigilio never did get kicked out of St. Mark's because, as he said, he "never broke the rules."

"By the time I was getting ready for college seminary, I had just had enough of the blatant heresy in the homilies, liturgical abuses you could not even dream of, and the promiscuity had reached an all-time high. I finally went to the bishop and begged him to send me to St. Charles Borromeo in Philadelphia for my college seminary years," explained Trigilio, who noted that Philadelphia's seminary was known to be of a much more conservative mentality.

But Bishop Michael Murphy[3] would hear nothing of it. "I don't send anybody to St. Charles, and I have a problem with anybody who wants to go to St. Charles," he told Trigilio in no uncertain terms.

"Along with a couple of fellow seminarians from another diocese, I was telling the bishop all the things that were going on at the minor seminary," Trigilio said, "and he merely looked at me and said, 'I haven't heard any of this before, and if something were going on at the seminary, don't you think I would know about it?' Instead of saying that he was sorry to hear of my bad experience—that priests are telling me that Mary wasn't a virgin, that Jesus didn't know he was God, that he had brothers and sisters—he didn't blink an eye. I told him of the apparent promiscuity, that some seminarians were sleeping with one another, that a few faculty members were allegedly preying on the younger students, and so forth. But these were the 'pre-lawsuit' days when no publicity had yet been given to any of these abuses. Since I had no physical evidence and no witnesses willing to come forward, I feared that nothing could be done. The bishop looked at us but said nothing. He didn't deny nor confirm our perceptions; perhaps it was too terrible to believe. How could the accusations of nineteen- and twenty-year-olds weigh more than the reputations of several men ordained longer than these boys were alive? Whether or not an investigation ever occurred, I don't know. In the end, it was our word against theirs. Without proof, there is little that can be done unless someone initiates a full-scale examination of all the facts, testimony, and involved persons."

Subsequently Trigilio started college seminary at St. Mark's, where he received his spiritual formation. For classes, the college seminarians were bused to nearby Gannon College in downtown Erie. It was there that Trigilio met his first "orthodox" priests. The formation team at St. Mark's had warned the seminarians not to take classes from several professors, including a couple of priests, because, they said, "they were bad news; avoid them like the plague." That was enough to pique Trigilio's interest. He headed immediately to the office of Father Robert Levis at Gannon to ask him why the St. Mark's formation team had warned the seminarians to stay away from him. He found out it was because Levis had a strong reputation for orthodoxy, a love for the traditions of the Church, and great respect for the papacy.

Life at Gannon was good, Trigilio recalled, but still each day he had to return to the situation at St. Mark's. During these years, he found that he was watched even more closely for his "gravitation to the 'Old Church model' promoted by John Paul II." He and his classmates were constantly reminded by the formation team that they had to "toe the line" since the priests on the team would be recommending whether they could continue on to theology studies. The formation priests constantly insinuated, Trigilio said, that even if he were approved for major seminary studies, they would "make life hell" for him by sending him to the most liberal institution they could manage.

One of the most memorable moments for Trigilio came during a rare benediction of the Blessed Sacrament[4] prayer service in the chapel. "The priest took the monstrance," Trigilio recounted, "and held it at waist level, walked over to the tabernacle, and replaced the Blessed Sacrament. Then he took a clay pot that looked like a Grecian urn, holding it much higher than he had held the monstrance, carried it over to the altar, and placed it in the spot where the Blessed Sacrament had been; he then incensed the pot and knelt before it, saying, 'Abba, you are the potter, we are the clay.' There was nothing in the pot, but the priest was incensing it, and praying to it, so I slammed down my prayer book and headed up to my room. About twenty minutes later this same priest came up to my room screaming at me, wanting to know just who the hell I thought I was to be so disrespectful and sacrilegious during a prayer service. The only way I could think to respond to him was by saying that 'maybe on a bad day, and with a golden calf perhaps, but never with a crock pot!' " This, said Trigilio, was the attitude of many of the formation team at St. Mark's: in short, idolatrous.

After five years of minor seminary (four years of high school and one year of college) studying for the Diocese of Erie, Trigilio decided to make a second request for transfer to St. Charles Borromeo Seminary in Overbrook (Archdiocese of Philadelphia) or to simply sever all ties and leave the diocese to join another one. The bishop again refused to let him go to Philadelphia and suggested that perhaps he would be better off in another diocese altogether. Ready for such a contingency, Trigilio immediately asked to be released to apply for the Diocese of Arlington.

Without much hassle, he found a home with the Diocese of Arlington and completed his studies at Gannon College under the spiritual direction of Father Levis, with whom he had become well acquainted. He no longer had to wrestle with the powers that be at St. Mark's; instead, Arlington's bishop Thomas J. Welsh[5] allowed him to live at home and report to Levis for his formation. This would be the most valuable part of Trigilio's twelve years of seminary education.

Once ready to graduate from college, Trigilio was delighted to find that Bishop Welsh had decided to send him to theology studies at Mount St. Mary's Seminary in Emmitsburg, Maryland, one of the few American seminaries with a robust reputation for orthodoxy at that time. That summer, however, Welsh was named bishop of Allentown, and with no bishop in Arlington, Trigilio's vocation director, who was "in cahoots," he said, with St. Mark's Seminary, sent him a terse letter informing him that he was no longer a seminarian for the Arlington diocese. The letter read: "Dear John, I am sorry to inform you that Mount St. Mary's will not accept you. I will be on the road for the next three weeks. God bless you!" So with only a few months left before the new school year would begin, John Trigilio was a man without a diocese. (Trigilio later found out that the vocations director had lied and that, without a bishop in Arlington, he had sent a similar letter to other seminarians he thought were too conservative.)[6]

Trigilio literally had his bags packed and was ready to move to Mount St. Mary's when he received the news that he had been ousted from the Arlington diocese. "There was never any indication to me," he said, "that there was any problem. I was getting great grades, so this really blew me out of the water."

After this abrupt turn of events, his pastor in Erie insisted he reapply to his native diocese, and he was surprised when the vocations director in Erie so readily accepted him. He was told he would begin his studies in the fall at Christ the King Seminary near Buffalo. But when Trigilio finally talked himself into the idea of being a seminarian again for his home diocese, he received another call from the vocations director. Trigilio was then told that the bishop had vetoed the decision to accept him as a seminarian.

"I was told that he threw up my file and allegedly said 'over my dead body,' " related Trigilio. With only weeks left before the fall semester, the vocations director advised him to take a few years off from seminary and work as a truck driver—then they might consider him for the permanent diaconate. He was told that since he had been turned down twice by Erie and once by Arlington that the "will of the Holy Spirit" was revealing that Trigilio did not have a vocation to the priesthood.

Trigilio, however, disagreed. He had felt called to the priesthood since he was a boy. He had never been more certain of anything, so he decided to apply to other dioceses, but since he had been rejected by Erie and Arlington, none would accept him. He then enrolled in Holy Apostles Seminary in Connecticut. It was the only major seminary that would accept candidates who were not yet sponsored by a diocese. He had to take out loans to complete his first year of theology, but he found that the Holy Apostles faculty was orthodox, the classes were very beneficial, and all in all it was a good year.

The following spring, in 1984, Trigilio applied to the Diocese of Harrisburg. As was required of all candidates, he had to meet with Bishop William H. Keeler[7] and the vocations admissions team.

"I drove down to Harrisburg for the appointment," Trigilio recounted. "There were about ten applicants there at the time, and we were taken up, one by one, to this huge table with the bishop and five priests seated on either side of him. Three guys went in before me, taking about twenty minutes apiece. They came out and said, 'This is easy.' They said they were asked if they believe in God, if they pray, and so forth. So I thought it would be a pretty easygoing interview. But when I went in there Bishop Keeler looked at me, and the first thing he said was, 'Can you quote for me—verbatim preferably, but paraphrase if you must—in *Presbyterorum Ordinis*,[8] paragraph four, what do the council fathers say about the primary duty of the priest?' And I'm thinking, 'They didn't tell me these were going to be comprehensive exams.' The bishop asked me five more very specific, very technical questions focusing on sections of Vatican II documents. I thought I gave them pretty good answers, but I wasn't prepared to quote anything verbatim at that point. When he asked what was the primary duty of the priest, I said the priest is supposed to offer the Holy Sacrifice of the Mass and forgive sins and so forth, and Keeler said, 'That's true, but the paragraph says the primary duty of the priest is to preach the Gospel.' And I responded by saying that one translator of the pertinent text (*primum officium*) says 'primary duty' whereas another translator says 'first task.' It seems to me that one is a matter of precedence ('primary' meaning most important) and the other a priority of time ('first' meaning the logical precursor to other things)—hence the question: is preaching the Gospel the *most important* task a priest does or is it the *first* task he does *before* the *most important*, i.e., offering the Holy Sacrifice of the Mass? So how do we know what the council fathers intended? The bishop looked at me and said, 'I was there!' meaning at the council when they drafted the document.

"So after the technical questions, the rest of them had a file the size of the New York phone directory and they asked me questions about my past seminary life at St. Mark's. It was like a feeding frenzy—question after question. And one priest finally asked, 'Why should we take you? Erie rejected you twice; Arlington said no.'

"I said, 'Look, Father, I just want to be a priest, and I'll go anywhere God wants me to go. So if it's God's will that I'm not going to be here, then I'll go elsewhere.' And another asked, 'What makes you think you are going to be a priest?' And I said, 'For the same reason you thought so.'

"So then it was goodbye. I went home thinking that was over. I'd never get accepted. That was in April, and I didn't hear until July. They did say they would take me, but the proviso was that I would have to take my first year of theology over, even though I had a 4.0 average at Holy Apostles. Thus, despite the interrogation, Bishop Keeler was kind enough to give me a chance to prove myself rather than just taking the word of my former superiors. He did in fact accept me as a seminarian for the Diocese of Harrisburg and would eventually ordain me a priest in 1988, for which I am most grateful."

Trigilio was sent to Mary Immaculate Seminary,[9] nicknamed "Mary Inaccurate," in Northampton, Pennsylvania, known as one of the most liberal institutions in the country at that time (1984), for the full four years of what Trigilio considered "indoctrination." At Mary Immaculate, Trigilio experienced more of the same heterodox education and formation as during his St. Mark's years. He was even subjected to the same techniques of harassment. Yet he was now more tightly watched because the student body (for five years of study, including pretheology) numbered only twenty, fewer than the number of faculty members! "It was so small," he said, "that they knew when we went to the bathroom, how long we were in there, and if we blew our nose."

There was a "siege mentality" at Mary Immaculate, he said, due to a big push to identify the conservatives and purge them from the seminary. By then the liberal faculty was "sick and tired" of John Paul II. "If you had a picture of the pope in your room," he explained, "they kept a close eye on you. If you wore black socks you were considered 'clerical,' even though we were required to wear the

Roman collar for Mass, class, and apostolate." Those who bucked the "party line" were labeled as mentally unbalanced. After enduring what Trigilio recognized as dissident theology for four years, he finally graduated, unlike many of his orthodox classmates who were either kicked out or driven out for being "too Catholic."

Trigilio's experience at Mary Immaculate was the complete opposite of his experience at Holy Apostles Seminary. "My only complaint about Holy Apostles was some of the 'old men' down the hallway who complained we were making too much noise.[10] At Mary Immaculate [MIS] I was the one complaining that others were making too much noise because they were giggling and laughing and fooling around too much," Trigilio lamented, hinting at the campy subculture that permeated the seminary atmosphere.

"We used to say, if you wore a cassock you were a reactionary 'daughter of Trent.' If you wore women's underwear, they'd make you seminarian of the year. We had a few guys who sometimes wore women's clothing, lingerie, makeup, etc., and some who were as effeminate as could be. These were guys who were into all kinds of funny stuff. The campy ones at MIS would call each other by female names—like Mary, Sally, or Hazel—or use the feminine pronoun to refer to one another—she, her, etc. As is common in other seminaries, the 'ladies' at MIS would organize themselves, confident that the faculty was either ignorant, apathetic, or supportive of them."

At the same time, he noted, out of the dozen or so seminarians he witnessed being driven away from or kicked out of MIS, rarely were any of them dismissed for immorality or impropriety. "Most of the time," Trigilio commented, "when a guy was expelled from the seminary it was because he was too Catholic. Of course, that wasn't the reason the seminary or vocations director told the bishops. All too often, academic and psychological reasons were given to dismiss a student who was too 'conservative' or 'traditional' as well as being completely orthodox. But the seminarians who were immoral or heterodox had no problem getting ordained, as their faculty and peer evaluations were as sterling as canonization briefs. And more often than not these same [dissident] guys would leave the priesthood after a few years. Many bishops and religious superiors are totally unaware of the doublespeak, propaganda, and deception that is used to identify, isolate, and remove seminarians deemed 'too Catholic.' "

There was one notable exception to the pattern of dismissal he witnessed at MIS: "We had the state police come in and arrest one of my classmates because he allegedly went to some fifteen-year-old kid's house during the afternoon and took pictures of him in his underwear. The rest of us never found out how he knew this poor kid, but we were having an evening class when the trooper arrived with a warrant for his arrest, cuffed him, and took him right then and there in front of everybody. The next day in the local newspaper ran a full story on a Catholic seminarian charged with corruption of the morals of a minor and other things."

Trigilio pointed out that up to the moment of that seminarian's arrest, the suspect was getting excellent evaluations because he was " 'tolerant, flexible, and liberal-minded'—i.e., he went along with the faculty on everything."

"I can say this," he explained, "but it's not an absolute: If a guy through his seminary career at MIS had never had any opposition from the faculty, there was something wrong with him. If you were anything near orthodox, you had to fight tooth and nail to keep your sanity and your faith, and it wasn't easy for us to remain there, let alone actually get ordained. The formation team would tell my bishop that 'He's having trouble adjusting to contemporary theology; he's clinging to archaic descriptions; he remains very rigid.' But for those who were openly homosexual, their bishops were not informed."

Almost as bad as the sexual improprieties at MIS were the blatant heretical teachings the seminarians received. Trigilio explained that by the time he started at Mary Immaculate, 80 percent of the seminarians were coming into seminary with virtually no background in philosophy or theology. "They were like clean slates," he said. "A lot of them hadn't even attended a Catholic high school, and almost no one had been at a high school seminary. So they were coming in there blank, and whatever the priests told them was, for the most part, uncritically accepted. If they came to Mary Immaculate for pretheology, and the priest-professor taught them there were only six sacraments, then they believed him because they didn't know otherwise. But my friends and I who had been in seminary previously were seen as a threat because we knew something about authentic Church teaching and discipline coming in."

Trigilio estimated that the proclaimed heresy at Mary Immaculate was bolder and more overt than at most seminaries: "At MIS they would come right out in the classroom and at the pulpit and deny dogmas of the Catholic faith or at least sow the seeds of doubt and dissent—from the divine personhood of Christ to inerrancy of Scripture to the infallibility of the ordinary magisterium and so on—whereas at other seminaries the heterodoxy would be much more subtle and covert, and spoken in a less obvious manner.

"All the classes were horrible from the standpoint of orthodoxy except our courses on canon law, which were taught by priests from Philadelphia. All the other theology courses were unbelievable. The *Catechism* was not yet published at that time, but almost everything they said contradicted the *Catechism*.

"We all got the new Bible theology that none of the Scriptures was really inspired, that Matthew, Mark, Luke, and John did not write anything themselves, that the Gospels were actually written centuries later by the 'Christian community,' that all the miracles attributed to Jesus in the New Testament were fabrications, and so forth. We also had a nun who taught us liturgy. She maintained that sacrifice is a pagan idea that needed to be expunged from the Mass. She also taught us that the Church has only six sacraments since she cannot receive [the Sacrament of Holy Orders]."

The orthodox seminarians, he said, were ridiculed and humiliated in front of the entire class when they would voice a traditional viewpoint, such as quoting St. Thomas Aquinas. "One day," Trigilio recalled, "in a moral theology course the priest was extolling O'Connell's principle of 'Do as little evil and as much good as possible.' I responded by pointing out that it seems to contradict natural law, where St. Thomas says we must 'do good and avoid evil.' Instead of answering my objection, the priest just said, 'Don't quote Thomas

Aquinas to me because all you're doing is quoting stuff you learned years ago, and now you're showing off to your classmates that you know something old, but you're really just too lazy to study anything new.' This was a typical response: They rarely, if ever, answered the points I brought forth, but would simply dismiss them in the name of exploring the latest novelty, however much that might contradict Church teaching."

The highlight of each year for Trigilio was attendance at an annual conference for seminarians sponsored by Opus Dei offered during Easter week. It attracted around 150 orthodox seminarians from all over the country. "We would get top-notch orthodox speakers for a whole week of unadulterated Catholicism," Trigilio explained.

It was also a chance for him and the few other orthodox seminarians from MIS to exchange "war stories" with other aspiring priests who were in much the same situation. "We found that guys at most of the other seminaries had to put up with the same," he said. "And we all got to hear teaching at this conference that we would never get in the seminary, not in our wildest dreams."

Each year, however, there was a bit of resentment in returning to Mary Immaculate Seminary, Trigilio admitted. The seminarians who had attended the conference would invariably ask themselves why they couldn't receive the inspiration they got at the conference, why they couldn't get the support for their vocations that they received from those whom they met there, and why they had to feel like they were returning to the "underground," as if they were living in Elizabethan England, just in order that their vocation could survive another year.

"Despite the fierce witch-hunt to ferret out orthodox seminarians and the bold campaign to indoctrinate the rest in heterodox theology," Trigilio reflected, "there were at both minor and major seminaries a few good men still left. Despite overwhelming odds, many orthodox seminarians were able to 'play the game' and get ordained. More ironic is that at almost every seminary there are some very good, holy, devout, orthodox, and extremely spiritual priests on the faculty who help you get through as best they can. Like the French resistance movement during World War II, there was some clandestine underground support to preserve tradition, piety, and orthodox teaching. Regrettably, the bad ones stand out and get the attention, but there were some fantastic priests at St. Mark's and at Mary Immaculate who put the others to shame. Their kindness, support, and fidelity should not be eclipsed even by the vocal majority who sought to remake the Catholic Church in their own image and likeness. More frustrating is that many good, devout, and orthodox bishops are too often shielded from the truth by certain faculty members, administrators, or vocation directors, or diocesan bureaucrats. The good guys don't know, the mediocre don't care, and the bad ones are calling the shots."

■ ■ ■

Although Father John Trigilio's experience may seem so sensational as to be an anomaly, unfortunately, it is not. Every year dozens of men are subjected to the same tactics in order to undermine their vocations. The ideal candidate for the priesthood in the eyes of many who are charged with forming them is the man, young or old, who comes to them as a blank slate, knowing little of substance about the Catholic faith. Obviously, these men are much easier to mold in the faculty's own image. Those who do understand the Catholic faith as taught by the magisterium of the Church are seen as a threat to the status quo of confusion and religious and moral liberalism.

Relatively few educated young men are willing or even able to endure the kind of unsupportive atmosphere found too often at certain seminaries in order to advance to the ordained priesthood. The vocational inquisition game can be brutal, say many orthodox priests and ex-seminarians. The younger and less mature the seminarian, the more difficult it is to take up the cross of white martyrdom for the purpose of living out one's calling.[11]

CHAPTER 10

Heads in the Sand

How Complaints about the Poor State of Seminaries Have Gone Unanswered

Complaints about doctrinal error, liturgical abuse and even personal misconduct in U.S. seminaries are now so common as to be routine.
—Francis X. Maier, former editor
of the **National Catholic Register**

If something is so obviously wrong with Catholic seminaries and the education of future priests, a logical question might be: Are the powers that be aware of this unjust and unorthodox situation, and if so, what is being done about it? The answer isn't as easy or direct as the question, but suffice it to say that many in positions of authority in the Catholic Church have long been aware that a self-inflicted pattern of ideological discrimination has taken root in Catholic seminaries. Others would rather not know too much or have taken an almost pathological approach to denial.

More than two decades ago Pope John Paul II seemed already to understand well the crisis of the seminaries in the United States. It is well known that as Karol Cardinal Wojtyla, he visited North American seminaries, purely out of concern for the formation of future priests, during a trip abroad just a little more than a year before he was elected to the See of Peter. Even so, it came as much of a shock to seminary incumbents that in September of 1981 John Paul ordered studies of the seminaries in the United States. At that time, only in the third year of his pontificate, the pope had already repeatedly emphasized the necessity for doctrinal conformity among Catholic theologians. During the previous year in a highly publicized case, the pope censured Swiss theologian Father Hans Küng for undermining certain dogmas of the Catholic faith, including papal infallibility. Thus, when Archbishop John R. Roach,[1] then president of the National Conference of Catholic Bishops, announced the Vatican investigation of American seminaries, the *New York Times* reported that the plan "alarmed some seminary heads who believe the study could result in an attempt to root out dissent and stifle academic freedom."[2] According to the *Times*, none of the critics of the Vatican's plan would permit his name to be used. But one seminary educator called the study a "witch-hunt," saying that *U.S. seminary officials* had not requested such an examination. Another anonymous critic predicted that the study would be used to coerce "doctrinal orthodoxy" and to "scare the hell out of everyone."[3] If the *New York Times* report revealed anything, it was that U.S. seminary educators were admitting they were doing whatever they pleased with willful disregard to orthodoxy and loyalty to the Church universal. And they did not want to be bothered by anyone from Rome.

The Vatican appointed Bishop John Marshall[4] of Burlington, Vermont, to coordinate the project in the United States, assisted by forty bishops, nineteen religious superiors, and fifty-seven priests who had worked as seminary educators. Reflecting years later, Archbishop Edwin O'Brien[5] offered an explanation for the planned visitations: "In the wake of Vatican II, greater emphasis was placed on the pastoral side of formation, on how effective a communicator the priest would be; whether he could reach people in their psychological needs; and whether he was aware of the social gospel of the Church."[6] Consequently, he said, some men were being ordained without being ready "for the long haul as priests."[7]

Many faithful Catholics had been furnishing conclusive evidence of heterodox thinking and poor liturgical training among newly ordained priests—products of the 1970s seminaries. In an October 1981 editorial in the *National Catholic Register,* Francis X. Maier explained that the study demonstrated growing concern by the Vatican that all was not well in American seminaries. "This will surprise no one," he wrote. "Complaints about doctrinal error, liturgical abuse and even personal misconduct in U.S. seminaries are now so common as to be routine."[8] Father Kenneth Baker, editor of *Homiletic and Pastoral Review,* also attested to the situation as perceived by Catholics in the early 1980s. "It is obvious to many priests and concerned lay people," he wrote, "that many seminaries have serious problems."[9] For years, he added, priests and concerned members of the laity had been writing to Rome and requesting that something be done about the sad state of affairs in U.S. seminaries. But Baker went further, identifying the connection between this poor state of affairs and the vocations crisis. Referring to an editorial he penned in 1973, he related that he had quizzed priests all over the country as to whether or not they encouraged young men to enter the seminary. What he found was startling: most priests, in fact, did not. The reasons, he explained, were: "1) the breakdown of discipline and morals in the seminary, and 2) the absence of solid Catholic teaching (not to mention the complaints about doctrinal errors, heresy and situation ethics)." In 1982, said Baker, he had no reason to change that view. "I am convinced that it was correct then and that it is still correct," he wrote.[10]

Maier, former editor of the *Register,* predicted that the result of the Vatican's study would be the closing of many seminaries, since in 1981 there were far too few seminarians for the number of such institutions. That would leave some of these worrying educators without a job. Thus, believing that orthodoxy would be the primary criteria for evaluation, naturally the dissidents fretted. With a hopeful outlook, the *Register,* as well as many American Catholics who had become fed up with the poor quality of priests coming out of the seminaries, viewed the Vatican initiative as an opportunity to purify the American seminaries that had fallen into ecclesiastical disrepair.

The visitation team, popularly called the Marshall Committee, drew up guidelines and questions to be asked. The preface of the 103-page study pointed out that "questions have been raised in various quarters concerning proper adherence to magisterial teaching with special reference to such subjects as the nature of the priesthood, celibacy, non-ordained ministry, social justice, formation of conscience and the like."[11] Each seminary first had a chance at "self-evaluation," an advanced written report in response to an extensive questionnaire. Then a five-man evaluation committee, including one bishop and a major religious superior, visited each seminary for three days, after which they gave an oral report to the seminary administration and local bishop. The committee then reported their findings to Bishop Marshall, who in turn reported back to Rome after consulting with the seminary in question.

"A lot of seminaries," admitted Archbishop O'Brien, "realized that they hadn't been giving spirituality and the interior life the emphasis that they should have."[12] Although O'Brien and other American bishops felt that the review process was very successful, in the end, others thought it was a whitewash.

Father John Trigilio said when he first heard that Marshall would be commandeering the visitation team, he held out much hope that the Vatican might finally do something about the serious problems besetting U.S. seminaries. Marshall was considered a "conservative" bishop, and Trigilio knew him as a guest speaker each year at an annual retreat and conference for seminarians run by Opus Dei near Boston. "A number of us seminarians went to him and we said, 'Bishop, if you want any information, we can give you some.' " Trigilio, however, was surprised by Marshall's response. "He said, 'Look, boys, this is not a witch-hunt. We're just going to visit the seminaries to find out what they're teaching,' " apparently in reference to the *New York Times* article. "The Vermont bishop was effectively saying, 'We don't want to find out *too* much,' " Trigilio lamented. He was also struck by the bishop's use of the term "witch-hunt," which he said was ironic considering that "seminaries and dioceses had instigated an all-out witch-hunt to identify, discredit, and remove orthodox seminarians who threatened the status quo of dissent." Looking back on the lack of results generated by the seminary visitations across the country, he regarded the Marshall Committee "as being analogous to the tobacco industry conducting its own medical tests on whether or not smoking causes cancer."

When the Vatican team came to Mary Immaculate, Trigilio's seminary in Northampton, Pennsylvania, "papal encyclicals mysteriously appeared," he said, "as if we were actually taught from them." Things that they never did, like benediction of the Blessed Sacrament, were all of a sudden done. It was a big show. And as soon as the delegation left, the encyclicals got placed back onto remote shelves; rosaries were put back into drawers; and clerics were stashed away in chiffoniers. "Like the *bella figura* the Nazis put on when the Red Cross visited their POW camps, seminary officials 'walked the walk and talked the talk' only while the committee was present," he said. "I went through four years of graduate study at Mary Immaculate and at no time were we ever exposed to papal encyclicals, the sixteen documents of Vatican II, or the *Summa Theologica*. In fact, 99 percent of my classmates and colleagues never heard of, nor did they ever use, Denzinger's *Enchiridion Symbolorum*,[13] despite the fact that even the *Catechism* today uses Denzinger references all over the place."

Father Eduard Perrone, a priest of the Detroit archdiocese, remembered when the Marshall Committee came to St. John's Seminary in Plymouth, Michigan. He was already several years ordained at the time but was still familiar with the school's major shortcomings. The seminary had run aground under the rectorship of Kenneth Untener, who was made bishop of Saginaw in 1980 at the age of forty-three. Some Detroit-area Catholics believe the main problem was rampant homosexuality among faculty and seminarians, he said, which led to a Pandora's box of other difficulties in line with the adage that "all heresy begins below the belt."

Former seminarians there report that the gay cliques would entertain themselves in the shadows of the seminary golf course, while everyone in the building knew what they were doing. This continuing nocturnal drama was dubbed "Spectrum Under the Stars."[14] A few weeks before the evaluation team was due to arrive, Perrone convinced two of his friends who were seminarians there to dictate to him the whole story of the moral and theological decadence that was strangling the school. Since seminary officials cleverly worked to minimize contact between the students and the visiting bishops, Perrone drew up an exposé document based on their story. "I wrote on the courses that were being taught, the faculty, the student life, liturgical shenanigans. It was very carefully outlined," he said.

Archbishop Ignatius J. Strecker[15] of Kansas City, Kansas, led the Vatican team to St. John's. One night at around 3 A.M., as the archbishop slept, Perrone entered the seminary building and slipped the document under Strecker's door. "I know he read it," recalled Perrone, "because Cardinal Szoka[16] was very upset that I had made this intervention. I had put my name to it.

"I also know that when the Vatican team came, St. John's tried to clean up and make everything look good. One of the professors hadn't worn a Roman collar in that seminary since before the council, and here he showed up to class during the evaluation wearing his clerics, collar and all. A number of the priest professors did the same. It was all show."[17]

Father Justice Wargrave* was a seminarian at the time of the four-day Vatican visit to St. John's. He too commented that it was strange to see the faculty wearing Roman collars.

Some of the concerned seminarians, he said, pushed hard for personal interviews with the visitation team, and some were held privately. Then, on the last day of the visit, apparently in response to the resounding complaints the visitors were hearing from seminarians, an "unplanned open forum" was held for about ninety minutes, recalled Wargrave. "About thirty attended, and there were no faculty present. The queens tried to defend the status quo," he said.

Jesuit Father Paul Mankowski, a lecturer in Old Testament Languages at the Pontifical Biblical Institute in Rome, was studying at the Weston School of Theology in Cambridge, Massachusetts, when the evaluation team came to the United States. "Some of us were hoping to see the visitors in private and give them the real story of what was going on there," he said. "They met two or three lapdog students preselected by the school and then announced they weren't giving any more interviews. And, of course, Weston got an absolutely glowing report," he added, explaining that Weston deserved not accolades but a strong rebuke.

Charles Wilson, founder and director of the St. Joseph Foundation, also remembers the Marshall Committee. He was working toward his Masters of Theological Studies degree at the Oblate School of Theology in San Antonio, Texas, at the time. Judging from the glowing report that Oblate received from the visitation, he too concluded that "the thing was a total sham." Aside from an obvious lack of attention to orthodoxy in classes, he said, Oblate's problems stemmed from the majority of its students being laity. In fact, the master of divinity degree, usually reserved for those being ordained to the priesthood, was offered to lay men and women.

Anthony Gonzales was a seminarian studying for the Diocese of Santa Rosa when the Marshall Committee team arrived at St. Patrick's in Menlo Park, California. "The faculty changed many things to prepare for it," he remembered. They replaced heterodox books with orthodox titles. The seminarians were made to dress in clerics, which was never done, and the classes were "toned down to give the impression that the seminary was orthodox when we definitely were not."

When the Vatican team visited Cincinnati's seminary at the Athenaeum of Ohio, Father William H. Hinds recalled hoping that they would "ride in on their white horses and save the seminary from itself." But, he said, it was more like they were riding mules. He also remembered that seminary officials made it difficult to speak personally with the visiting bishops. "We had to go to the office to sign up for an appointment, and then we were told that we'd get to speak to one of the bishops 'if there was enough time.' " Most of the seminarians who wanted to speak their minds to the evaluation team about the "deplorable" conditions of the moral and spiritual climate there were intimidated. If you signed up, he explained, it would be frowned upon by seminary officials, and they'd ask why you wanted a secret meeting and "were you going to tell them your own sins or the seminary's?"

Hinds did get to meet with a bishop. Hoping he would be greeted by a Savonarola type who would make some heads roll, he met instead with a soft-spoken elderly bishop from Pennsylvania. "He seemed just like an average priest who was checking out something that didn't really need to be checked on," Hinds recalled. The whole visitation was highly bureaucratic and perfunctory, he said. "When the bishop found out that I could speak Latin, he conducted the whole interview in Latin," which Hinds said was bizarre and comical. "I was as blunt as I could be in Latin," he joked. In the end, he could tell that the visitors would not be able to figure out what was really going on at the seminary and probably didn't really want to. "They asked the seminary officials how they were doing, and they said 'great,' and the evaluation team was glad to hear it."

When Father Norman Weslin heard a Vatican visitation team would be visiting Sacred Heart Seminary in Hales Corner, Wisconsin, he held out similar hope that the bishops would take some interest in seeing some major problems resolved. While a seminarian there, Weslin had a reputation of being outspoken. He openly challenged professors who were at odds with the magisterium. Other seminarians, he related in his autobiography, were surreptitious about their own orthodoxy: "I asked them, that, if they planned to stay submerged, then document information on the heretical teachings to me with dates, times, places, and teacher. I told them that I would then write a report for the pope's Seminary Investigation Team."[18]

When the visitation team arrived, said Weslin, the seminary officials "had spotters, most of them homosexuals, watching the corridors to determine who went in to see the pope's investigation team."[19] Weslin first went to see the seminary rector and told him that he intended to expose the teachings of the seminary to the team as well as the fake syllabi used in deceiving the team, giving them the false impression that the theology they were teaching was of the orthodox stripe. The fake syllabi for the year listed sound Catholic textbooks and other references, but, wrote Weslin, the seminarians were given photocopies of the works of Andrew Greeley[20] and other well-known dissenters. "The orthodox material was rarely, if ever, used."

At the conclusion of the protracted process of gathering information from all of the nation's seminaries, the Vatican issued several guarded reports that expressed general satisfaction with the state of most U.S. seminaries, yet expressing a faint hope that certain failings or oversights would be corrected in short order. The study, however, was never made public. In October of 1986, William Cardinal Baum,[21] the prefect for the Vatican's Congregation for Catholic Education—an American—issued a statement that a few seminaries "have one or more serious deficiencies," but offered no details other than to say he was concerned about "weaker scholarship," the use of lay men and women as spiritual directors, and the presence of nonseminarians in all too many courses. His deepest concern was for the proper development of the identity of the priest in the seminary. In his statement, he wrote:

> Our most serious recommendations have been about the need to develop a clear concept of the ordained priesthood, to promote the specialized nature of the priestly formation in accordance with Vatican Council II's affirmation of seminaries, to deepen the academic formation so that it becomes more properly and adequately theological (with more convinced and convincing attention to the magisterium in some courses), and to ensure that the seminarians develop a good grasp of the specific contribution that the priest has to make to each pastoral situation.

In 1988, Bishop Marshall delivered the most comprehensive report on the Vatican-commissioned investigation to the U.S. bishops. Although he cited that the study revealed some glaring deficiencies, including dissent from key Church teachings, the American bishops ultimately interpreted the Vatican's findings as a vindication of the American-style approach to educating Catholic priests in postconciliar times.

What was thought of as a "Vatican investigation" had precious little to do with the Vatican, it seems. Although the Holy See had commissioned the visitation project, those chosen to do the snooping appeared to be working more to satisfy the American bishops than to furnish facts to Rome. Ralph McInerny, a philosophy professor at the University of Notre Dame, summed up the process well:

> For decades we have been hearing stories about priestly training and religious houses that would have made Boccaccio blush. And yet a task force formed by the U.S. bishops during the 1980s to look into the seminaries found that everything was just fine. Here indeed was a failure, and by churchmen, who had to make a determined effort not to acquaint themselves with the facts they were supposedly investigating.[22]

One possible positive outcome of the Marshall Committee findings—whatever they were—was that they may have led to the 1990 Synod of Bishops. That year Pope John Paul II devoted the theme to "The Formation of Priests in Circumstances of the Present Day." The proceedings from the Synod eventually led to the publication of the *Directory of the Life and Ministry of Priests* and Pope John Paul's *Pastores Dabo Vobis*, both of which provided concrete direction for authentic reform of the seminaries of the world.

The 1980s—the years of the Vatican-commissioned seminary evaluation—were arguably the worst of times for most American seminaries. During the confusion of the 1970s, the progressive theologies and experimental approaches to liturgy were at least sometimes balanced by intelligent and conservative "holdovers" who were trained before the Council. But by 1980, the revolution had completely taken hold in most of the seminaries.[23] The 1980s were the crest of a wave of the liberals' rise to power. By then, liturgical experimentation was systematized into a series of abuses that had become "norms" in the seminaries; moral theology had been confused, and was reflected practically in the moral lives of faculty and students.

One of the most important points, however, was that by the 1980s, career seminary officials had worked out—independently of one another perhaps—ways of identifying and weeding out seminarians with whom they disagreed. These men who were unjustly discriminated against were seminarians, as Archbishop Curtiss would point out a decade later, who accept and defend Church teachings, especially on sexual morality and the priesthood.

Despite the liberals' efforts, in the early 1990s somewhat more conservative priests emerged from the seminary. Historian James Hitchcock theorizes that since many of these priests ordained in the 1990s saw firsthand the destruction wrought by the crisis of the priesthood that followed the council, they desired a priesthood regrounded in the authentic tradition of the Church.

"While many older priests continue to insist that everything which has happened since 1965 is true renewal, as they continue to rail against the forces of orthodoxy, younger men see with a clear eye the destruction done in renewal's name and that the path to a healthy and vibrant Church lies in quite a different direction," he wrote in 1999.[24] A sort of inverted generation gap began to widen throughout the Clinton years: the younger, more conservative men who seek to live the priestly life as the Church defines the ministry versus the middle-aged, "radical" priests of days past who seek to reenvision the priesthood and the entire Church based on a misguided sense of renewal. Hitchcock describes these old radicals:

> The clergy whose lives now seem blighted, and who kick back almost compulsively against all signs of renewed orthodoxy, were mostly victims of a process they did not begin to understand, swept along by cultural forces they had in no way anticipated.... But this is the generation of priests which now controls many dioceses and most religious orders, and they are often ruthless. Having successfully rebelled thirty years ago, having destroyed the traditional system of authority, they now often employ tactics of control and intimidation which preconciliar religious superiors, carefully following the rules, would never have dreamed of using. In all but a few blessed places, orthodox younger clergy will now

have to endure varying degrees of suffering until the day comes—if it does—when they are finally in a position to shape the direction of their communities.[25]

Part of their "ruthlessness" has been long evidenced in seminary formation programs. These tactics of control and intimidation are used systematically in seminaries and vocations offices to identify and root out the orthodox vocations, precisely so that the young conservative can't take root in their diocese or religious order. Hitchcock compared this state of affairs with the conditions of the Counter-Reformation years. Authentic reform, he said, was not achieved by the older clergy, whose memories stretched back before the emergence of Protestantism, "many of whom were confused, passive, and locked into patterns of immoral living."[26] It fell to a new generation of priests, those with no memory of life before Protestantism, to bring about genuine reform. And so one pities the aging radicals who thought they offered such progress but are living to see that Holy Mother Church still knows best, and that younger generations of priests aren't interested in their dated ideas and agendas.

Slowly, as the 1990s progressed, Catholics saw more and more genuine reform in the Church, a shift away from the experimental "spirit of Vatican II" to a practical regrounding of Catholic faith and culture. Likewise, certain pockets of the United States, as mentioned in Chapter 1, began seeing a significant increase in vocations to the priesthood and a healthy number of ordinations each year. The newest vocations in fact are often products of new or revitalized Catholic colleges such as Ave Maria, Christendom, Franciscan University of Steubenville, and Thomas Aquinas College. They often come from countercultural families that homeschool or that are involved in the many orthodox "movements" that place an emphasis on the dynamic faithfulness of the lay vocation.

Another related phenomenon that emerged in the 1990s was a sort of "brain drain" away from liberal dioceses toward orthodox ones. In part because of a growing awareness of the culture wars being played out in the Church, some young men, often guided by orthodox parents or priests, began to seek out dioceses that would support their vocations instead of discouraging them or burying them. Speaking to this point, the late Jesuit theologian Father John Hardon identified the primary cause of the vocations crisis as a lack of authentic Catholic life. Hardon, who worked for the Holy See for decades, said, "In dioceses and religious orders where young men can witness authentic Catholic life, vocations will flourish. In others, vocations to the priesthood and religious life will languish."[27] Hardon's "survival of the fittest" theory explains why orthodox dioceses have a disproportionately higher number of vocations and priests than others. It is a natural and logical process.

CHAPTER 11

A Self-Fulfilling Prophecy

How a Death Wish for the Male, Celibate Priesthood Created an Artificial Priest Shortage

First, many of [our present seminarians] have had multiple sex experiences. Their backgrounds are different from ours. I'm also surprised at the frankness with which they discuss their personal lives. This is great.
—Rembert Weakland, Archbishop of Milwaukee

I have in earlier chapters referred more than a few times to the desire on the part of many well-placed priests and nuns, as well as others, to "reenvision" the Catholic priesthood. This reenvisioning plays a crucial role in the crisis of ideological discrimination, whereby good men, orthodox and loyal to the Catholic Church, are dismissed as unfit for the priesthood. It is important to understand this "reenvisioned" role: who is promoting such an idea, and why? As Archbishop Curtiss wrote, "the vocations 'crisis' is precipitated by people who want to change the Church's agenda"; they therefore strive to eliminate candidates to the priesthood who do not support their political views, views which, it is instructive to note, are not those of the Church. Curtiss specifically mentioned those directly responsible for promoting and fostering vocations as having a "death wish" for the male, celibate priesthood.

These "death wishers" also happen to be the doomsayers who have been predicting a dire priest shortage for decades. At the same time they've viewed the priest shortage and vocations crisis as a prophetic call to institute widespread change in the Church. Dominican Father Frank Norris, for example, writing in *Ligourian* magazine in 1997, believed the vocations situation to be so bleak at that time that he asked, "Should we weather the storm, or is it time to abandon ship and reenvision our perspective on vocations to the priesthood?"[1] Norris admits that the doomsayers have "discerned" that the present dearth of vocations "represents a movement of the Holy Spirit to expand the pool of candidates" for priestly ministry.[2] Many, a majority of whom are priests and nuns, surmise that the priest shortage is not a crisis of faith but rather an institutional crisis fueled by the Church's strictures on celibacy. Predictably, they call for an end to such a discipline; they request that priests be allowed to marry and that resigned priests be fully reinstated in order to solve the crisis. The same crowd also believes that the Church's ability to attract vocations is hampered by the fallout from the unhealthy sexual repression that results from "imposed" celibacy: pedophilia scandals and a priesthood that is said to be dominated by homosexuals.

Many of those who promote the fulfillment of this death wish for the male, celibate priesthood have long appealed to the "spirit of Vatican II," despite the glaring contradiction the council itself provides. In fact, the Second Vatican Council clearly reiterated the importance of priestly celibacy in the Latin rite. According to *Presbyterorum Ordinis*,

> Through virginity or celibacy observed for the sake of the kingdom of heaven, priests are consecrated to Christ in a new and distinguished way. They more easily hold fast to Him with undivided heart. They more freely devote themselves in Him and through Him to the service of God and men. They more readily minister to His

kingdom and to the work of heavenly regeneration, and
thus become more apt to exercise paternity in Christ,
and do so to a greater extent.[3]

Nevertheless, the male, celibate priesthood turned into one of the
most controversial issues facing the Church in the late twentieth
century. Before the Second Vatican Council, the role of celibacy in
the life of the priest was not often questioned or dwelt upon by
Catholics. It was not an issue that concerned the laity; it was not seen
as a deterrent to attracting priestly vocations. Yet, since the 1960s,
celibacy has evolved into a complicated issue linked to the issues of
homosexuality and the ordination of women.

Those pushing for opening priestly ordination to married men
rely heavily upon the assumption that dispensing with the Church's
discipline of clerical celibacy would greatly increase the number and
quality of those men who would serve the Church as priests. With
the severe shortage of priests and seminarians in certain parts of the
U.S. over the past three decades, this argument becomes all the more
attractive. Some, such as sociologist and ex-priest Richard Schoenherr, author of *Full Pews, Empty Altars*, argue that "mandatory
celibacy" is the driving force behind the priest shortage, despite the
fact that our seminaries were filled beyond capacity forty years ago
when the discipline of celibacy was exactly the same as it is today. "To
be authentically religious," he maintains, "Catholic ministry must
open itself to the charismatic transformative power of marriages as
well as celibacy."[4] One could argue—indeed, many do—that ordaining women would also help swell the ranks of the priesthood.
For the feminist contingent the priest shortage promises to pave the
way for women's ordination. The restriction of the priesthood to
celibate men is seen as the last vestige of patriarchy, a system of
power, control, and sexism that must inevitably collapse—they hope.

The link between celibacy and women's ordination is consistently
drawn by national organizations such as the Women's Ordination
Conference, Call to Action, and Catholics Speak Out. They see ordination as a right rather than a privilege. Celibacy, however, sets

apart a certain class of people as "different," and to the mind of those agitating for such things as the ordination of women to the priesthood and diaconate, such a class of people is unjust and patriarchal.

Much of the sting has been taken out of the rhetoric surrounding the issue of women's ordination since Pope John Paul II issued the apostolic exhortation *Ordinatio Sacerdotalis*, which declared that "the Church has no authority whatsoever to confer priestly ordination on women," and that this judgment is "to be definitively held by all the Church's faithful."[5] Nevertheless, certain elements in the Church—including in seminaries and vocations offices—continue to champion the cause.

It has also been popular to suggest, as Father Norris pointed out, that since countries like the United States have experienced dwindling numbers of priests, "maybe the Holy Spirit is telling us something." Catholic News Service columnist Father Peter Daly, for instance, wrote:

> Whenever I have a conversation with young men about the possibility of priesthood, I hear the same remark: "Father, I would think about it except for the requirement of celibacy." Over the years I have been a defender of celibacy as a spiritually valuable discipline and an important witness. But the Eucharist and preaching the Gospel are more valuable.[6]

Then the often repeated suggestion comes: "It could be that the Holy Spirit is telling us something...."[7] Daly then suggests the Church should allow married men to be ordained to serve as parish priests.[8] The same reasoning has been applied by other prominent Catholic columnists such as Father Richard McBrien, Sister Joan Chittister, and Tim Unsworth.

Even some U.S. bishops have expressed these sentiments. Bishop Raymond Lucker[9] of New Ulm, Minnesota, wrote in an October 1998 issue of his diocesan newspaper that, considering the shortage of priests and seminarians, he strongly endorsed married priests.

The celibacy requirement for priests, he wrote, is an obstruction "in the way of our fulfilling the law of God." Celibacy, he reassured, is not a doctrinal issue, but a matter of Church discipline suited perhaps for the Middle Ages but not for our post–Sexual Revolution culture. Again, he is assuming that the discipline of celibacy is *the* cause of the priest shortage, and therefore that its elimination would eliminate the vocations crisis. Lucker's sentiments again seem to confirm Archbishop Curtiss's claim that vocations directors and others, even bishops, have a "death wish" for the male, celibate priesthood. Not coincidentally, the Diocese of New Ulm had one of the lowest rates of ordination during the years Lucker served as its shepherd. His diocese also "boasts" the highest percentage of parishes without a priest-pastor.

Milwaukee's archbishop, Rembert Weakland,[10] also believes that the Holy Spirit is telling us that the male, celibate priesthood is unworkable. In a 1996 editorial published in the *Milwaukee Journal-Sentinel*, Weakland sang the praises of a married priesthood, suggesting that an end to celibacy would solve the problem of lonely priests and ultimately the priest shortage.

In a follow-up editorial in the same venue, Catholic lay-activist Margo Szews asked if it were not the ultimate in hypocrisy for the archbishop to "promote and implement policies that have resulted in the current priest shortage, and then deplore the problem as though he had no hand in it?" The problem is not celibacy, wrote Szews, but rather the archbishop's own policies, which deter young men from serving as priests in the Milwaukee archdiocese, known as one of the most liberal areas of the nation. Szews rhetorically asked:

> Isn't it the archbishop who has allowed/encouraged priests to move out of the rectories and into apartments, thus causing the loneliness he laments? Isn't it the archbishop who has allowed potential seminarians, whose loyalty to Church teaching is viewed as "rigid and inflexible," to be rejected? Isn't it the archbishop who has permitted/encouraged the use of altar girls, when it is

known that service as altar boys has inspired many priestly vocations? Isn't it the archbishop who has encouraged women to attend the seminary, a place for priestly formation, where they have outnumbered men for years? Isn't it the archbishop who has, through forced early retirement, rejected the services of able-bodied priests who are also seen as "rigid and inflexible"?[11]

In a *Green Bay Press-Gazette* article in 2000, Weakland confirmed his sympathies on the issue of priestly celibacy. He sees signs of hope in the younger generation coming into the priesthood, he said. "First, many of them have had multiple sex experiences. Their backgrounds are different from ours. I'm also surprised at the frankness with which they discuss their personal lives. This is great," he added.[12]

The Milwaukee archbishop's comment brings up another aspect of the celibacy cause-and-effect theory: Celibacy, especially during the 1990s, has been linked to various scandals in the priesthood, mainly those relating to pedophilia and homosexuality, but also to old-fashioned heterosexual adultery. Public opinion maker Father Andrew Greeley, for instance, made the point that the image of the priesthood has been dealt a savage blow by well-publicized resignations, by the pedophile crisis, and by the fact that the priesthood is increasingly becoming a gay group, a gay occupation—all of which may be true. Yet Greeley consistently claims that the celibate priesthood is what led to a clergy depleted by such scandals. In short, he claims that the primary cause of all this scandal is the Church's discipline of priestly celibacy. However correct Greeley is to say that the image of the priesthood has been tainted by certain scandals, the link between celibacy and sexual misconduct remains unsubstantiated. But then Greeley has long been a publicly outspoken proponent of a married priesthood.

In a 1999 editorial, the *National Catholic Reporter* (*NCR*) identified, also without substantiation, the same link between celibacy and sexual scandal, essentially concluding that celibacy is killing Catholicism. *NCR* editor Tom Fox wrote: "Mandatory celibacy has . . . corrosive effects. In the past 15 years, the U.S. Church has spent an estimated $1 billion to cover court costs, attorney fees, settlements and victim/survivor awards in clergy sexual abuse cases. Again, this is a complex phenomenon, but surely one factor in the crisis of sexual misconduct within the clergy is the inability of priests to form open, healthy sexual relationships."[13] In other words, according to *NCR*, obligatory priestly celibacy for the Latin rite is the chief enemy of a healthy priesthood and a thriving Church.

Pulitzer Prize–winning author Garry Wills made a similar claim in his book *Papal Sin: Structures of Deceit*. Wills boldly asserts that Pope John Paul II's determination to maintain the Latin Church's discipline on clerical celibacy is a "ludicrous and compromising argument." He even claims that John Paul's real legacy to the Church, despite all the pope's outstanding accomplishments, is a gay priesthood. This, he implies in his book, is a direct result of the pope's maintaining the practice of clerical celibacy amid all the clamor to cave in to the sexual revolution. Wills, it seems, bases his conclusion on the argument, again without substantiation, that most of the heterosexual men want to marry, while the homosexuals are virtually the only men drawn to the priesthood. Like many people, Wills is suspicious of celibacy and does not seem to understand the intense nature of the consecration to the priesthood upon which the whole idea of celibacy rests.

Anglican author Elizabeth Abbott exemplifies this same thinking in her study on celibacy published in 2000 as *The History of Celibacy*. Abbott, dean of women at Trinity College at the University of Toronto, has a mocking attitude toward celibacy in Catholicism. The revelation of sexual abuse of children by the Christian Brothers in Ontario was one of the events that prompted Abbott to begin her research into celibacy. Abbott essentially implies that the Christian Brothers (a Catholic religious order), driven to madness by "imposed" celibacy,[14] victimized children under their institutional care. According to Abbott's line of reasoning, the brothers were just as much victims as the children. That is, the Christian Brothers were victims of the Catholic Church and her discipline of clerical celibacy. She, of course, fails to recognize the thousands of Catholic celibates—nuns as well as priests and religious brothers—who have

made extraordinary contributions to the Western world. Nor does
she recognize that it was the Catholic Church that has upheld
human rights throughout history by opposing sexual aberrations
such as polygamy, castration, female genital mutilation, pederasty,
and prostitution. Nor does Abbott examine the evidence that suggests that bad philosophy, not celibacy, is the cause of such heinous
crimes. This is a point that commentators such as Wills, Fox, and
Greeley fail even to consider. This "bad philosophy"—which un-
dermines both the Catholic priesthood and the mission of the
Church—can be traced to the experimentation with humanistic psychology by well-placed Church leaders.

Around the time of the Second Vatican Council, humanistic psychology had already become popular, and on top of that a philosophy
of personal development and interpersonal relationships called the
"human potentials movement" was flowering. Its pioneers were psychologists Abraham Maslow and Carl Rogers. The latter is considered the father of the "encounter group," otherwise known as "group
sensitivity training." In 1970, Dr. William Coulson, a disciple and
coworker of Carl Rogers, began to see the destruction wrought by
Rogerian psychology both in the Catholic Church and in society in
general. Coulson, now director of the Research Council on Ethnopsychology in California, realized that a "self-fulfillment" model was
replacing the traditional "self-sacrifice" model in the priesthood and
religious life, and humanistic psychology played a large role in this.
Catholics in the late 1960s were led to believe that truth no longer
rested in the Catholic Church, but rather in experience, he said, and
the Church was a suppressor or preventer of "experience" as pro-
pounded by John Dewey.[15] This was the beginning of the "religion
of the self" which was picked up quickly by seminary educators and
applied to their coursework and formation programs.

Coulson worked to train "facilitators" at the Western Behavioral
Science Institute (WBSI) in La Jolla, California, during the late
1960s, and this work continued without him throughout the 1970s.
The purpose of the workshops was to train others to conduct encounter groups. "Our biggest single vocational group coming for facilitator training for a number of years, into the late 1970s," he

explained, "was Catholic priests and nuns and teaching brothers, all of whom thought that Rogers's methods of nondirective therapy applied to group work would be a very useful vehicle for making deeper contact with their students, and for helping them to become better Catholics." What it helped them do in actuality, he added, was to become non-Catholics. In fact, most of the priests, in his recollection, who came to the program, later dropped out of the priesthood. These nuns and priests, who were among the "experts" who would later wreak havoc in seminaries, colleges, and novitiates, were trained to lead sessions of truth-telling and ice-breaking group exercises that broke down social inhibition, fostered an illusory sense of intimacy, and opened the way for the engineering of consent through small group peer pressure.[16]

In a 1994 address at the Franciscan University of Steubenville, Coulson explained how the Rogerian theories destroyed St. Anthony Seminary,[17] run by the Franciscans in Santa Barbara. The Franciscan province in California had recently concluded an inquiry into a major sex scandal at the seminary, one that warranted front-page treatment in the *New York Times* on December 1, 1993. The runover headline on page A-12 sums up the story: "Friars Sexually Molested Boys at California Seminary, Church Inquiry Says." The Franciscans had requested and paid for the inquiry, and their provincial superior called the findings "horrific." Eerily similar to the Christian Brothers pedophilia scandal in Ontario, thirty-four high-school-age boys were said to have been molested over a twenty-three-year period, involving nearly one fourth of faculty members.

Coulson was at the WBSI when the California Franciscans invited him to deliver a series of programs on the human potentials movement at their seminary. In 1968, shortly after the presentations, Coulson received a letter from one of the Franciscan friars. The priest-professor noted that his vocation had changed direction after hearing about human potentials and participating in the sensitivity training of the encounter group. "I am behaving like mad," he wrote, "with true self blossoming all over the place. Killing me." Coulson took his remarks as tongue-in-cheek at the time, but later realized that the friar had spoken more truth than he could bear to face. "Was the behaving-like-mad friar one of the notorious eleven child-abusers reported in the *New York Times*?" he wondered. We'll probably never know. Except for the two who have gone to jail, the names of the men are being held secret. "Something was wrong with the very idea of huggy-kissy priests in the first place, something wrong with applying heavy-duty human potentials lessons to religion."[18]

Coulson explained to his audience how the destruction was wrought at St. Anthony's Seminary:

> For years there had been catalogues of rules in friaries. Some were designed to make the exchange of intimacies unlikely. That the rules were of "long standing" made them *eo ipso* invalid from a human potentials perspective. The protective framework got set aside at St. Anthony's. It seems to have been seen as a form of oppression. Among the unspoken corollaries of the discarding of old-time rules were that everybody could now have sex. Or if they didn't feel like having sex, at least they could practice acceptance, understanding, and permissiveness about other people having sex. According to the investigative report of the situation at St. Anthony's: "The board of inquiry was assured that no student was ever allowed into the private rooms of the friars. But time and again in the course of the investigation, we learned that the opposite was actually true. Doors and rules were intended as physical and psychological barriers. But they were ignored. The perpetrators often brought students into their private rooms to molest them there. One offender had taken a private room in a house next to the seminary. There he had children in his room overnight. The board of inquiry learned that on several occasions, two young boys who were not seminarians, were brought by him to the table occupied by the friars in the refectory. They were there for dinner and they were there for breakfast the next morning."[19]

The independent report concluded that "a cancerous evil existed in the institution which exerted, and continues to exert, its pernicious effects in the lives of those who were abused and in the life of the province."[20] Out of the eleven offending priests or brothers, related Coulson, only two of these were evaluated as certifiable pedophiles. The others, he said, were not under the influence of a mental illness but of bad philosophy—specifically, an application of humanistic psychology.

By 1970 Coulson came to the realization that the human potentials movement, and especially the encounter groups, were destroying long-standing institutions in the Church—seminaries, convents, and the like. He was distressed by the number of priests and nuns who were losing their faith, dispensing with sexual mores, and abandoning their vocations after being introduced to the theories of humanistic psychology. Thus, in Coulson's informed opinion, it is not celibacy that drives priests and religious to pedophilia and other sexual perversions, but "bad philosophy," a philosophy that dispensed with chastity. Celibacy was a casualty, not a cause.

This point is highly relevant to the controversy surrounding the male, celibate priesthood. But unfortunately it is too often overlooked or dismissed in order to keep the focus on celibacy as the culprit. Indeed, most proponents of dispensing with clerical celibacy fail to see certain essential points that do not support their cause.

It is neither celibacy nor the Church's teaching on human sexuality that leads to sexual scandal among priests. Rather, it is loss of faith and lack of a prayer life. What is the source of this loss of faith or lack of prayer life that leads to sexual aberration? Those who contend that celibacy is the cause of all the ills in the priesthood do not often consider the actions of bishops and others in positions of authority in Catholic dioceses that potentially lead to destructive behaviors among their priests.

Consider someone such as Archbishop Weakland. As we read earlier, Weakland believes that one of the great assets of his seminarians today—the few that he has—is that they have had "multiple sex experiences" before they even enter the seminary. This might easily be construed as indicative of his contempt for priestly celibacy. Also consider that the archbishop routinely allowed seminary students to view what any normal person would consider a pornographic program, entitled *Sexual Attitude Reassessment*, so seminarians could "rethink" their views on sexuality to conform with what the archbishop considered to be his more positive attitude. The program's registration form promised to examine "how we were trained (or not trained) to hold restricting attitudes about our sexuality."[21] For at least ten years (1978–88), seminarians and many others attending the sex workshops viewed a series of explicit movies produced by Multi-Focus, Inc. (a distributor of other "educational movies" such as *Plain and Fancy Penises*, *Hookers*, and *Women in Love: Strategies of Black Lesbians*), in San Francisco. These showcased on the big screen male and female masturbation, heterosexual and homosexual intercourse, and variations in oral sex. One particular film, entitled *A Ripple of Time*, depicted a fifty-six-year-old woman and a sixty-three-year-old man engaging in sexual games with a vibrator. The program was protested for years, but it was not until 1988, when a local Christian television station exposed the program during Milwaukee's prime time, that the court of public opinion forced the archdiocese to shut it down.

Weakland also endorsed and permitted, at least since 1980, a four-week series titled "Homosexuality and Its Impact on the Family," to be taught in his archdiocese for many years, even after being repeatedly asked to cancel the program, which did not at all reflect a Catholic understanding or response to the issues of homosexuality. This sex workshop was taught by Milwaukee priest Father James Arimond, who also served as the chaplain of the Milwaukee Dignity[22] chapter and was a regular columnist for *Wisconsin Light*, a member publication of the Gay and Lesbian Press Association. A two-page promotional flyer coauthored by Arimond and Leon Konieczny stated that the Catholic Church's moral theologians held "differing viewpoints on the morality of homosexual acts. When making a moral decision . . . ultimately it is the individual's conscience which must be his or her guide. A Catholic may in good conscience make a decision not in total agreement with Church teaching and still remain within the Church if they do not deny any point of divine and Catholic faith and do not reject the teaching authority of the Church. An example of this is the millions of American Catholics who have decided on a moral stance different from the teaching of the Church and use artificial means of birth control, yet remain Catholics in good standing."[23]

Then, in 1990, Arimond[24] pleaded no contest to charges that he had molested a teenage boy.[25] Was the offending priest victimized by the Church's teaching on celibacy, or was he so immersed in homosexual propaganda that he thought more about sex and perversion than about God? The Archdiocese of Milwaukee's nonjudgmental, amoral sexual education programs clearly deadened the conscience to chastity. In fact, during Weakland's tenure, sexual abuse lawsuits resulting from Milwaukee priests abusing teenage boys cost the diocese at least $5.5 million, in addition to countless vocations. By 1993, there were seven known priests involved in sex abuse scandals in the Milwaukee archdiocese with over a hundred young victims. By 1997, even more cases of priest pedophilia had surfaced. Celibacy was not the cause.

The problem of "sexual reassessment" (or desensitizing) of seminarians was unfortunately not limited to Weakland's archdiocese, nor was he the first to introduce such degrading sex workshops. In the late 1970s the same type of pornographic films were shown at St. John Provincial Seminary in Plymouth, Michigan, when Fathers Kenneth Untener and Robert Rose were seminary administrators. Untener was named bishop of Saginaw in 1980 and Rose was named bishop of Gaylord in 1981, and later bishop of Grand Rapids. Shortly after the Vatican announced that Untener was going to lead the Saginaw diocese, the *Detroit Free Press* and the *National Catholic Register* reported that he was summoned to Rome to "explain" his sex desensitization program. With the help of Detroit's John Cardinal Dearden, he apparently argued successfully in defense of the seminary porno program.

According to Detroit priest Father Eduard Perrone, the "porno flicks" were shown at the seminary as part of a class on morality. "They showed a man masturbating, a woman masturbating, couples copulating, homosexuals humping," he recalled. The crudely produced films, he said, were supposedly put together by doctors who worked for clinical sex-study institutes. "There were ladies in the class too," explained Perrone, "because at that time they were already teaching seminarians and laity together."

He also remembered a controversial sex-ed textbook being used in classes. *Human Sexuality: New Directions in American Catholic Thought*, authored by Detroit priests Ronald Modras[26] and Anthony Kosnik,[27] was first published by Paulist Press in 1976. Billed as a "handbook for confessors," the textbook took the same desensitizing approach to sexual morality. In sum, it amounted to a broad attack on Catholic Church teaching. It even incurred the wrath of the Vatican, which formally denounced it in a rare statement issued by the Congregation for the Doctrine of the Faith. Of the countless criticisms of the book, perhaps the pithiest came from Monsignor Hubert Maino, former editor of the *Michigan Catholic*, who said on a local radio talk show that it was "soft on bestiality."[28]

This is not at all unlike the "sex text" scandal at Mount Angel Seminary in Oregon, brought to light by Father John Lewandowski. The entire course presentation on human sexuality, said Lewandowski, was an offense against chastity. Neither the professor nor his chosen textbook spoke positively about celibacy, nor were seminarians by any means encouraged to remain chaste. Quite the contrary.

The often repeated contention that young men take no interest in the priesthood because of the celibacy requirement is put to rest by the fact that so many men who enter the seminary (or at least apply) do so with the understanding that celibacy is an integral part of the priestly life. What many of these men have found, however, when they enter the seminary, is that the role of celibacy is not taken seriously, or it is undermined, as in the case of Mount Angel or St. John's. In 2000, Dominican Father Brian Mullady explained that "seminarians in the recent past had to contend with the popular but mistaken notion that the Church was probably going to change this discipline, and so they were practically expected to oppose celibacy."[29] This is not nearly so much the case at the dawn of the twenty-first century as it was in the 1970s and 1980s. According to a nationwide survey of priests by the National Opinion Research Center in Chicago, the youngest and oldest priests share similar views supporting celibacy in the priesthood and rejecting the cause of women's ordination. But the generation in the middle—those who are in positions of authority in most dioceses now—is still much more in favor of dispensing with celibacy and ordaining priestesses. The popular opinion, truly a conjured myth, that Rome was going to dispense with celibacy in the wake of Vatican II was mainly propagated via theologians and seminary educators, many of whom have since left the priesthood and the Church. Most Catholics in the pews *never* expected a married priesthood and still do not.

Once these theologians and seminary educators realized that the Vatican was not going to capitulate on this issue, they soon got the idea—how conscious it was, we will never know—that if seminarians were put into positions where priestly celibacy was undermined and their own chastity was jeopardized, they could "prove" that celibacy was a deterrent to priestly vocations. First, in many instances, seminarians were not provided with examples of chastity by men in the seminary who showed balance, self-mastery, and affective maturity. Second, the teaching many seminarians received in courses did not support celibacy, or even chastity of any sort. Third, many seminarians were actually encouraged to date and carry on sexual relationships. One wise man once said, "If you can get a seminarian into bed with a woman, you'll destroy his vocation." In fact, many, many vocations were destroyed through the undermining of chastity. Once desensitized in sex workshops or by poring through sexually explicit material in seminary textbooks, the prospect of dating and carrying on a straightforward sexual relationship with a woman (as opposed to a perverted sexual relationship) probably struck many seminarians as rather reasonable. Be that as it may, the saints have repeatedly taught that it is difficult to remain faithful to the Church if one cannot remain chaste.

What happened to the Seminary of St. Pius X in the Diocese of Covington, Kentucky, provides an illustrative example of how vocations were systematically undermined in one diocese. In 1979, Bishop William Hughes[30] succeeded conservative prelate Richard

Ackerman.[31] The seminary was still flourishing in Covington. In fact, it was one of the few seminaries in the country that had maintained orthodoxy, discipline, and high numbers of seminarians. The young men still wore cassocks or clericals to classes until 1982. By that year the new bishop had decided that he did not like what he called the "monastic environment" there and, according to Father Joseph Jenkins, president of the student body for the seminary's last graduating class there, Hughes told the seminarians point-blank that he wanted them out of clericals and dating girls on a co-ed campus. Hughes, however, told the public that he sought to close the seminary for economic reasons. He claimed it was costing the Diocese of Covington $25,000 in subsidies for each man at the school, which Jenkins believed was not the case. "Money was not an issue. In fact, Bishop Glennon Flavin[32] of Lincoln, Nebraska, offered Hughes a blank check, if only he would leave the seminary undisturbed."[33] Hughes would not, added Jenkins. Since Roman guidelines required him to get another bishop to concur with his decision to close the school, he enlisted Bishop Walter Sullivan of Richmond, Virginia, who did not even send students to St. Pius X. "Sullivan arrived at the seminary wearing shorts, an undershirt and sandals, badmouthing the school while looking for dirt," wrote Jenkins.

When Jenkins, as class president in 1982, tried to get a graduation speaker, Bishop Hughes rejected three in a row. "We had selected men orthodox in faith and loyal to the pope," said Jenkins. "He wanted none of them. He even turned down Bishop Ackerman, the former shepherd of Covington." The rector of the seminary, Father William Brown, however, convinced Hughes to reconsider the choice of Ackerman. The latter had been informed of the snub and was furious. At the graduation ceremony, Ackerman spoke of his love for the seminary and how integral it was in the life of the diocese. Nevertheless, Hughes had his way. The thriving seminary of St. Pius X was closed and the seminarians were sent to co-ed Thomas More College to date and "gain life experiences." Numbers went from more than 140 seminarians to about eighteen men in the 1982–83 academic year.

But even before some men make it to the seminary, they are able to sense that their diocese or religious order does not take the role of clerical celibacy too seriously. John Horton, for instance, remembers attending a vocations conference for prospective seminarians in the Archdiocese of Seattle in 1996. One question at the meeting with Archbishop Thomas Murphy[34] was posed by the youngest prospect, a senior in high school. "Should I be dating?" he asked. Murphy answered that seminarians were expected to be involved in "serious relationships" with women and that seminarians who were not would be considered unsuitable for the priesthood—unfortunate wording. Even if Murphy did not mean "sexual" by the term "serious relationships," "the words 'chastity' and 'celibacy' were never mentioned during the course of the evening conference," recalled Horton, who believed that is exactly what the high school senior wanted to hear about. The other prospective candidates looked dumbfounded. The four other priests present added nothing. They all remained silent, even as everyone else in the room looked perplexed. (It is worth noting that the "Program of Priestly Formation" published by the National Conference of Catholic Bishops specifically states that prospective seminarians and seminarians should have a commitment to celibacy and the observance of perfect chastity, which would preclude any romantic or sexual relationships.)

A few years earlier, in 1990, Horton applied to enter the seminary for the Archdiocese of Seattle. At that time, Archbishop Raymond G. Hunthausen,[35] an outspoken proponent of women's ordination, was still head of the archdiocese. The vocations director said that Horton would have to participate in the "Channel Program" for one year in order to be eligible for admission as a candidate for the priesthood. The program was the diocese's version of the Peace Corps. As instructed, he met with the directress of the program in an old house in the neighborhood of the University of Washington. They talked for a few minutes, said Horton, "about 'diversity' and 'inclusiveness' and all the old mantras of the liberal feminist establishment." The director showed him photographs of the participants for the previous three years of the program, and he was surprised to find that there were around twenty college-age women participating each year, and only one man during the entire three-year period. He was also stupefied by the homogeneity of the archdiocese's "diversity" program. They all looked like "rich suburban white girls," remembered Horton, a Hispanic who grew up in modest surroundings.

He was more surprised, however, to find that he was expected to live under the same roof with the twenty young females over the course of the one-year program. When Horton asked the directress how this sort of arrangement was supposed to be preparing him for a life of celibacy in the priesthood, she told him she didn't think celibacy was all that important, especially before he was ordained.

Horton objected. The interview lasted just twenty minutes, and by the time Horton left the house, the Channel Program directress was thoroughly displeased with him. A month later, he contacted the Seattle vocations director about the status of his application and was informed that he had received a bad review from the Channel Program directress; she did not find him worthy of her program. The vocations director had no choice then, he said, but to reject Horton's application to the seminary—purely on the basis that he objected to living for a year in co-ed quarters.

As Horton reflected, he believes the Channel Program and the attitude of the vocations office at the time were reflections of Hunthausen's feminist viewpoint. "Although he talked a lot about diversity and inclusiveness, he seemed to try to pack diocesan offices and programs with nearly 100 percent white females."

In fact, in March of 1990, Hunthausen discontinued the archdiocese's deacon training program until, as he explained to Seattle priests, the Church further addressed the role of women.[36] Hunthausen, who wanted to ordain priestesses and deaconesses, defended his decision by saying that "the diaconate creates another all-male clerical caste that excludes women."[37] In a December 1989 letter to his priests, Hunthausen, along with Murphy, suggested that discussion about the role of women in the Church should include discussing issues such as "women's ordination, optional celibacy for priests and creation of a more positive environment for vocations to the priesthood."[38]

The logical result of this advocacy in Seattle is that, first, very few healthy men are going to apply to serve an archdiocese whose leaders believe that the priesthood is nothing more than an "all-male clerical caste that excludes women." And second, when such men do apply to the seminary, it would not be hard to believe that the "recruiting" staff would expect applicants to be open to women's ordination and optional celibacy. Such a scenario again harks back to Archbishop Curtiss's contention that many of those who are directly responsible for promoting vocations actually have a death wish for the male, celibate priesthood.

Not all bishops are as direct and self-incriminating as Hunthausen. But many have supported similar campaigns in order to "create facts" so that they might in turn present Rome with a fait accompli: "Since we are not getting vocations, the Church needs to open priestly orders up to everyone, male or female, single or married, heterosexual or homosexual"—so the reasoning goes.[39] In other words, in many places applicants or seminarians who embraced the male, celibate priesthood were rejected from the seminary program. Countless others, as has been stated, simply would not answer the call to the priesthood at all.

■ ■ ■

Another group sees the vocations crisis as "presaging a revolution and the demise of the hierarchical structure of the Church."[40] This is the contingent that has long been promoting "lay ecclesial ministry," the laicization of the clergy, and the clericalization of the laity. Simply put, they would like to see the laity take over the leadership of the Church at the parish level and beyond, from teaching and preaching to administering the sacraments. This program would effectively entail eliminating the priesthood rather than just "reenvisioning" it.

Indeed, in many places, the lack of priestly vocations is embraced as a way to promote a new vocation to "lay ecclesial ministry," that is, nonordained, paid church professionals. Some bishops, priests, and other diocesan and seminary authorities actually seem to rejoice over decreasing priestly vocations as an opportunity for creating a "new model of Church" in which the laity can "take their rightful place." In a pastoral letter released in April 2000, for instance, Roger Cardinal Mahony[41] of Los Angeles described the drop in ordinations since 1970 as "one of the fruits of the Second Vatican Council."[42] It has taken "the shortage of priestly and religious vocations," Mahony wrote, "to awaken in us an appreciation of a broadly based shared ministry and a realization that it is in the nature of the Church as the Body of Christ to be endowed with many gifts, ministries and offices."[43]

Archbishop Daniel E. Pilarczyk[44] of Cincinnati has similar sentiments. In a 1997 presentation on Church authority, he emphasized what he calls the "upside" of the priest shortage: lay ministry. "We have learned that a lot of other people can do a lot of other things," he said. In the "good old days" a large parish might have had as many as four or five priests, he explained, but now one priest is sufficient when he is supported by dozens of lay parish employees. Although Pilarczyk admitted that we still need priests, he said "we probably don't need as many as we think we need. We certainly don't need as many as we used to have."[45]

This philosophy, drawn out by many over the last decade of the twentieth century, betrays a peculiar attitude—the priesthood as a barrier to the emergence of the laity in their own dignity and mission. After Bishop Robert Muench,[46] then of Covington, Kentucky, met Pope John Paul II during the 1998 *ad limina*[47] visit in Rome, the Kentucky prelate explained that the visit was an opportunity for him to explain what a "vibrant" church he had in Covington. "I bragged about our local Church," he said. "I told the Holy Father that God has blessed us and the people of this diocese have been very responsive." Muench mentioned specifically that the pope asked him about vocations in his diocese. "I talked to him about the programs we have in place," explained Muench. "We are so fortunate with the explosion of vocations within the laity to service in the Church. We don't want to isolate one aspect—both are very important."[48] Was this the bishop's way of sidestepping the pope's question, since the Holy Father was obviously inquiring about priestly and religious vocations, not vocations to the newly arrived "lay ecclesial ministry"? Or was he more honestly propounding his own philosophy—that lay ministry vocations were as important as priestly vocations?

Father Marty Heinz of Rockford, Illinois, who was rejected by the Milwaukee archdiocese, is one of the most successful vocations directors in the country. While he thinks lay ministry is important, he wondered if sometimes a parish or diocese trains the laity for ecclesial roles to substitute for a shortage of priests. Such a solution to the priest shortage, he observed, ends up becoming a "self-fulfilling prophecy."[49] In other words, where lay ministry is overemphasized, the priesthood becomes devalued. Priests are reduced to sacramental ministers, their ministry defined (alongside so-called music ministers, youth ministers, hospitality ministers, et al.) by what they *do* rather than what they *are*—an *alter Christus*. Such a devaluation of the priestly ministry further discourages priestly vocations. In fact, this devaluation is part of a vicious circle that looks like this: Catholics in key positions of authority (bishop, vocations director, or pastor, for example) actively discourage vocations to the priesthood in order to promote lay ministry. Yet at the same time, lay ecclesial ministry is proposed as the answer to the dearth of priestly vocations, as if this were a permanent and perhaps ideal situation. Parishes run by lay ministers are likely to foster little, if any, interest in vocations to the priesthood. The result is that the number of priests will continue to decline further, necessitating more lay ministers to fill their places. This is the obvious self-fulfilling prophecy that Heinz mentioned—a vicious circle perpetuated by a few who have a death wish for the male, celibate priesthood.

■ ■ ■

This self-fulfilling prophecy evidences itself in the "task force" committee approach to learning to live without priests in a particular diocese. Throughout the 1990s bishops issued reports warning of the coming priest crunch in their dioceses. The problem, they said, was that in the coming years there just wouldn't be enough priests to serve the number of parishes adequately. In November 2000, for instance, Bishop Thomas V. Daily of Brooklyn issued a pastoral letter addressing this issue. Proclaiming the priest shortage in his diocese "urgent and serious," he called for an increased emphasis on the parish "cluster" system through which neighboring churches shared resources and personnel, including a pastor. Daily's letter followed up on recommendations he received in 1998 from a task force he appointed to study the effects of the vocations dearth.[50]

Citing "burnout" and health problems among his overworked priests, Bishop James A. Griffin of Columbus, Ohio, issued guidelines that same year to cope with the present and projected priest shortage in his diocese. He reluctantly acknowledged that in the near future there might be no Mass on Sunday in a given parish. His guidelines addressed ways in which laity should respond to situations when no priest is available, including celebrating Sunday and holy day liturgies without a priest.

In Green Bay, Wisconsin, Bishop Robert Banks projected that by 2005 only twenty to twenty-five of his 198 parishes would be "independent," that is, having a pastor who was not shared with other parishes. These independent parishes are expected to have no fewer than 4,000 households each. In 2000, 102 parishes were sharing pastors and in some places a priest was pastor of as many as six parishes. Mark Mogilka, the chairman of Green Bay's diocesan planning committee, described the situation to the *Green Bay Press-Gazette* as a "paradigm shift in terms of what is leadership in the Catholic Church."[51] Not surprisingly, the committee is focusing on forming "lay ministry teams" to replace priests. Mogilka's admission that his committee's work represents not a temporary solution to a temporary problem but a "paradigm shift" is important. The Diocese of Green Bay, one assumes, is committed to the new paradigm of the lay-run Church. In other words, it is more interested in learning to live without priests than in attracting vocations to the priesthood. The problem, again, is self-perpetuating.

The Diocese of Lexington, Kentucky, is of similar mind but is perhaps even more committed to this new paradigm than most American dioceses experiencing the ballyhooed vocation crisis. In 1998, Bishop J. Kendrick Williams concluded a similar task force evaluation. Drawing from the information culled by the "New

Faces of Ministry" task force, he produced a plan in which deacons, nuns, and laypeople will function as the heads of parishes. These "heads" will contract with priests for their "sacramental services." Thus, priests will normally serve various parishes run by non-priests, even though the bishop, in order to comply with Canon Law, will designate the priest as the official pastor. In initial proposals published in the diocesan paper, *Crossroads*, the ordination of women and married men was also considered. Yet, according to at least one parish in the Lexington diocese, the task force simply discarded ideas it did not agree with.

Even though the New Faces of Ministry task force claimed that each parish would be listened to, parishioners at Sacred Heart Church in Corbin, Kentucky, claimed their ideas were never published alongside the push for lay ministry, women priests, and dispensation from priestly celibacy. In a 1998 letter to Bishop Williams, Sacred Heart's pastor, Father Roger Arnsparger, expressed his regret that his parish's suggestions, representing a good number of active Catholics, never made it to the printed and published draft report. Nor did he believe that the published report reflected the wishes and desires of common, working-class, grassroots Catholics of the diocese. Instead, he suggested, the task force had its own ideas of a new model of Church that it wanted to see promoted and eventually implemented. Arnsparger wrote:

> The process needed to include for discussion and planning the only permanent solution for leadership in a Catholic parish: a priest in every parish and mission with the Holy Sacrifice of the Mass in every parish or mission. A program of recruitment as vast as New Faces of Ministry would be good: manual, meetings, and so forth. We were not permitted to look at various options to attain the only permanent solution for the goal. . . . In this process we have restricted [the laity's] leadership to mimicking that of priests and in that way have set the stage for a Protestant conception of the priesthood and the exodus of our own men who think

they have a vocation to the priesthood to other dioceses
and religious orders.

During the New Faces of Ministry process (the name alone suggests that priests are the "old faces"), Sacred Heart Church determined that it would do all in its power to secure a priest-pastor. Its
committee concluded that it did not want to have a lay administrator
as its leader or have communion services in lieu of Mass. "It has been
strongly recommended," wrote Arnsparger, "that in the eventuality
the Diocese of Lexington is unable to assign a priest pastor to Sacred
Heart Church, parishioners would form an Ad Hoc committee to secure a priest pastor." His parish drew up a list of ways they could recruit a pastor:

• Advertising outside the diocese
• Recruiting from religious orders
• Supporting a priest from a Third World country

In fact, the Sacred Heart committee concluded that "if there is not
regular Sunday Mass at Sacred Heart, the parish should not exist."
Parishioners said they would rather travel to the nearest church that offered Sunday Mass than attend communion services at Sacred Heart.[52]
The most important part of Sacred Heart's plan was that it was
predicated on the assumption that the *only permanent solution* for
leadership in a Catholic parish was a priest-pastor offering the Holy
Sacrifice of the Mass, at the very least each Sunday. The diocese,
however, did not share this assumption. Instead, the Lexington task
force revealed that it really didn't want priests—at least not male,
celibate priests.[53]
One of the most aggressive moves toward the lay-run Church
came north of the border from Archbishop Marcel Gervais of Ottawa. In December 2000, Gervais appointed lay men and women and
nuns to perform marriages, baptisms, and funerals in his diocese—
functions that are specifically reserved to priests and deacons. His ac-

tion came after several years of appointing lay members and religious as "pastoral coordinators" of parishes. The prelate, evidently believing that there can be a Catholic Church without a Catholic priesthood, vaunted his decision as "not just solving problems" arising from a shortage of priests, but as "a new model of Church."[54] Similar to Green Bay's emphatic embrace of a new paradigm in Church leadership, Gervais also revealed that the lay-run Church was more than a temporary solution, it was the wave of the future Church.

In the Archdiocese of Cincinnati during the late 1990s, each deanery was charged with making recommendations to Archbishop Daniel Pilarczyk regarding what to do about the diminishing number of priests. One deanery recommended that they canonically dissolve all twenty-three current parishes in the deanery and reestablish nine new parishes, with the current parishes becoming "faith communities" within each new parish. Each faith community would maintain itself, but would have a nonresident parish administrative staff and pastor. The proposal called for Mass to be celebrated in every community on a rotating schedule to be worked out by each of the new parishes, with prayer services held on Sundays in the communities where a priest was not present.

Here too, then, is another example of a new model of Church wherein priests serve as little more than as perfunctory sacramental ministers. Priestless "faith communities"[55] over time are likely to become simply congregational communities centered on the reading of the Scriptures, the homily, and on sharing bread and wine— devoid of the act of perfect worship, the Holy Sacrifice of the Mass—based on the model of a Protestant community.

Likewise, many other American and Canadian bishops have appointed "task forces" and "planning commissions" to study the projected shortage of priests in the near future and to propose solutions to deal with the crisis. Remarkably, solutions to solve the priest shortage often center around reducing the number of parishes served rather than increasing the number of priests. Much time and energy is being expended on determining how Catholics will get along without priests. The results are closed parishes, parish mergers, and cluster arrangements in which the parishes are largely run by nuns and "lay pastoral associates."

In short, the evidence suggests that some dioceses don't want an increase of priests. The so-called shortage suits them just fine, precisely because they can use the crisis to justify radical changes in the local Church—changes that will affect the Mass, the sacraments, the parish structure, and Church leadership. In dioceses such as New Ulm, Minnesota, and Saginaw, Michigan, under the leadership of Bishops Raymond Lucker and Kenneth Untener, respectively, parishes are already commonly run by nuns and "lay pastors."

This "new model of Church" is not really about solving the priest shortage. Prelates such as Archbishop Gervais see it as advancing their agenda of a politically correct Church, one kowtowing to feminism and the other sacred cows of liberalism. The results of these task force proposals will only perpetuate the exodus of men who think they have a vocation to the priesthood. They will naturally seek dioceses that support the ministry of the priest as defined by the Church. As mentioned earlier, such dioceses do exist. And it is instructive to note that they are the ones that have been affected little, if at all, by any vocations crisis or priest shortage. Nor are the bishops of such dioceses issuing pastoral letters introducing parish "clusters" or instructions on how to celebrate Mass in the absence of a priest.

In summary, it is worth emphasizing that the vocations crisis and the resultant priest shortage is exacerbated and exploited by Catholics who do not accept the Church's understanding of the ordained priesthood. Their ideologically inspired views on the male, celibate model are a crucial part of the ferment that has been bubbling around the present and projected priest shortage. They have a death wish for the male, celibate priesthood.

CHAPTER 12

The Right Stuff

How to Live Up to the Church's Expectations for Seminary Life

Since the training of seminarians hinges, to a very large extent, on wise regulations and on suitable teachers, seminary directors should be chosen from among the best, and be painstakingly prepared by solid doctrine, appropriate pastoral experience, and special spiritual and pedagogical training.
—Optatam Totius, *Pope Paul VI, from Vatican II*

It is probably worth repeating that the "reenvisioned" priesthood and a lay-run Church both run directly counter to the priesthood as the Church defines the ordained ministry and the hierarchical structure of the Church. More to the point, however, is that when those who have a "death wish" for the male, celibate priesthood run the vocations offices and the seminary formation programs for future priests, the seminaries cannot possibly discharge their proper duties.

What, then, is the precise function of a seminary? What purpose ought it serve? To be sure, few Catholics really know very much about the nature of the institutions upon which they depend to provide them with the leaders of their Church.

The seminary as it exists today—or, rather *ought* to exist—owes its origins to the sixteenth-century Council of Trent (1543–63). That important council defined a seminary as "a fertile nursery for priests." The word "seminary" itself, derived from the Latin *seminarium*, describes a place where seedlings are prepared for eventual transplanting into the ground. In ecclesiastical terms a seminary is a place where a young man is prepared to live out his priestly vocation in fidelity and holiness in service to the Church. Father Benedict Groeschel, founder of the Franciscan Friars of the Renewal in the South Bronx, defines a seminarian as "one studying for the priesthood, forming himself and being formed, to one day be ordained to the service of God, his Church and His people as a priest of Jesus Christ."[1]

Following the turmoil of the Protestant Reformation, the Catholic bishops and priests were greatly concerned with the proper formation of priests. In 1563, the final year of the Council of Trent, *Cum Adulescentium Aetas* decreed that specialized institutions of formation for those aspiring to be priests be established in every diocese.[2] Cardinal Pallavicini, a prominent council father, called this the most important reform enacted by the Tridentine council. The new system would rely more on discipline in spiritual and character formation than past methods of training priests.[3] This system of discipline, characterized by asceticism, was used in order to train the student's will and to develop habits of regularity, self-control, and self-sacrifice, habits that would help him to grow in holiness of life. The seminarians were to follow a rule of life which determined what they would do throughout the course of each day: prayer, Mass, classes, study, recreation, and devotion follow one another at regular intervals— leaving nothing to caprice.

Two great saints led the way in the establishment of seminaries during this period of the Catholic Counter-Reformation. St. Ignatius, the founder of the Jesuits, established the Collegium Germanum in Rome for the education of German clergy. His model was used to establish other national colleges in Rome exclusively for the education and spiritual formation of diocesan priests. St. Charles Borromeo, the cardinal archbishop of Milan, was also a key personality in the development of the modern seminary system. Perhaps the most renowned father of the Tridentine Council, he enthusiastically enforced its decrees against determined opposition. He quickly established three seminaries in his large archdiocese in northern Italy. The first was founded to educate clergy who would serve in urban parishes, and the second to form those who would become country priests. The third was conceived as a sort of remedial institution to provide courses and spiritual direction for priests who were already ordained but needed to make up the deficiencies of their previous training. St. Charles drafted a set of regulations for his three seminaries, and these have provided inspiration to almost all seminary founders since. His contribution to the foundation of seminaries in Europe after the Council of Trent was so significant he is often called the "father of the seminary."

The model provided by St. Charles called for an eight- to ten-day retreat at the start of each academic year. During this week of initiation, the minds and hearts of the seminarians would be brought under the influence of the great truths of the Christian faith. They would participate in meditations, spiritual conferences, recitation of the Divine Office,[4] visits to the Blessed Sacrament, and consultations with their spiritual director. Once the normal routine of seminary life began, the seminarians would spend their days in prayer, study, and recreation primarily in the confines of the seminary environment. It was deemed essential that in order to properly form a priest, especially in the spiritual life, the seminary needed to be removed from the world. One day each week, however, was set apart for visiting hospitals and other institutions, where the candidates were to gain some experience of their future work among the poor and the sick.

An important part of the formation experience was that it was undertaken in community with fellow students animated by the same purpose and love of God; they each entered with the understanding that they were being formed so that they might one day be capable of bearing the burden of the priesthood with humility and perseverance.

Some nations faced serious obstacles to the full implementation of the Tridentine ideal with respect to the establishment of seminaries. War and the progress of heresy, for instance, hampered the German bishops. In England and Ireland, religious persecution prevented the foundation of any kind of seminaries. English Catholics were trained at Douai,[5] a Flemish college in northern France, while the Irish left for colleges in Paris, Louvain,[6] and Salamanca[7] to receive their priestly formation. In France, the French Revolution decimated the seminaries St. Vincent de Paul and Father Jean Jacques Olier had successfully established during the violent persecutions that killed off an enormous number of the loyal French clergy. Even the theology faculty at Paris's Sorbonne was wiped out by the Revolution, which had essentially declared war on all things Christian.

In the United States, one of the chief concerns of John Carroll, America's first bishop (1790), was to provide the means for training a native clergy. At that time, he had twenty-four priests, all of them foreign-born, to serve a Catholic population of twenty-five thousand—a priest-to-people ratio of roughly 1:1,000. The Order of St. Sulpice (the Sulpicians), founded by Olier, sent four of its priests to Baltimore to help Carroll open St. Mary's Seminary, which still remains today. Because of the lack of priestly candidates, the seminary accepted lay students, including Protestants. In 1793, Carroll ordained Stephen Badin, his first priest in the New World. St. Mary's enrolled just sixteen students in its first dozen years.

According to Tim Unsworth, author of *The Last Priests in America*, "the paucity of candidates stemmed from a deep-seated suspicion of Irish candidates, who would someday account for 80 percent of the American hierarchy. The Irish were viewed as crude and more interested in just getting an education and moving out. There was a decided preference for candidates with a more refined background."[8] This discrimination against Irish vocations by the French- and English-born clergy resulted in only 110 ordinations between 1793 and 1848. In 1829, there were 232 priests serving 500,000 Catholics. The priest-to-people ratio had fallen to 1:2,150. In some areas of the country, the priest shortage was even more severe. In New York, for instance, when John Hughes became bishop of New York, he had only forty priests ministering to 200,000 Catholics, a 1:5,000 ratio.

During the next century seminaries were established in the U.S. as quickly as new dioceses were formed. By the end of the Civil War, fifty seminaries enrolled nearly a thousand men studying to be priests. Just a few decades later, at the turn of the century, nearly one hundred seminaries were educating five thousand candidates.[9] Eventually the Irish were deemed acceptable candidates for the priesthood. Irish immigrants—and Germans less so—dominated the American priesthood in the latter half of the nineteenth century. By the twentieth century, Italian vocations were discriminated against, and later the Poles were turned away from seminaries.

Many of the new U.S. seminaries met the Tridentine ideals, educating seminarians in the academic (high school), collegiate, and theological courses. The earliest of these were St. Patrick's in Menlo Park, California, and St. Charles Borromeo near Philadelphia, both of which exist today.

The Third Council of Baltimore in 1884 established further standards for the operation of seminaries in the United States. These would set the tone for seminary education until the Second Vatican Council: Parents and parish priests were urged to encourage young men "who by their intelligence and piety give hope that they are called to the priesthood." It was established that the seminarian was to study Christian doctrine, Latin and Greek, rhetoric and elocution, history and geography, math and science, Gregorian chant and bookkeeping, Scripture and philosophy, dogmatic, moral, and pastoral theology, liturgy, and canon law. The Baltimore Council also stipulated that students should learn the virtues by example of their instructors and spiritual directors, who should be "conspicuous for ability, learning, piety, and seriousness of life. They should devote their life to study, bear cheerfully the burden of seminary rule and of a busy life; by word and example teach the students the observance of seminary discipline, humility, unworldliness, love of work and retirement, and fidelity to prayer."[10] The importance of the council's decree was reiterated in Pope Pius X's first encyclical, promulgated in 1903. In *E Supremi* the Holy Father reminds bishops that their first care, to which every other must yield, is "to form Christ in those who are destined from the duty of their vocation to form Christ in others. We speak of priests."[11]

Here at the dawn of America's "golden age" of the priesthood (1900–60), the U.S. was experiencing rapid growth in the Catholic population. From 1880 to 1924[12] more than twenty million immigrants stepped ashore. Most were Catholics from Italy and eastern Europe. During the 1920s the number of priests grew by 28 percent, twice the rate of the Catholic population. In the 1930s the number of U.S. Catholics increased by just 6 percent while the number of priests grew by 26 percent. The result was that by 1940 there were 36,000 priests ordained to serve a Catholic population of twenty-two million. The priest-to-people ratio dropped to 1:630, the lowest in U.S. history.[13]

During the 1950s the Catholic population grew by an astounding 47 percent and the priest-to-people ratio climbed slightly to 1:711. At the opening of the Second Vatican Council in 1962, the U.S. Church was supporting 5,000 seminarians in graduate theology programs, 3,300 in philosophy studies, and more than 16,000 in minor seminaries in high school and junior college programs.

Through the first half of the twentieth century the priesthood became a well-respected and well-defined institution in the United States. Addressing a meeting of the National Conference of Catholic Bishops in 1986, Archbishop Daniel Pilarczyk recalled his image of the priesthood in 1948 at the age of fourteen when he entered Cincinnati's St. Gregory's Seminary: "To be a priest was the highest life a boy could aspire to."[14] The priest had a clearly defined doctrinal role, authoritative leadership, personal esteem, and status. The standards for ordination during those years were high and seminarians were carefully selected and trained. Expectations were high and priests generally had a strong following among faithful Catholics. Such a clearly defined identity of the priest was one of the strengths that attracted intelligent and pious young men to the seminary. The Catholic priesthood was an elite group with clearly defined behavior.

■ ■ ■

During the years of Vatican II, the number of seminarians and priests continued to increase and reached a peak in 1966. But in the following year, at the beginning of the "implementation" of revolutionary changes that were not even a part of the council, the seminarian population dropped by 878 students. At that time there were some six hundred seminaries and religious houses of formation in the United States that educated future priests. The steep decline in vocation numbers began in 1967. That year more than three thousand seminarians left their studies, and their places remained unfilled. Consequently, thirty-two seminaries closed. By 1970, the seminary population had dropped to 28,000, and seventy-four more seminaries shut their doors. Within five years the decline had escalated: 11,000 seminarians had left their studies, many of them confused about the nature and purpose of the priesthood. Many of the seminaries that closed during this period were high school seminaries, some of which had already devolved into college-prep high schools that did not see their students as young men discerning a call to the priesthood, but rather as teenagers preparing for college studies. Others had merely sunk into decadence and killed themselves off. By 1999, the total number of seminarians dropped to 4,826, studying in 192 seminaries.[15]

Although the steep decline began at the end of the council, "Vatican II was intended to renew the priesthood, not lead to a denial of the nature of the priesthood or the denigration of the priestly role."[16] As happened with other aspects of the council's teachings, the media and often Catholic theologians with a predetermined agenda emphasized their own interpretation of the council documents rather than what the council fathers actually called for.

Optatam Totius, Vatican II's document on priestly formation, was no different. In keeping with the spirit of the times, interpreters reported that the Church was calling for a dramatic renovation of the priesthood and the system used to educate priests. Although the wording of the document does suggest that some areas of priestly formation needed refinement, it generally reiterated the principles already laid out by the Trent and Baltimore councils. *Optatam Totius* reiterated, for instance, the grave importance of having instructors and directors of the highest repute: "Since the training of seminarians hinges, to a very large extent, on wise regulations and on suitable teachers, seminary directors should be chosen from among the best, and be painstakingly prepared by solid doctrine, appropriate pastoral experience, and special spiritual and pedagogical training."[17] While calling for the same general course of studies, including the study of Latin, it clearly emphasized Scripture as the foundation and center of the theological curriculum. The decree also urged a "better integration of philosophy and theology."[18]

But these pronouncements were not exactly revolutionary or even particularly controversial. In almost every way, *Optatam Totius* ratified the existing structure and focus of the seminary, in order to safeguard the institution from the capricious whims of those tempted to think they knew better how to educate and form priests for the late twentieth century and beyond. In summary, the seminarian was to be "trained in priestly obedience in a program of humble living, and in the spirit of self-denial."[19] By priestly celibacy, which was emphatically reiterated and promoted, the seminarian was to devote himself to the Lord with an undivided love.[20] An objective reading of the decree does not reveal a desire on the part of the council fathers to eliminate the discipline of the seminary. On the contrary, it seems to be consistent with the Council of Trent in its call for an environment that was suited especially to form holy priests in humility and self-sacrifice.

In 1969, the Vatican's Sacred Congregation for Catholic Education published the *Ratio Fundamentalis Institutionis Sacerdotalis*, a basic plan for priestly formation, and asked each national bishops' conference to draft its own program for priestly formation in light of particular regional or national pastoral needs. The National Conference of Catholic Bishops in the U.S. first approved its *Program of Priestly Formation* in 1971. Most recently, Pope John Paul II addressed the topic of priestly formation "in the circumstances of the present day" in his 1992 apostolic exhortation *Pastores Dabo Vobis*, which begins by quoting Jeremiah: "I will give you shepherds after my own heart" (Jer. 3:15). This pastoral letter summarized the discussion during the Synod of Bishops on the Priesthood in 1990.

John Paul addressed four areas of priestly formation: human, spiritual, intellectual, and pastoral. Human formation, he wrote, is the basis of all priestly formation. Quoting from the Second Vatican Council, the pope called for seminarians to be "educated in truth, to

be loyal, to respect every person, to have a sense of justice, to be true
to their word, to be genuinely compassionate, to be men of integrity
and, especially, to be balanced in judgment and behavior."[21] To this
end the Holy Father explained that the seminarian must be formed
to responsible freedom and the moral conscience. "His affective maturity must build upon the awareness that love has a central role in
human life. Especially in light of a priest's charism of celibacy, he
must be formed by a suitable education to true friendship and must
freely and lovingly respond to God's demands."[22]

Spiritual formation, the second aspect of total formation of the
seminarian, "introduces him to a deep communion with Jesus Christ,
the good shepherd, and leads to the total submission of one's life to
the Spirit, in a filial attitude toward the Father and a trustful attach-
ment to the Church."[23] Again the Holy Father referred to *Optatam
Totius*, which requires that spiritual formation

> be conducted in such a way that the students may learn
> to live in intimate and unceasing union with God the
> Father through his Son Jesus Christ, in the Holy Spirit.
> Those who are to take on the likeness of Christ the
> priest by sacred ordination should form the habit of
> drawing close to him as friends in every detail of their
> lives. They should live the paschal mystery in such a
> way that they will know how to initiate into it the
> people committed to their charge. They should be
> taught to seek Christ in faithful meditation on the word
> of God and in active participation in the sacred mys-
> teries of the Church, especially the Eucharist and the
> Divine Office, to seek him in the bishop by whom they
> are sent and in the people to whom they are sent, espe-
> cially the poor, little children, the weak, sinners, and
> unbelievers.[24]

Spiritual formation is necessary if, as the pope notes, the seminarian is to one day *be* a priest rather than simply *act* as a priest.
Without a developed spiritual life grounded in the perennial tradition

of the Church, the priest cannot function properly as a pastor of souls. His "pastoral formation would be left without foundation." In other words, the future priest's spirituality must be grounded in prayer and in *lectio divina*, reading the word of God. It has as its "source and summit" the Eucharist.

Intellectual formation involves understanding the Faith. According to Pope John Paul, it can be seen as a necessary expression of both human and spiritual formation. Proper intellectual formation enables the priest to proclaim the changeless Gospel of Christ and to make it credible to the legitimate demands of human reason in a world marked by religious indifference and a disbelief in objective truth. Specifically through the study of theology and philosophy, the seminarian "assents to the word of God, grows in his spiritual life, and prepares himself to fulfill his pastoral ministry."[25]

Pastoral formation is built upon the previous three. It must aim to make candidates to the priesthood true shepherds of souls after the example of Jesus Christ. The seminary, instructs the Holy Father, must seek to initiate the candidate into "the sensitivity of being a shepherd, in conscious and mature assumption of his responsibilities, in the interior habit of evaluating problems and establishing priorities and looking for solutions on the basis of honest motivations of faith and according to the theological demands inherent in pastoral work.

John Paul's apostolic exhortation also clearly defined the purpose of the seminary, "an ecclesial community" designed to form future priests, who are primarily pastors of the Church. To this end, those who are involved in the nurturing of vocations and formation of priests must have a true love and sincere respect for each seminarian who, in conditions very personal, is proceeding toward priestly ordination. *Pastores Dabo Vobis* explains that the seminary is built around those involved with formation: the rector, the spiritual director, the superiors, and the professors. Each of these people represents the bishop, who has primary responsibility for the seminary environment. The effectiveness of the training offered at any given seminary depends almost entirely upon the maturity and strength of those entrusted with formation, "both from the human and the Gospel points of view."[26] It is important, the pope stressed, that the rector, spiritual director, and course instructors be selected carefully. They should be intimately joined to the bishop, who is primarily responsible for the formation of priests. For this ministry, "priests of exemplary life should be chosen," men who exhibit human and spiritual maturity, pastoral experience, professional competence, and stability in their own vocation. These priests may be aided by the lay faithful, both men and women, in the work of training future priests. They must also be chosen with great care.

■ ■ ■

It is necessary to know what the Church expects from seminary training in order to measure it against what has actually happened at American seminaries since the end of the Second Vatican Council. No discussion of seminaries and its students, however, would be complete without an understanding of the priesthood. If a seminary is a place where a man learns what it means to *be* a priest and to do what a priest *does*, it will be helpful to understand these things. Empirical evidence reveals that a large segment of the Catholic population in the U.S. has no real understanding of what a priest *is*, let alone what a priest *does*, aside from celebrating the sacraments. Consequently, the priesthood suffers from what many would call an "identity crisis." Such a crisis can hardly encourage vocations to the priesthood. In a sense the priesthood has become a battleground for ideologies contrary to the Church's teaching.

In the face of this controversy, St. Jean-Marie Vianney, better known as the Curé of Ars, provides an excellent example of what a priest does and what it means to be a priest. When Jean-Marie was canonized in 1925, Pope Pius XI dubbed him the "patron saint of parish priests." Interestingly enough, he was not known to excel at his studies in seminary. In a sense, though, this holy and simple peasant *was* good at his studies, but not according to the methods in which theology was being taught in his day. He was far advanced in spiritual matters and in the practice of the virtues long before he came to the seminary to study these things *in theory*. He was a humble man, innocent and pure of heart. His teachers, on the other hand, were condescending. In fact, many of them were Jansenists who were teaching theological error.

Jean-Marie was twenty-nine years old when he was ordained, his superiors having decided that his great zeal for souls made up for his lack of learning. Even then he was not allowed to hear confessions because of his supposed lack of knowledge in moral theology. (It is doubtful that Jean-Marie truly lacked knowledge in moral theology. Historians indicate that his bishop and superiors in seminary were distrustful of his anti-Jansenist views.) The bishop did not grant him this faculty until several years later. First assigned to assist an older priest, when that priest died Jean-Marie was sent to Ars, a small village about thirty miles from Lyon, where he became well known for performing his duties as a parish priest. Upon his assignment there in 1818 he wrote down this prayer: "My God, grant me the conversion of my parish. I am willing to suffer all my life whatsoever it may please you to lay upon me. Yes, even for a hundred years I am prepared to endure the sharpest pains; only let my people be converted." Jean-Marie prayed earnestly for the conversion of his parish not only because it was his duty to do so, but because Ars had been without a priest for many years, and its people had become wholly ignorant of the faith. The years following the bloody French Revolution (1789–99) saw the persecution and execution of much of the clergy in France. Thus, there was a severe man-made priest shortage in that once Catholic country known fondly throughout Christendom as the "land of saints." The holy Curé of Ars lamented, "Leave a parish without a priest for twenty years and it will worship the beasts." That's what he judged had happened in the parish of Ars.

The Curé was granted his prayer: he suffered nonstop for forty-one years until his death at age seventy-three. Some of his suffering was of his own choosing. He slept in a small, bare bedroom, selling all his furniture except for a few pieces. He ate crusts of bread for his breakfast, and no more than a potato for his dinner. He slept but an hour or so each night. These mortifications that Jean-Marie practiced for more than four decades attested to the miraculous nature of the saint's entire life. His food and sleep, humanly speaking, were not enough to sustain a man.

The second type of suffering endured by the Curé was inflicted upon him by his people. They mocked him in obscene songs, wrote him threatening letters, and nailed slanderous postcards to his rectory door. Some villagers even told him he must leave Ars at once. Yet he continued to preach fearlessly from the pulpit of his small country church. "If a priest is determined not to lose his soul," he said, "he must not allow anything to bar his way in the discharge of his duty, even were he certain of being murdered on coming down from his pulpit." His sufferings quickly began to bear fruit. The more sufferings he endured, the more people converted. The greater the sufferings he endured, the greater the sinners that converted. His long hours in the confessional—sometimes sixteen to eighteen hours a day—earned him a reputation as a brilliant confessor. In fact, as the years went by, his preaching and his spiritual direction attracted people from other parishes. Thousands began to pilgrimage from all over Europe to hear him preach and to confess their sins to him. When one priest from a neighboring village asked him the secret to giving out proper penances in the confessional, the Curé answered, "Give them light penances, and perform the rest yourself."

Jean-Marie continued to lead souls to the sacraments, something that caused a stir even among some Church leaders. A popular heresy of his day was that of the Jansenists, who believed with false humility that they were unworthy to receive the sacraments frequently (e.g., every Sunday). But the Curé would preach against them, some of whom were French bishops and priests, instructing his people properly about the sacraments. "We have the sacraments at our disposal," he said, "because we belong to the religion of salvation. We are bound to give thanks to God for them from our hearts, for the sacraments are the sources of salvation. The Jansenists have the sacraments, it is true, but they are of no use to them, for they imagine that only the perfect can receive them." He explained that, of course, no one will ever be "worthy" to receive Jesus in the

Holy Eucharist, for instance, but if Jesus had in view our worthiness, he never would have instituted the Eucharist. He had in view our "wants," and the Curé made his people want to partake in the sacraments, which, if faithfully received, would lead them to salvation.

The number of pilgrims who visited St. Jean-Marie Vianney increased to 20,000 every day. They came to hear his preaching, to listen to his catechism instruction, and to confess their sins to him. Day in and day out he did nothing other than function as a parish priest, accomplishing the simple duties assigned to him.

When, in 1947, as a seminarian, Karol Wojtyla, the future John Paul II, visited the home of St. Jean-Marie, he came away convinced that the Sacrament of Penance was an "indispensable part of the drama of a Christian life," and that as a priest he would imitate the saintly Curé by making himself a "prisoner of the confessional."[27] The future pope imitated this patron saint of parish priests in many ways as Pope Pius XI had meant for his priests to do. It was this French peasant, who was first persecuted in seminary and then later as a young priest for his fidelity to Christ and the Church that Pius XI held up as the model for the parish priest. The Curé of Ars preached the truth fearlessly, he celebrated the sacraments with great reverence, he catechized, he performed acts of mortification, all with a self-sacrificial spirit that enabled him to achieve his ultimate goal as a pastor of souls: to convert his parish.

Obviously if the Church believes that Jean-Marie ought to be imitated as a model priest, we can by studying his life better understand what it is a priest *does*. Judging from the Curé of Ars, the most important thing a priest does is to lead a life of self-sacrifice. Before the Vatican II years, the priestly vocation was always presented as sacrificial, which brought deep and satisfying rewards. "Vocations appeals," wrote Church historian James Hitchcock, "always emphasized the spirit of self-denial expected of the priest, and many communities, such as those of cloistered monks and foreign missionaries, attracted vocations by offering almost nothing but a life of self-sacrifice."[28]

Jesuit theologian Father John Hardon went so far as to say that every vocation is born of sacrifice, is maintained by sacrifice, and is measured in the apostolate by the sacrifice of those whom God calls to the priesthood or the religious life.[29] In fact, he added, "the more intimate one's vocation to the service of Christ, the more demanding will be the sacrifices required."[30] The experience of self-denial in the use and enjoyment of material things is the normal predisposition for a life of self-sacrifice in the priestly ministry. Hardon calls sacrifice in childhood and young adulthood the "seedbed of vocations," and sacrifice in the priesthood the norm of apostolic work.

This ideal is further reflected in the writings of the Vatican Council. In the Decree on Priestly Formation, the seminarian, it states, "must be trained in priestly obedience, in a program of humble living, and in the spirit of self-denial."[31] Despite the clear and demanding teachings of this decree and *Presbyterorum Ordinis*,[32] Vatican II's decree on the ministry and life of priests, the emphasis on self-sacrifice and self-denial almost evaporated following the council. Yet nothing in the council's decrees even suggested such a change. Through self-appointed "interpreters," the teachings of Vatican II were sufficiently distorted to convince Catholics that in living out the Christian vocation, the Church had called for a shift away from the self-sacrifice model to the self-fulfillment model. In other words, pew Catholics were persuaded that the Church was now telling them to stop being sacrificial in order to concentrate on fulfilling themselves. Such a perceived change in emphasis deeply wounded the priesthood. Its effects were felt in parishes slowly, yet the change in seminaries came almost immediately.

At the same time—and not unrelated, by any measure—a crisis of priestly identity progressively followed on the heels of the council and the reform of the Mass instituted by Pope Paul VI. One great help the Church has provided in remedying this identity crisis, in addition to John Paul II's *Pastores Dabo Vobis*, is the *Directory for the Life and Ministry of Priests*, issued in 1994 by the Vatican's Congregation for the Clergy under the direction of José Cardinal Sanchez. The *Directory*, authorized by Pope John Paul II, clearly defines the identity of the priest and provides a lucid explanation of what a priest *does* and what a priest *is*. The document collects Church teaching on the subject from Pope Leo XIII down to the writings of John Paul II.

Not surprisingly, the document looks to the example of the Curé of Ars as a model to imitate. The *Directory* begins by defining the priesthood as a "gift which was instituted by Christ to continue his own salvific mission." This gift was "conferred upon the Apostles and remains in the Church through the bishops and their successors." Thus, the identity of the priest centers on the participation in the priesthood of Christ. The priest, in other words, acts *in persona Christi*. He is consecrated to preach the Gospel and shepherd the faithful, and above all to celebrate the Holy Sacrifice of the Mass.

The *Directory* also spells out what a priest *does* and what he ought to do in order to grow in holiness and be fruitful in his apostolic ministry, including attracting vocations to the priesthood. Seven habits to be cultivated are:

- daily celebration of the Mass
- frequent confession and spiritual direction
- daily examination of conscience
- daily reading of Scripture and other spiritual reading
- days of recollection and retreats
- Marian devotions
- meditation on the Passion of Our Lord

These habits of life are necessary for the priest to carry out the work he was ordained to do. The contrast between these and the actual habits cultivated in today's seminaries and evidenced in many priests ordained over the past three decades is sobering.

CHAPTER 13

Where the Men Are

Why Orthodoxy Begets Vocations (or, How to Learn from the Successful Dioceses and Seminaries)

Vocations are out there, but a vocation is like a plant; it needs to be nourished and supported. You reap what you sow.
   —Father David Misbrener, Diocese of Youngstown, Ohio

We know what the problem is, and what the causes of the problem are. The next natural question is: "What then is the solution?" Both *Pastores Dabo Vobis* and the *Directory of the Life and Ministry of Priests* provide ample direction for Catholics seminaries. But those alone are probably not enough. These documents, as with most Church documents, risk being reduced to theoretical ideals—even though they are certainly much more than that. Never is there a shortage of those who will dismiss Church pronouncements as "unrealistic" or "outmoded" solutions.

The popularly pessimistic proclamation that "vocations just aren't out there" can easily be contradicted by empirical evidence to the contrary. As Archbishop Curtiss mentioned in his seminal article that exposed the problem of discrimination against orthodox candidates, there are several notable dioceses that have a disproportionately large number of seminary candidates and recently ordained priests.

Thus, bishops and others charged with fostering vocations can easily look to the dioceses that are having success and try to model their own programs after these.

Unfortunately, it seems that although most bishops are aware of the success stories and well understand what it takes to attract vocations, there appears to be a willful incapacity on the part of diocesan leaders to learn from their own past mistakes. They are unable to admit that the vocations shortage is not a naturally occurring phenomenon but rather a man-made crisis. Those who have the "death wish" for the male, celibate priesthood and who, further, promote agendas that are counterproductive to the mission of the Catholic Church simply do not want the candidates that present themselves with a willingness to serve the Church. It boils down to a generation gap of sorts, one that pits the aging radical reformer against the young, pious conservative.

An interesting exchange from Youngstown, Ohio, illustrates this point. The May 29, 1998, issue of Youngstown's diocesan newspaper, the *Catholic Exponent*, ran a full back-page ad with the headline: "Were you looking for coverage of the Diocese of Youngstown's ordinations to the priesthood for 1998?" Beneath a silhouetted caricature of a priest bearing a question mark on his chest is the answer: "There are no ordinations to the priesthood in our diocese this year or next. Please pray for vocations!" That same month, in a lengthy letter to the editor of the same paper, Father Kenneth E. Miller provided some insight into possible reasons for the lack of seminarians studying for the priesthood in the Youngstown diocese. Miller, who had recently concluded nearly ten years as the vocations director for the diocese, wrote, "The bishops are under tremendous pressure to staff parishes with an aging and dwindling supply of priests. And despite what some say, they [the seminarians] aren't 'out there' if we try hard enough."[1] Miller testified that he and other vocations directors across the country have been trying "very hard" to recruit candidates, but with minimal success.

"For the most part," he claimed, "dioceses today often admit candidates who do not and probably will not have the intellectual and psychological skills necessary to lead a well-educated Catholic laity in the next millennium. Many present seminarians have a fondness for good 'old-fashioned' practices of Catholic piety (which they are too young to remember first hand), without having a true and authentically Catholic spirituality."

Miller believes that seminarians—those whom Archbishop Curtiss would characterize as "orthodox"—who focus on personal piety as an integral component of their priestly formation might avoid the social justice mandate of the Church. In an illogical argument, he somehow finds personal piety and social justice mutually incompatible.

According to Miller—remember that he was a highly *un*successful vocations director for nearly a decade—devotion to the Blessed Sacrament is also problematic for these "conservative" and "pious" seminarians. Their "focus on the Blessed Sacrament" is, for Miller, "disturbing." He maintains that this "resurgence of Eucharistic piety by many future leaders of the Church ... denies, at least implicitly, the Incarnation" because, he says, "the Risen Jesus cannot be contained."

In Miller's final observation he states, "I see many dioceses around the country 'importing' priests and seminarians from other countries and dioceses." Miller does not approve. "A diocesan presbyterate suffers when priests are brought in to fill spaces left vacant from a lack of local diocesan clergy. [Tell that to the great missionary saints.] There are, after all," he wrote, "other models of parish leadership and staffing that don't necessitate this growing trend of importing clergy and seminarians." Is it any wonder then, with observations such as these from a former vocations director, that the Diocese of Youngstown during the Bishop James W. Malone years (1968–95) produced scant priestly vocations?[2]

First, Miller admits his awareness of dioceses that are having tremendous success with recruiting vocations and ordaining priests, year after year. Yet, instead of trying to learn from these successes, he summarily dismisses them. In doing so he further admits that vocations are indeed "out there"—roundly contradicting himself in the process—but they apparently aren't to his liking. They are too dumb or too pious or too young or too focused on the Blessed Sacrament. Then he criticizes the successful dioceses for accepting candidates who were rejected by vocations directors like him for being too

"orthodox." Not only that, he justifies not "importing" vocations because there are alternatives to priest-pastors in Catholic parishes,
thereby implying that Catholics really don't need priests in today's
Church because they now have a progressive new model of Church
that relies on lay ministry and priestless parishes.

Fortunately Miller's letter with its self-condemning admissions set
off a flurry of responses in the weeks that followed. Many were from
his fellow priests who pointed out that "you reap what you sow."

Monsignor Thomas Acklin, O.S.B., rector of St. Vincent Seminary in Latrobe, Pennsylvania, was one of the first to respond. In his
letter published in a later issue of Youngstown's *Catholic Exponent*, he
identified himself as one of those who believes that vocations "are
out there." It is the lack of support, Acklin offered in rejoinder, "not
only of our culture but often even of Catholics, that has caused a
great many of those entering the seminary to experience strong challenges to their vocation."[3]

The Latrobe rector defended today's "pious" and "conservative"
seminarians against the former Youngstown vocations director's accusations. He stated that he finds today's seminarians to be, above all, authentic. He wrote: "What has been strikingly refreshing to me is their
passionate desire to personally appropriate the Catholic faith and its
tradition.... It is interesting to see how many people in the pew are
deeply appreciative of the seminarians whom they meet, especially regarding their emphasis on prayer, but also regarding an openness to
devotion which some priests seem to lack or even oppose."

From his experience as a seminary rector, Acklin believes the
priests of tomorrow "will place a definite priority upon liturgical
praying and personal prayer, seeking an experience of intimacy with
Him who calls into the priesthood a man who is then able to witness
to this intimacy and share it with others."

Father David M. Misbrener, associate pastor of Immaculate Con-
ception Church in Ravenna, Ohio, also wrote to defend the personal
piety and devotion of young priests such as himself. "It is through
devotion to the Blessed Sacrament," he wrote, "that I am able to witness to the people and truly be a part of the social ministries and
other aspects of the Church. It also helps me face my frailties and

gives me strength to try to overcome them."[4] Misbrener affirmed that "vocations are out there," but, he said, "a vocation is like a plant; it needs to be nourished and supported. You reap what you sow."

With that in mind, it is worth returning to Archbishop Curtiss's explication of the simple formula that his successful archdiocese follows: "Our vocation strategy is drawn from successful ones in other dioceses: a strong, orthodox base that promotes loyalty to the pope and bishop; a vocations director and team who clearly supports a male, celibate priesthood and religious communities loyal to magisterial teaching; a presbyterate that takes personal ownership of vocations ministry in the archdiocese; . . . [and] eucharistic devotion in parishes, with an emphasis on prayer for vocations."[5]

In short, orthodoxy begets vocations: the formula with proven success is based on fidelity to the Church's magisterium.

Nevertheless, the dioceses that have been experiencing the greatest problems with vocations have ignored this formula. In fact, a certain degree of helpless desperation on the part of so many American dioceses is evidenced clearly by the methods to which they are resorting to "encourage" or "promote" vocations, eschewing the proven formula for success. Gimmicks, including comic books, basketball games, billboards, and television advertisements, replace authentic vocations outreach that demands fidelity to the Church's teaching and especially to the priesthood.

The Diocese of Des Moines, Iowa, for instance, holds basketball games with a traveling team of priests called "The Running Revs," and advertises on billboards with messages like "White Collar Workers Needed: Priesthood" and "Priesthood: It's Awesome."

The billboard approach was also adopted by the Diocese of Providence, one of the more liberal East Coast dioceses, when they initiated a major media blitz to "target" potential candidates to the priesthood. The campaign, explained Providence vocations director Father Marcel L. Taillon, "will bring Christ to the young people of [Rhode Island] by meeting them where they are."[6] In addition to billboards, a Web site, and newspaper advertisements, the diocese has been running television commercials on MTV, a crass rock music-video cable channel that doesn't by any stretch promote

Catholic life, thought, or teaching. Taillon explained that "the best place to reach potential candidates would be on MTV and the Comedy Channel," presumably because studied viewing patterns show that these are the two most popular networks with men ages eighteen to thirty-five.

Skeptics wonder why a Catholic diocese would advertise to an audience that sits on the couch tuned into video music from bands such as Marilyn Manson, Godsmack, Limp Bizkit, and Porno for Pyros—the ultimate in "cold call" marketing techniques that makes faithful Catholics wonder if the diocese is trying to attract "unchurched" men that they can then mold easily into their "reenvisioned" image of the priest.

An editorial in the *Providence Visitor*, however, claims that the media campaign "isn't an endorsement of the MTV-style of life, but rather an attempt to deliver the message of Jesus Christ to our young people in the midst of it."[7]

Patrick Simmons,* who said he "wouldn't be caught dead watching MTV," wonders who the diocese would find suitable. "Maybe there's a reason why they're advertising on MTV instead of more suitable venues," he suggested. Simmons, an orthodox Catholic, applied to the priestly formation program in the Diocese of Providence in 1999 around the time the media blitz hit the streets and airwaves in Rhode Island. After being interviewed by a woman he described as a "radical ex-nun," he was declared "rigid," "hostile," and "reactionary," for holding to Church teaching on essential issues of the faith. In other words, he said, he was not a "suitable" candidate. He soon received a rejection notice. Thus, amidst an expensive media campaign to attract "suitable" candidates, the Diocese of Providence rejected as "unsuitable" a young man who watches EWTN instead of MTV. This perhaps partly explains why this diocese of 700,000 Catholics had just twenty-five seminarians in 2001 and will be ordaining not even one man to the priesthood in 2002.

Also in 1999, the *Washington Post* and the *Milwaukee Journal-Sentinel* reported on the Archdiocese of Milwaukee's similar media campaign. Billboards in and around Milwaukee presented kitsch messages like "Wanted: Doctor of Souls" and "Work with the World's Greatest Boss." (Milwaukee Catholics were unsure if the billboard was referring to God or Archbishop Rembert Weakland.)

In April 2000, NBC News discussed a similar Madison Avenue–style advertising campaign launched by the Archdiocese of Chicago, long troubled by a dearth of vocations, to attract candidates for the priesthood. The campaign is founded on the same premise as in Des Moines, Providence, and Milwaukee: that men can be lured into answering the call by billboard slogans. Chicago's marketing team came up with these:

- "Minimize your wardrobe, maximize your potential"
- "Dreaming of a white-collar job?"
- "Help Wanted: Inquire within yourself"
- "If you are waiting for a sign from God, this is it"
- "Some people who care donate clothes, others donate their lives"

But sensible Catholics wonder why the Church is spending thousands of dollars to advertise like a secular corporation, commercializing the priesthood as a product you might want, before fixing the well-known problems that exist in the nation's seminaries and vocations offices.

The fact is that no diocese that has successfully attracted vocations has enlisted marketing professionals to make the priesthood attractive to mainstream consumers. The media blitz is more of an embarrassment to the Catholic Church than anything else. Resources need to be put not toward marketing, but toward a demanding seminary program and an orthodox educational curriculum. At the same time, vocations offices and seminary staff need to be supportive of authentic priestly vocations from orthodox men.

■ ■ ■

Returning to those dioceses that have a proven record of success—Arlington, Lincoln, Peoria, Wichita, Bridgeport, Omaha, Atlanta, and Rockford, for starters—one common denominator is that these dioceses *primarily*, although not exclusively, send their seminarians to one particular seminary: Mount St. Mary's Seminary in Emmitsburg, Maryland. A natural conclusion might be that if the conservative and successful bishops are all sending their men to the same seminaries, and one in particular, it might be helpful to look to that institution to see what it is doing right.

Mount St. Mary's—not to be confused with Baltimore's St. Mary's Seminary—was in the late 1990s the subject of several prominent news articles in places like *Crisis Magazine* and the *New York Times Magazine*.

Father Thomas Kocik is a recently ordained priest and graduate of the Mount, as it is fondly known. For two years, while attending St. Mary's Seminary in Baltimore, he struggled bitterly with faculty and fellow students as a seminarian for his home diocese of Syracuse, New York. When he switched dioceses to Fall River, Massachusetts, Bishop Sean O'Malley decided to send him to Emmitsburg's Mount St. Mary's, which, although geographically close to the Baltimore seminary, has a decidedly different outlook.

After just a month at the Mount, Kocik says he could tell that life in Emmitsburg was going to be far more encouraging to his vocation. In stark contrast to life at Baltimore's "Pink Palace," Kocik characterized life for seminarians at Mount St. Mary's with these eight observations:

1. Zeal for Catholic orthodoxy and traditions, including traditional devotions, e.g., public rosary, regular Eucharistic adoration, and Benediction of the Blessed Sacrament
2. Emphasis on personal prayer, holiness, and sanctification through the sacraments, especially the Eucharist and Penance
3. Preaching that reinforces and expounds upon the whole of the Catholic faith, including distinctively Catholic doctrines
4. Strong devotion to the Blessed Virgin Mary, particularly through the rosary and scapular
5. No flagrant liturgical abuses
6. Active involvement in pro-life efforts

7. Enthusiasm for evangelization—for example, a seminarian Legion of Mary group frequently visits the college students door-to-door, reaching out to Catholics who have fallen away from the practice of the faith and to interested non-Catholics

8. A clear priestly identity as the Catholic Church defines the ordained ministry in all its sacredness and solemnity

According to Kocik, "Given the crisis of faith and the climate of dissent in the American Church today, I believe that Mount St. Mary's ranks among the finest in the nation."

Interestingly, according to rector Father Kevin Rhoades, "Mount St. Mary's does *no* recruiting because the school is operating above capacity...and there is need for expansion."[8] Echoing Archbishop Curtiss's words, Rhoades believes that his seminary's success can be attributed to orthodoxy: "We are faithful to the magisterium and carefully follow all the Vatican documents on priestly formation. No one is in dissent here."

Seminarians and recent graduates speak just as highly of Mount St. Mary's as does their rector. They all seem to agree that the Mount has that formula for success that Archbishop Curtiss outlined, and that is the fundamental reason that many of the successful dioceses in the Midwest go out of their way to send their seminarians to Maryland rather than somewhere much closer to home.

Life at Mount St. Mary's, according to seminarians there, can be summarized like this:

Prayer life: Seminarians come together for community prayer at least four times each day, for Morning Prayer, daily Mass, an hour of adoration, and Evening Prayer.

Faculty and staff: Seminarians have an academic advisor, a spiritual advisor, and a formation advisor. The faculty and staff are known for their orthodoxy and their availability to students.

Fraternity: On Wednesday evenings seminarians come together for prayer with other seminarians from their diocese or nearby dioceses. For example, all the seminarians from New Jersey would come together, or all those from New England would be clustered together.

Atmosphere: Unlike in other seminaries across the United States, the students from the Mount do not typically feel as if they are being closely scrutinized, monitored for political correctness, or placed under psychological pressure.

Apostolate: The Mount is located in a rural area but within an hour's drive of both Baltimore and Washington. Each seminarian has an assigned apostolate each year, such as working in a hospice or a prison.

Campus modality: The seminary is attached to Mount St. Mary's College, which the seminarians see as important. Their daily routine allows the seminarians not only to come together as men studying for the ordained priesthood, but also to interact with "everyday people."

Manly recreation: A significant stress is placed on manly recreation. The overwhelming majority of seminarians are into athletics of one kind or another. The athletic facilities at the college are some of the best in the country.

Spanish: Many of the seminarians are involved with Spanish language groups, meeting regularly for a Spanish liturgy.

Full schedule: A seminarian's schedule is full each day, including prayer, academics, social service, and recreation.

Much the same might be said about a few of the other seminaries to which the successful dioceses send their seminarians: Holy Apostles College and Seminary in Cromwell, Connecticut, and St. Charles Borromeo Seminary in Overbrook, Pennsylvania, are two excellent examples. Another is the North American College (NAC) in Rome, known as the West Point for Catholic seminarians. Brian Murphy, an Associated Press writer, wrote a book about the NAC in 1997. In *The New Men*, Murphy describes the atmosphere there. "The North American College is a serious place. The rector makes it clear before the [seminarians'] pew seats are even warm on arrival day. 'I'm not interested in halfway seminarians looking to become bend-the-rules priests,' he says. 'Not these days with the Roman Catholic Church being routinely bashed as a haven for maladjusted pastors with retrograde thinking. Not with the congregations back home shriveling up.' "[9]

Probably the most promising development in the past thirty years is the opening of two new diocesan seminaries, one in Lincoln, Nebraska, and the other in Denver, Colorado. The relatively small Diocese of Lincoln, which has consistently had one of the highest rates of ordination in the country over the past several decades, has never experienced a shortage of priests. Under the leadership of Bishop Glennon Flavin, the diocese attracted orthodox seminarians who accepted the teachings of the Church, looked up to their bishop and the pope, and embraced the male, celibate priesthood. Flavin had a reputation as being a strong Vatican supporter and an impeccably orthodox bishop. He was succeeded by Bishop Fabian Bruskewitz, one of only a few remaining orthodox pastors from the Milwaukee diocese under Archbishop Rembert Weakland.

Bruskewitz made national news when he opened up a new diocesan college seminary. Although a shepherd to only 85,000 Catholics, Bruskewitz had forty-four seminarians when the Seminary of St. Gregory the Great opened in August of 1998, making it the first freestanding diocesan seminary to be opened in the United States for many decades. "They are a healthy bunch, very active and energetic both intellectually and physically," marveled rector Father John Folda of the Lincoln seminarians.[10] When asked what made these men enroll, he answered, "The love of the Church and the examples set by Pope John Paul II and Bishop Bruskewitz."

Two years later Our Lady of Guadalupe Seminary, the sixty-student seminary of the U.S. branch of the Priestly Fraternity of St. Peter, moved to the Diocese of Lincoln, precisely because of the orthodoxy of Bishop Fabian Bruskewitz, who welcomed them, something that other bishops have refused to do in the past.

In Denver, since Archbishop Charles Chaput was appointed in 1997 to lead the Catholic Church in northern Colorado, vocations have seen a remarkable increase, going from twenty-six seminarians in 1991 to sixty-eight in 1999, with an additional twenty studying for religious orders.

The Archdiocese of Denver has taken a unique approach to the issue of reforming a seminary. Several years ago, Chaput's predecessor, then archbishop Francis Stafford,[11] bought the forty-acre campus of St. Thomas Theological Seminary after the Vincentian-run institution closed in 1995 allegedly due to a dwindling student body. But the problems there, moral and pedagogical, were well known and documented. In 1999, Chaput reopened the seminary under a new name and with a new faculty. The new St. John Vianney Theological Seminary is not only decidedly rooted in the theology of Pope John Paul II and Joseph Cardinal Ratzinger, it is connected with the two-hundred-year-old Pontifical Lateran University. Officials at the Lateran, which is known as the Pope's University because it is directly under the pope's authority, approved the Denver faculty and its curriculum. Moreover, the university's students and faculty are overtly and joyfully supportive of the Catholic priesthood and the authentic mission of the Catholic Church to save souls. Its mission from inception is clearly to form holy and healthy priests for the "new evangelization." Rather than reading texts penned by dissidents who rose to notoriety in the 1960s, the Vianney curriculum emphasizes the philosophy of St. Thomas Aquinas and the "great books" of Western civilization.

Just as with Bishop Bruskewitz in Lincoln, many more seminarians are attracted to serve the Archdiocese of Denver precisely because of Charles Chaput's orthodoxy, his enthusiasm, and his encouragement. Even new Catholic communities and established religious orders have contacted the archdiocese to inquire about the possibility of relocating their groups there. Father John Hilton, former director of vocations in Denver, explained that, above all, the rapid rise in seminarians can be attributed to "the relentless efforts of Archbishop Chaput in promoting vocations."[12] Francis X. Maier, chancellor for the archdiocese, similarly explained that "what the archbishop does through his personal witness is to make the priesthood attractive to a lot of people. . . . It's his highest priority. He raises the issue of vocations to the priesthood and the religious life every time he's with young people." But more importantly, he added, Chaput is "a good masculine role model," and the archbishop's example spills over to the clergy and laity alike. His appeal is not due to progressive ideas and reform-minded schemes. Rather, it is his obvious love for the Church, the sacraments, the papacy, and the priesthood.

Another reason for Denver's success, says Hilton, is the preparatory "spirituality year" program, which was modeled after the successful program developed by Jean-Marie Cardinal Lustiger in Paris. This "preseminary" year in Denver allows prospective seminarians to study, pray, and discern God's will in their lives before diving into the hectic life of a seminarian. Each day of the spiritual year begins and ends with the Liturgy of the Hours, the prayer of the Church that all priests are required to recite or sing daily. The candidates also attend daily Mass and Benediction, and participate in Eucharistic adoration at least weekly. The study component of the year program consists of reading the entire Bible, both Old and New Testaments, the *Catechism of the Catholic Church*, and a generous selection of spiritual classics written by the Fathers and Doctors of the Church. Apostolic work, such as visiting AIDS patients or working with the homeless, is the third component of the triad.

Another "re-formed" institution is St. Joseph's in Yonkers, New York, the seminary operated by the Archdiocese of New York. Shortly after being named the archbishop of New York in 2000, Edward Cardinal Egan asked for and accepted the resignations of a great number of faculty members at St. Joseph's Seminary, more commonly known as Dunwoodie, though it must be said that the New York seminary was not one of those commonly listed as problematic; seminarians there say it is for the most part an orthodox institution, if a little too bureaucratic and political sometimes. If Egan's action proves nothing else—some critics say he "pruned" some of the wrong faculty—it demonstrates that the local bishop has the authority and opportunity to quickly "re-form" his seminary. It can be done. And it needs to be done in most seminaries across the U.S. and beyond.

Again the solution harks back to Archbishop Curtiss's formula for success: he recognizes—and so should others—that orthodoxy begets vocations. Then, to reiterate, he candidly suggests that it is time to pay close attention to the dioceses that have not suffered the priest shortage and vocations crisis. If diocesan bishops and seminary officials are unwilling to recognize the reasons for the successes, he says, "then we allow ourselves to become supporters of a self-fulfilling prophecy about the shortage of vocations."

The archbishop has done everyone a favor by identifying the successful dioceses as those that promote orthodoxy and loyalty to the Church, are unambiguous about the ordained priesthood as the Church defines that ministry, have bishops who are willing and able to confront dissent, and are willing to call forth candidates who share their loyalty to the pope. "When this formula, based on total fidelity to Church teaching, is followed in dioceses and religious communities," he wrote, "then vocations will increase."

The orthodox seminarian naturally wants to be supported in his vocation, not coerced into accepting theological opinions that the Church does not accept. He wants to be formed in an environment that does not hold him in contempt for his adherence to Church teaching and does not present obstacles such as a "gay subculture" to his growth in personal holiness. He wants to be surrounded by classmates and instructors who share his vision—which is not an idiosyncratic vision but the universal vision of the Church, working in unity for the salvation of souls.

Bishops would do well to take the advice of Archbishop Curtiss and look at successful dioceses and seminary programs to see what they are doing. They would do well to look to the dioceses which are not presently experiencing either a vocations crisis or a priest shortage. Reform of the nation's seminaries and vocations offices is key. If that reform is not undertaken, the self-imposed priest shortage will occupy Catholic resources which would be better spent on evangelization, spiritual formation, and performing spiritual and corporal works of mercy.

Notes

Introduction

1. J. M. Hirsch, "Bishops' Committee Members Accused," Associated Press, April 12, 2002.
2. Arthur Austin, "I Say...My Anguish Does Not End, Ever," *Boston Globe*, April 9, 2002.
3. As I employ the term, "orthodox" (with the small *o*) connotes adherence to the magisterium of the Church (i.e., the official teaching office of the Catholic Church) and a full acceptance of authentic Church teaching.
4. Pope John Paul II, "Holy Thursday Letter to Priests," March 21, 2002.

Chapter 1: A Man-Made Crisis

1. Robert E. McNally, "Priesthood in Crisis," *America*, June 25, 1966.
2. "In the United States the period from 1900 to 1960 can be considered a golden age of the priesthood, not merely in modern times but throughout all the Catholic centuries. While priests of that era certainly had their faults, by all measurable standards there was less ignorance, less immorality, less neglect of duty, and less disobedience than at almost any time in the history of the Church. More positively, priests of that era were generally pious and zealous, and those who were not at least had to pretend to be." James Hitchcock, "He's the Last One I Would Have Expected," *San Francisco Faith*, September 1999.
3. *Catholic Almanac* (Huntington, IN: Our Sunday Visitor Books, 2000).
4. *The CARA Report*, Summer 1998, as published by the United States Conference of Catholic Bishops at: http://www.nccbuscc.org/vocations/statistics.htm.
5. "Dire pronouncements of this sort appear with great frequency in the pages of the *National Catholic Reporter* and periodically in *America* and *Commonweal* as well. Indeed, one columnist for the *Reporter*, Tim Unsworth, was so troubled by this question that he put together a book about it and gave it a suitable apocalyptic title: *The Last Priests in America*." John F. Quinn, "Priest Shortage Panic," *Crisis*, October 1996.

6. Archbishop Elden F. Curtiss, "Crisis in Vocations? What Crisis?" *Our Sunday Visitor*, October 8, 1995.

7. Dale Vree, "Why Is a Good Priest So Hard to Find?" *New Oxford Review*, January 1996.

8. Archbishop Elden F. Curtiss, "Vocations to the Priesthood and Religious Life: The Formula That Works Is Based on Fidelity to the Church's Magisterium," *Social Justice Review*, November–December 1995.

9. Ibid.

10. The dioceses of Lincoln and Arlington are the only two dioceses in the United States that do not permit female altar servers. In 1994, the Vatican gave permission to bishops to permit female altar servers in their dioceses at their discretion. Some have cited Lincoln and Arlington's policy as a significant contributing factor in their disproportionately successful vocations numbers.

11. The *National Catholic Reporter*, lamenting the success of Arlington, describes the diocese as "a conservative bastion with a conservative bishop and many senior clergy who gravitated there after the diocese was split from Richmond" (May 6, 1994). The Diocese of Richmond, considered a "bastion of liberal Catholicism," pales in comparison to Arlington's vocation numbers.

12. Curtiss, "Vocations to the Priesthood and Religious Life."

13. The *National Catholic Reporter* disparagingly referred to the Diocese of Peoria as "an island of archconservativism presided over by [Bishop] John J. Myers, ordinary of the diocese since 1990. . . . Myers recruits both in area elementary schools and nationwide, accepting rejects from other seminaries" (May 6, 1994). Prior to being named bishop of Peoria, Myers was vocations director for the Peoria diocese. He is now the archbishop of Newark, New Jersey.

14. Curtiss, "Crisis in Vocations? What Crisis?"

15. *The Official Catholic Directory* (New Providence, NJ: P. J. Kennedy & Sons, 1999), 777.

16. Ibid., 1,039.

17. Pamela Schaeffer, "Vocation Directors Reject Archbishop Curtiss's Attack," *National Catholic Reporter*, October 20, 1995.

18. Ibid.

19. Quinn, "Priest Shortage Panic."

20. Schaeffer, "Vocation Directors Reject Archbishop Curtiss's Attack."

Chapter 2: Stifling the Call

1. Pope St. Pius X, *Haerent Animo*, 1908.

2. A "chancery" is the central administrative office of an archdiocese or diocese.

3. Joseph Illo, "Letter to the Editor," *Catholic World Report*, January 2001.

4. Alessandra Staley, "Pope in Austria to Heal a Troubled Church," *New York Times*, June 20, 1998.

5. Catholic News Service, "Bishop Resigns Over Relationship with Priest," *Catholic New York*, July 29, 1999.

6. The term "scholastic" is used by the Jesuits to identify a member who has completed his novitiate (formation program) and has entered into the preparatory stages for the priesthood. As a scholastic the priesthood candidate is a full-fledged Jesuit and often teaches high school religion or college philosophy or theology courses as part of his preparation for the priesthood.

7. George Neumayr, "The Walls Came Down," *San Francisco Faith*, October 1997.

8. Ibid.

9. Ibid.

10. Ibid.

11. Ibid.

12. George Neumayr, "Jesuits Implode," *American Prowler*, March 13, 2002.

13. Garry Wills, "Jesuits in Disarray," *New York Review of Books*, March 28, 2002.

14. Donald B. Cozzens, *The Changing Face of the Priesthood: A Reflection on the Priest's Crisis of Soul* (Collegeville MN: The Liturgical Press, 2000), 18.

15. Philip F. Lawler, "Suffer the Children," *Catholic World Report*, November 1993.

16. Cf. Michael Rezenfez, "Church Allowed Abuse by Priest for Years," *Boston Globe*, January 6, 2002.

17. Gerald Coleman, "Is Proposition 22 Discriminatory?" *San Jose Valley Catholic*, January 18, 2000.

18. Dawn Fallik, "Ex-Seminarian's Charges Lead to Removal of Priest," *St. Louis Post-Dispatch*, March 8, 2002.

Chapter 3: The Gatekeeper Phenomenon

1. Cozzens, *The Changing Face of the Priesthood*, x–xi.

2. Thomas Fath, "Our Vocations Crisis Is Manmade," *New Oxford Review*, April 1998.

3. Ibid.

4. Charles Curran, a former seminary professor in Rochester, New York, and professor of moral theology at the Catholic University of America, led the public dissent in the United States against *Humanae Vitae*, Pope Paul VI's 1968 encyclical on artificial contraception. On July 25, 1986, the Vatican ruled that Curran could "no longer be considered suitable or eligible to exercise the function of a professor of Catholic theology."

5. Paul Likoudis, "From the Mail," *The Wanderer*, June 20, 2000.

6. Gregory Flannery, "Masonic Master Screens City's Catholic Priests," *Mt. Washington Press*, May 8, 1991.

7. Ibid.

8. Ibid.

9. "Sex Abuse Cases Not New Locally," *Cincinnati Enquirer*, March 16, 2002.

10. Elizabeth Altham, "The Religion of Self: An Interview with Dr. William Coulson," *The Latin Mass*, Fall 1999.

11. Remarks taken from a videotaped school board meeting of March 3, 1998, available at: http://www.diocesereport.com/diocese_report/news/ajd_homo_part2.shtml.

12. "Position Statement of the Catholic Medical Association on Inpatient Treatment and Outpatient Psychiatric Evaluations for Priests and Religious," 1999.

13. Ibid.

14. Ibid.

15. This Latin expression, which literally means "from the throne," is used to refer to the most solemn and authoritative papal pronouncements. Teachings pronounced *ex cathedra* are infallible. According to the First Vatican Council, the pope teaches *ex cathedra* when he speaks as the supreme shepherd of the universal Church in matters of faith and morals that he proposes should be definitively held by all Catholics.

Chapter 4: The Gay Subculture

1. Ralph McInerny, "Priests with AIDS," Belief.net, February 7, 2000.

2. Cozzens, *The Changing Face of the Priesthood*, 101.

3. Ibid.

4. Andrew Greeley, "Priests and AIDS," *American Catholic*, March 2000.

5. Known as Broadway's first "homosexual musical," *La Cage aux Folles* tells the story of two middle-aged homosexual lovers who run a transvestite nightclub in St. Tropez.

6. Paul Likoudis, "Seminarians Were 'Fresh Meat' for Faculty," *The Wanderer*, May 9, 1996.

7. Ibid.

8. Jason Berry, *Lead Us Not into Temptation* (New York: Doubleday, 1992), 271–72.

9. Ibid., 245.

10. Ibid., 247.

11. Ibid., cf. 248.

12. "Under an extraordinary cloak of secrecy, the Archdiocese of Boston in the last 10 years has quietly settled child molestation claims against at least 70 priests, according to an investigation by the Globe Spotlight Team.... One law firm alone won financial settlements for its clients against at least 45 priests and five brothers from religious orders, according to the lead

attorney in those cases, Roderick MacLeish, Jr." "Scores of Priests Involved in Sex Abuse Cases," *Boston Globe*, January 31, 2002.

13. The restraining order was filed at Brighton District Court (Massachusetts) on Friday, April 2, 1999.

14. Joe Fitzgerald, "Priest Fears Gays in Ranks Pose Threat to Church," *Boston Herald*, March 6, 2002.

15. Taken from the written peer evaluation of Joseph Kellenyi, which is included in the "Theology I Assessment," April 25, 2000.

16. Taken from written comments in the peer evaluation of Joseph Kellenyi by Wolfgang Dietrich, which was also included in the "Theology I Assessment," April 25, 2000.

17. Rev. Kevin A. Codd, "Formation Advisor's Evaluation of Joseph Kellenyi," March 8, 2000.

18. Letter from David Windsor to Joseph Kellenyi, August 25, 2000.

19. Seminarians who are members of religious orders ordinarily live in community at a "religious house" where they receive their spiritual formation.

20. Pamela Schaeffer, "Court OKs Harassment Suit," *National Catholic Reporter*, December 17, 1999.

21. Mother Angelica is a conservative nun who founded the Eternal Word Television Network (EWTN).

22. "Postulancy" is a period of prenovitiate formation for candidates for a religious order.

23. Norman Weslin, *The Gathering of the Lambs* (Boulder, CO: Weslin, 2000), 102.

24. Ibid.

25. Ibid.

26. Cozzens, *The Changing Face of the Priesthood*, 102.

Chapter 5: The Heterodoxy Downer

1. Aaron Milavec, *Rediscovered Discipleship: Exploring Scriptural Sources* (New York: Sheed & Ward, 1994), 1.

2. *Catechism of the Catholic Church*, paragraph 390.

3. Gregory Flannery, "Seminary Fires Professor after Complaint to Vatican," *Hamilton Journal-News*, July 16, 1996.

4. Milavec's textbook supports this notion. For example, he writes: "While Mark 14:24 and other associated texts (e.g., Rom. 3:24–25, 1 Cor. 1:30, Eph. 1:7, Col. 1:14, 1 Tim. 2:6, Heb. 9:15) have habitually been bent in the direction of supporting the medieval theology of Jesus' atoning death, all of these texts taken together fail to take seriously the prevailing attitude of Jesus that God is abundantly ready to forgive sins now without any association with the intended or future death of Jesus," and later: "... it was necessary for you to be coldly aware of just how far the medieval theology and mindset had to go beyond the expressed

meaning of the Gospels in order to assert the atoning death of Jesus as the central mystery of salvation."

5. Rudolf Bultmann (1884–1976) was a Protestant New Testament scholar. According to Richard McBrien's *Encyclopedia of Catholicism* (San Francisco: Harper Collins, 1995), "Bultmann assumed the world was a closed causal system in which God had no influence; no miracles were possible, no Incarnation, atonement, or Resurrection. All these were myths no longer believable in the modern age" (201).

6. In an April 9, 1996, "Review of Fr. McBrien's *Catholicism*," issued by the National Conference of Catholic Bishops' Committee on Doctrine, the problems that *Catholicism* poses as an introductory text fall into three categories: "First, some statements are inaccurate or at least misleading. Second, there is in the book an overemphasis on the plurality of opinion within the Catholic theological tradition that makes it difficult at times for the reader to discern the normative core of that tradition. Third, *Catholicism* overstates the significance of recent developments within the Catholic tradition, implying that the past appears to be markedly inferior to the present and obscuring the continuity of the tradition. Falling within the latter two categories are difficulties that reappear throughout the work; they constitute a pattern that could be overlooked by an exclusive focus on particular passages."

As an example the bishops' doctrine committee gave several examples drawn from McBrien's text, including: "*Catholicism* insists that it is possible to hold the faith of the church while maintaining that Jesus Christ could have sinned.... *Catholicism* presents the virgin birth of Jesus as being of uncertain and perhaps even doubtful historicity.... The book stresses that the New Testament says nothing about the perpetual virginity of Mary (rather, it speaks of brothers and sisters of Jesus) and asserts that even in the second century there is no evidence for this belief.... While *Catholicism* is concerned to include a wide range of voices in the theological conversation, the teaching of the pope and bishops is often reduced to just another voice alongside those of private theologians.... The overall direction of the text of *Catholicism* is toward reducing to an absolute minimum the church teachings and beliefs that are to be considered essential to the Catholic faith.... On a number of important issues, most notably in the field of moral theology, the reader will see without difficulty that the book regards the 'official church position' as simply in error."

7. Levada served as archbishop of Portland from 1986 to 1995, when he was installed as archbishop of San Francisco.

8. Paul Likoudis, "Northwest Seminary's Required Sex Textbook Attacks Church and Encourages Deviant Behavior," *The Wanderer*, October 13, 1991.

9. Al Matt Jr., "Another Seminary Scandal," *The Wanderer*, October 13, 1991.

10. She legally changed her name to Frodo Okulam when she was ordained a minister for the Metropolitan Community Church. "Frodo" is derived from Tolkien's *Lord of the Rings* character of that name, because, she says, her first experience of the Divine came when praying to Elbereth, Queen of the Stars, also a figure from Tolkien's classic novel. Elbereth, she told an audience at a 1998 lesbian spirituality conference (CLOUT), spoke to her when she was thirteen, affirming her sexual orientation. "Okulam" she took from a children's book of Native American tales called *Kutkos, Chinook Tyee*. Okulam means "sound of the sea."

11. Cf. SisterSpirit Web site at http://home.teleport.com/~sistersp.

12. The Vatican's Congregation for the Doctrine of the Faith censured the writings of the late Indian-born Jesuit Father Anthony DeMello in 1998. The congregation said the priest's writings contain omissions and references to contradictions to Catholic doctrine.

13. "Progress 2000," *Quad City Online* (Iowa), http://www.qconline.com/progress2000/religion.shtml.

14. Starhawk is one of the most prominent promoters of "Goddess worship" and the feminist aspects of Wicca (witchcraft). The plot of her book, *The Fifth Sacred Thing*, is marketed thus: "A city of eco-feminist witches must stand up to the violence of an army bred on a repressive Christian ideology."

15. According to promotional literature for this book, "Fox was defrocked by the Roman Catholic Church for the ideologies he supports in this text." In his spiritual autobiography, Fox calls himself a "post-denominational priest."

16. Charles Fiore, "Seeds, Weeds, Seminaries, and Gardeners," *The Wanderer*, November 14, 1995.

Chapter 6: Pooh-Poohing Piety

1. Pope John Paul II, *Pastores Dabo Vobis*, March 25, 1992, paragraphs 47–48.

2. For example, Pope John Paul II, as bishop of Rome, does not allow Holy Communion to be distributed "in the hand" in the Diocese of Rome.

3. Katarina Schuth, *Seminaries, Theologates, and the Future of Church Ministry* (Collegeville MN: The Liturgical Press, 1999), 92.

4. *Catechism of the Catholic Church*, no. 1,374, drawing on sources from St. Thomas Aquinas, the Council of Trent, and Pope Paul VI.

5. Quoted from a handout distributed during the quasi-liturgy.

6. Weslin, *The Gathering of the Lambs*, 103.

Chapter 7: Go See the Shrink!

1. Lesley Payne, "Salt for Their Wounds," *Catholic World Report*, February 1997.

2. Ibid.

3. Ibid.

4. Ibid.
5. Ibid.
6. Ibid.
7. John Fraunces, "Vocations Crisis: The Self-Inflicted Wound," *Homiletic and Pastoral Review*, July 1997.
8. Ibid.
9. "Position Statement of the Catholic Medical Association on Inpatient Treatment and Outpatient Psychiatric Evaluations for Priests and Religious."

Chapter 8: The Vocational Inquisition

1. *Catechism of the Catholic Church*, no. 2,352, states: "By *masturbation* is to be understood the deliberate stimulation of the genital organs in order to derive sexual pleasure. Both the Magisterium of the Church, in the course of a constant tradition, and the moral sense of the faithful have been in no doubt and have firmly maintained that masturbation is an intrinsically and gravely disordered action. The deliberate use of the sexual faculty, for whatever reason, outside of marriage is essentially contrary to its purpose."
2. In summarizing his response to the common objections to Pope Paul VI's *Humanae Vitae*, Hinds wrote: "I have made this attempt to enter into the conversation concerning the issues of *Humanae Vitae* in this modest way. My feelings about the subject are expressed in the responses; they are I think nuanced, reasonably well-considered, and in accord with the tradition of the Church. The best thing about the situation is the positive assessment of conjugal sex which the document proposes. The worst thing is that the contraceptive mentality which the Pope has deplored and suggested would accompany a widespread use of artificial contraception has in fact become extremely widespread in the United States. Because of this mentality, or at least, along with this mentality, we are immersed in a tremendous increase in venereal disease, abortions, and sexual aggression. I find that the use of artificiality in the relationship has a logical connection with other abuses, rather than a helpful effect."
3. Sacred Congregation for the Doctrine of the Faith, *Declaration on Sexual Ethics* (Washington, DC: United States Catholic Conference, 1976), 15.
4. The Athenaeum did in fact later issue guidelines to strongly encourage the use of "inclusive, non-sexist" language. These "Inclusive Language" guidelines were published in the 1996–98 Athenaeum course catalog: "Gospel values and contemporary social consciousness urge us to recognize and change those attitudes and practices which are unjust. Christian tradition holds that all people are created in the image of God and that attitudes against anyone because of sex, age, race, or handicap diminish us all. Therefore, it is the policy of the Athenaeum to foster the use of inclusive language in academic endeavors and to work to

eliminate attitudes and customs that stereotype and separate persons from one another."

5. "Supervisor's Evaluation," April 7, 1986.
6. "Pastoral Staff Report," March 23, 1986.
7. Letter from Dr. Joseph Wicker to Father Roger Kriege, August 28, 1986.

Chapter 9: Confronting the Obstacles

1. "Breviary" is the popular name for the book containing the fixed cycle of official daily prayers called the Liturgy of the Hours.
2. *The Code of Canon Law* is the book that contains the fundamental laws of the Catholic Church. It was first published in 1917 and later reissued in a revised form in 1983.
3. Bishop Michael J. Murphy was bishop of Erie, Pennsylvania, from 1982 to 1990.
4. "Benediction of the Blessed Sacrament" is a liturgical practice in which the consecrated Host (also called the "Blessed Sacrament") is placed in a monstrance for exposition. Typically the prayer service includes time for silent prayer, hymns, and reading of Scripture. At the end of the service the congregation is blessed by the priest, who traces the sign of the cross over the congregation. This whole practice is grounded in Catholic Eucharistic theology, which holds that the Blessed Sacrament is the body, blood, soul, and divinity of Jesus Christ.
5. Bishop Thomas J. Welsh was bishop of Arlington, Virginia, from 1974 to 1983 and bishop of Allentown, Pennsylvania, from 1983 to 1997.
6. It must be noted that this preceded the "boom" in priestly vocations experienced by the Arlington diocese beginning a few years later under Bishop John Keating and vocations director Father James Gould.
7. William H. Keeler was secretary to Bishop Leech at Vatican II, where he was named *peritus* by Pope John XXIII. He was bishop of Harrisburg from 1984 to 1989, when he became the archbishop of Baltimore. He was made a cardinal by Pope John Paul II in 1994.
8. *Presbyterorum Ordinis* is the Second Vatican Council's "Decree on the Ministry and Life of Priests," issued by Pope Paul VI, December 7, 1965.
9. Mary Immaculate Seminary eventually closed and the property was later purchased by the Archdiocese of Philadelphia. The campus is now used for the "spirituality year" program for Philadelphia seminarians.
10. Holy Apostles Seminary in Cromwell, Connecticut, caters in some respects to "late vocations"—those seminarians who do not enter into studies for the priesthood in their twenties. Trigilio's use of "old men" is rather tongue-in-cheek.
11. Some readers may erroneously infer that the alleged incidents, behavior, activity, and persons involved in this chapter are currently present at St. Mark's Seminary in Erie. Father Trigilio wishes to state unequivocally

that his experiences as related in this chapter refer to the *former* St. Mark High School Seminary and have no connection whatsoever to the current St. Mark Seminary College Formation Program, which is a reputable and responsible institution. Neither Bishop Donald Trautman of Erie nor the current faculty and seminarians of St. Mark's are responsible, nor were they even present during the time in question. Likewise, any and all references to Mary Immaculate Seminary are directed exclusively to the former interdiocesan major seminary in Northampton (when it was run by the Vincentians), and no association, allegation, or accusation should be inferred to the Spirituality Year Program in Northampton that is now part of St. Charles Borromeo Seminary system.

Chapter 10: Heads in the Sand

1. Archbishop John R. Roach was archbishop of St. Paul–Minneapolis from 1975 to 1995. He was president of the NCCB from 1980 to 1983.
2. Kenneth A. Briggs, "Vatican Will Investigate U.S. Seminaries with Aid of Bishops," *New York Times*, September 23, 1981.
3. Ibid.
4. Bishop Marshall went on to become the bishop of Springfield, Massachusetts, in 1991. He died in 1994.
5. Archbishop O'Brien was rector of St. Joseph Seminary in Yonkers, New York, at the time of the Marshall Committee visitations. He was appointed auxiliary bishop of New York in 1996 and later archbishop of the military archdiocese. The Yonkers seminary, nicknamed "Dunwoodie" after the area of Yonkers, has been long regarded as a center of orthodoxy, yet perhaps because of its location in New York City it also has a reputation of being a bit provincial.
6. Joop Koopman, "Priestly Formation Returns to the Basics," *National Catholic Register*, August 11, 1996.
7. Ibid.
8. Francis X. Maier, "American Seminaries," *National Catholic Register*, October 4, 1981.
9. Kenneth Baker, S.J., "Papal Study of American Seminaries," *Homiletic and Pastoral Review*, January 1982.
10. Ibid.
11. Mark Nelson, "U.S. Seminaries Subject of Vatican Investigation," *National Catholic Reporter*, January 1, 1982.
12. Koopman, "Priestly Formation Returns to Basics."
13. The *Enchiridion Symbolorum*, published in 1854, was a comprehensive collection of official Church statements. It served the Church as the standard reference work on magisterial teaching until the *Catechism of the Catholic Church* was released in 1992.
14. In the 1980s the Archdiocese of Detroit hosted an annual conference

attended by more than two thousand Catholic educators from schools and parishes. The conference was called the "Spectrum." "Spectrum Under the Stars" was a takeoff on the popular religious education conference.

15. Archbishop Ignatius J. Strecker was archbishop of Kansas City, Kansas, from 1969 to 1993.

16. Edmund Cardinal Szoka was archbishop of Detroit from 1981 to 1990. He then became the president of the Pontifical Commission for Vatican City State.

17. In 1986, St. John's Seminary closed. The official reason given was economic, but Catholics in Detroit who were following the situation at the time suspect it was closed because of issues outlined in Perrone's report.

18. Weslin, *The Gathering of the Lambs*, 102.

19. Ibid.

20. Greeley is a priest ordained for the Archdiocese of Chicago in 1954. He is one of the best-known voices of Catholic dissent in the United States. His many books and columns have expressed opinions that differ markedly from authentic Catholic teaching, especially on the subject of the male, celibate priesthood. He has long argued that the Church's restriction against married priests has created a clergy that is largely gay and dysfunctional.

21. Cardinal Baum was archbishop of Washington, D.C., from 1973 to 1980. He then served as the prefect of the Vatican's Congregation for Catholic Education until 1990, when he was appointed the Vatican's Major Penitentiary.

22. McInerny, "Priests with AIDS."

23. There were some seminaries such as Mount St. Mary's in Emmitsburg, Maryland, that never capitulated to the emerging zeitgeist and maintained orthodoxy amid much of the confusion of the 1970s and 1980s.

24. Hitchcock, "He's the Last One I Would Have Expected."

25. Ibid.

26. Ibid.

27. Interview with the author, June 2000.

Chapter 11: A Self-Fulfilling Prophecy

1. Frank Norris, "The Vocations Crisis: Where Do We Go from Here?" *Ligourian*, October 1997.

2. Ibid.

3. Pope Paul VI, *Presbyterorum Ordinis*, Decree on the Ministry and Life of Priests, Second Vatican Council, 1965, no. 16.

4. Pamela Schaeffer, "Vocations Crisis Artificial, Says Bishop," *National Catholic Reporter*, October 20, 1995.

5. Pope John Paul II, *Ordinatio Sacerdotalis*, 1994.
6. Peter Daly, "Those Declining Priesthood Statistics," *Catholic Telegraph*, January 5, 2001.
7. Ibid.
8. Responding to Father Daly's column, George Dragan, a former seminarian now married, asked: "Since when has the Holy Spirit told us to follow the path of least resistance? With all the sin in the world, maybe the Holy Spirit is also telling us we should just give into the world's declining moral values, too. Maybe the Holy Spirit is saying that abortion isn't really all that bad after all, either. In fact, maybe the Church should just be disbanded as an archaic construct of extremist 1st Century Messianism. I'm being sarcastic, of course, but Fr. Daly's illogical conclusion assumes that because we have a crisis, the Holy Spirit wants the Church to cave into the spirit of the world. More likely is that the Holy Spirit wants priests to take a more courageous stand from the pulpit. The *sensus fidei* has been saying that for years but so many priests continue to ignore it. Well, isn't the path of least resistance exactly what Satan would want? Fr. Daly also fails to consider the great damage done by the culture and by the American Church's failure to challenge its congregations and provide priests who take boys under their wings in healthy, solid spiritual formation. For those orders and societies that do, their vocations are blossoming at rates as high as ten times that as much as the orders that are self-absorbed with homosexual activism and spiritually digressive ecclesiastical agendas." "Letter to the Editor," *Catholic Telegraph*, January 12, 2001.
9. Bishop Raymond Lucker died in 2001. He was one of the few bishops that identified himself as a member of the dissident Catholic group Call to Action.
10. Archbishop Weakland has been the archbishop of Milwaukee since 1977. From 1967 to 1977 he served as abbot-primate of the Benedictines.
11. Margo Szews, "Married Priests: The Debate Continues," *Milwaukee Journal-Sentinel*, November 17, 1996.
12. Jean Peerenboom, "U.S. Catholic Church Grows Up," *Green Bay Press-Gazette*, September 9, 2000.
13. Tom Fox, "Costs of Clerical Celibacy Are Rising," *National Catholic Reporter*, September 3, 1999.
14. Much of the talk about celibacy assumes that this practice is unnatural, or at least unnatural when it is "imposed." The Catholic Church, however, cannot be said to impose anything. A man is ordained to the priesthood with the full knowledge of what is to be expected of him. "Celibacy, therefore, is not an external effect placed upon the priestly ministry, nor can it be simply considered an institution laid down by law, because those who receive the Sacrament of Holy Orders do so with full

freedom and conscience, after years of preparation, and profound reflection, and diligent prayer." *Directory for the Life and Ministry of Priests*, Vatican Congregation for the Clergy, 1994, no. 58.

15. Altham, "The Religion of Self: An Interview with Dr. William Coulson."

16. E. Michael Jones, "Carl Rogers and the IHM Nuns: Sensitivity Training, Psychological Warfare, and the Catholic Problem," *Culture Wars*, October 1999.

17. From 1898 until 1987, St. Anthony's Seminary of Santa Barbara, California, was a minor seminary operated by the Province of St. Barbara of the Order of Friars Minor. It operated as a boarding school for high school boys who aspired to become Franciscan priests or brothers. The school was closed in 1987.

18. William Coulson, "Full Hearts and Empty Heads: The Price of Certain Recent Programs in Humanistic Psychology." This paper was read on October 20, 1994, to a conference at Franciscan University of Steubenville on "The Nature and Tasks of Personalist Psychology."

19. Report to Father Joseph P. Chinnici, OFM, Provincial Master, Province of St. Barbara, Independent Board of Inquiry (November 22, 1993), 46.

20. Ibid., 1

21. Flyers and registration form from 1988 "Reassessment of Sexual Attitudes" workshop conducted at the Archdiocesan Cousins Center in Milwaukee.

22. Dignity is a prohomosexual group that was banned by the Vatican in 1986 because the group failed to adhere to Catholic teaching on sexual morality.

23. "To Answer Some Questions," a mailer authored by Reverend James Arimond and Leon Konieczny, in conjunction with the Spouse and Parents Support Committee through Adult and Family Ministry of the Archdiocese of Milwaukee, envelope postmarked March 18, 1988.

24. In 1980, Father Arimond led his four-part series on "Homosexuality and Its Impact on the Family." In the *Milwaukee Journal*'s promotional article for the series, Arimond was quoted as saying that "a pervert is someone who goes against his or her sexual tendency. If a heterosexual acted homosexually, that would be perversion. Similarly, if a homosexual acted heterosexually, that would be a perversion" (September 20, 1980).

25. Marie Rohde, "Convicted Priest Working as Counselor in Racine," *Milwaukee Journal-Sentinel*, April 30, 2002.

26. Modras was formerly a faculty member at St. John's Provincial Seminary in Plymouth, Michigan. He left the priesthood to marry.

27. Kosnik was formerly a faculty member at Sts. Cyril and Methodius Seminary in Orchard Lake, Michigan. He was also a member of the Catholic Coalition for Gay Civil Rights, "a national Catholic network of pro-homosexuals" (Enrique Rueda, *The Homosexual Network: Private*

Lives and Public Policy [Old Greenwich, CT: The Devin Air Co., 1982], 334).

28. The critiques continued into 2002. On April 11, William Donohue, president of the Catholic League, issued the following statement regarding Paul Shanley, a former priest of the Archdiocese of Boston who "was a serial child molester" and who "publicly justified" pedophilia and "endorsed bestiality": "Shanley's twisted views on sexuality were not an anomaly. In a 1977 book published by the Catholic Theological Society of America, *Human Sexuality: New Directions in American Catholic Thought*, author Father Anthony Kosnik argued against traditional Catholic teaching on sexuality. He maintained that we must jettison the view that holds fornication, adultery, homosexuality, sodomy and bestiality to be intrinsically evil acts. Showing the wide cultural variance in sexual taboos, Kosnik concluded that priests must understand that 'God is surely present' in homosexual relations that are marked by 'sincere affection.' This book was widely used in seminaries at the time but was condemned in 1979 by the bishops. Kosnik, however, remained teaching in a seminary until 1982. It is time we connected the dots between dissidence and deviance. While the latter is not always caused by the former, it provides intellectual cover." William Donohue, "Dissidence and Deviance in the Church: Connecting the Dots," April 11, 2002, available at: http://catholicleague.org/02press_releases/pr0202.htm.

29. Rich Rinaldi, "Celibacy, More Ancient Than Many Think, Is Also Surprisingly Popular," *National Catholic Register*, March 12–18, 2000.

30. Bishop Hughes retired in 1995.

31. Ackerman was bishop of Covington from 1960 to 1978.

32. Flavin was bishop of Lincoln from 1969 to 1992.

33. Joseph A. Jenkins, "Letter to the Editor," *St. Catherine Review*, September–October 1997.

34. Murphy was archbishop of Seattle from 1991 to 1997. He died in 1997.

35. Hunthausen was archbishop of Seattle from 1975 to 1991.

36. The diaconate program was reinstated a decade later by Archbishop Alexander J. Brunnett, who succeeded Thomas Murphy as archbishop of Seattle.

37. Terry McGuire, "Archbishop Puts Deacon Program on Hold Until Women's Issues Addressed," *The Progress*, March 8, 1990.

38. Ibid.

39. Recall that other Christian churches are now ordaining women and openly active homosexuals.

40. Helen Hull Hitchcock, "I Will Give You Shepherds," *Adoremus Bulletin*, September 1999.

41. Cardinal Mahony has been archbishop of Los Angeles since 1985.

42. Roger Cardinal Mahony, *As I Have Done for You: A Pastoral Letter on Ministry*, April 20, 2000.

43. Ibid.

44. Pilarczyk has been archbishop of Cincinnati since 1982.

45. Michael S. Rose, "Archbishop Pilarczyk Shares Vision of Church," *St. Catherine Review*, March–April 1998.

46. Muench was bishop of Covington from 1996 to 2002. He was installed as bishop of Baton Rouge in 2002.

47. Diocesan bishops are required to make a visit to Rome every five years in order to give an accounting of what is going on in their diocese. It is considered a pilgrimage *ad limina apostolorum*, to the threshold of the apostles. It is called the *ad limina* visit, for short.

48. Jerry Enderle, "Bishop Describes Highlights of 'Ad Limina' Visit," *Messenger*, April 10, 1998.

49. Brian McGuire, "Reversing the Vocations Crisis," *National Catholic Register*, July 9, 2000.

50. Paul Moses, "Daily: Consider Cutting Masses—Priest Shortage Getting Worse," *New York Newsday*, November 12, 2000.

51. Mike Blecha, "Catholic Diocese Faces Dramatic Change," *Green Bay Press-Gazette*, April 23, 2000.

52. According to a study by Cornelius Hughes published in a 1992 issue of *Review of Religious Research*, Catholics in the southwestern United States are largely unwilling to attend communion services in lieu of Mass with a priest: "The official response of Church authorities to the absence of a priest for Sunday services has been to make provision for a communion service to take the place of the Mass. The first question in this section [of the study] therefore asked, 'If your parish were unable to provide Mass on a Sunday, which of the following would you be most likely to do?' The alternatives to attending a communion service were made deliberately unattractive in order to facilitate the selection of the official solution.... [T]wo-thirds chose options other than the official alternative."

53. Lexington is home to outspoken women's ordination proponent Janice Sevre Duszynska. Dressed in alb and stole, she presented herself to Bishop Williams for ordination during the 1997 ordination service at Christ the King Cathedral in Lexington. "Bishop Williams! Bishop Williams!" she cried out. "I am called by the Holy Spirit to present myself for ordination. My name is Janice. I ask this for myself and for all women." Although Williams did not ordain her that day, he remains sympathetic to the ordination of women as well as promotion of the lay-run Church.

54. Bob Harvey, "Introducing a 'New Model of Church,' " *Ottawa Citizen*, December 16, 2000.

55. Catholics are members of the Body of Christ, not members of any faith community. In the words of columnist George Weigel, faith community is "an ultramundane concept of the Church that blinds us to our union with the community of saints."

Chapter 12: The Right Stuff

1. Benedict J. Groeschel, "A Seminarian Reflects," *The Priest*, June 1998.
2. These were stipulations for the education and formation of diocesan clergy, not religious priests. Scholasticates and novitiates for religious priests differed in their approach to spiritual and intellectual formation.
3. Prior to the Council of Trent there were several models used in the education and formation of priests, including individual instruction by bishops, university study, and monastic or cathedral schools. Each of these models proved to be inadequate in providing a strong intellectual, spiritual, and practical (professional) formation for clerics.
4. The "Divine Office" is the former name of the public daily liturgical prayer of the Catholic Church. Since Vatican II, the Divine Office has been known as the Liturgy of the Hours.
5. Philip II of Spain established a university in Douai (also spelled Douay) in 1562. Six years later the English cardinal William Allen opened a seminary for English Catholics there. Allen was one of many Catholic alumni of the University of Oxford who fled to Douai from England following the Church of England's adoption of the Thirty-nine Articles, the theological manifesto imposed upon the English clergy. The Douai-Rheims Bible, an English translation of the Latin Vulgate, was begun in the town by members of the seminary; the Old Testament was published in Douai in 1609. The seminary was suppressed in 1793 during the French Revolution.
6. Université Catholique de Louvain, near Brussels in Belgium.
7. Universidad Literaria de Salamanca, in central Spain.
8. Tim Unsworth, "U.S. Seminarians: Dedicated and Different," *National Catholic Reporter*, May 6, 1994.
9. George Kelly, *The Battle for the American Church* (New York: Image Books, 1981), 306.
10. Council of Baltimore, 1884, article 159.
11. Pope St. Pius X, *E Supremi*, 1903.
12. In 1924, the U.S. Congress enacted the Immigration Act, which severely curtailed the entry of Italians, Poles, Hungarians, and Russians.
13. Quinn, "Priest Shortage Panic."
14. Daniel Pilarczyk, "The Changing Image of the Priest," *Origins*, July 3, 1986.
15. *Catholic Almanac.*
16. Kelly, *The Battle for the American Church*, 309.
17. Paul VI, *Optatam Totius*, Decree on Priestly Formation, Second Vatican Council, October 28, 1965, article 5.
18. Ibid., article 14.
19. Ibid., article 9.
20. Ibid., article 10.
21. John Paul II, *Pastores Dabo Vobis*, March 25, 1992, article 43.

22. Ibid.
23. Ibid., article 45.
24. Ibid., article 45, cf. *Optatam Totius,* article 8.
25. Ibid., article 51.
26. Ibid., article 66.
27. George Weigel, *Witness to Hope* (New York: Harper Collins, 1999), 84.
28. Hitchcock, "He's the Last One I Would Have Expected."
29. Father John Hardon, "Sacrifice and Vocations," *Religious Life,* September–October 1984.
30. Ibid.
31. Paul VI, *Optatam Totius.*
32. According to *Presbyterorum Ordinis,* issued on December 7, 1965, priests are to seek "not what is to their own advantage but what will benefit the many for salvation" (article 13).

Chapter 13: Where the Men Are

1. Kenneth E. Miller, "Letter to the Editor," *Catholic Exponent,* May 15, 1998.
2. In 1995, Bishop Thomas Tobin, known to be an orthodox bishop, was appointed to replace Bishop James Malone as the head of the Youngstown diocese. In 1998, responding to the dwindling number of active priests within the Diocese of Youngstown, Tobin urged members of his northeastern Ohio diocese to continue to promote vocations to the priesthood. This will continue to be "one of the primary priorities of this Diocese," wrote Tobin that year in an October 2 letter addressed to all the faithful of his diocese. "It is encouraging to point out that the vocation picture for the priesthood in this Diocese is beginning to turn around," he wrote. "At the present moment we have 10 men—very fine candidates—studying for the priesthood, and we are in contact with several more actively considering entrance into the seminary. In the years 2000–2001, we may have as many as seven men ordained for the priesthood, as many as were ordained in the previous five years combined!"
3. Thomas Acklin, "Letter to the Editor," *Catholic Exponent,* June 12, 1998.
4. David Misbrener, "Letter to the Editor," *Catholic Exponent,* May 29, 1998.
5. Curtiss, "Vocations to the Priesthood and Religious Life."
6. Cynthia G. Smith, "Vocations Launches Media Blitz," *Providence Visitor,* January 7, 1999.
7. "Media Blitz Aside, All Need to Boost Vocations," *Providence Visitor,* January 14, 1999.
8. Robert McClory, "Some Seminaries Thrive, Others Struggle," *National Catholic Reporter,* April 3, 2000.
9. Brian Murphy, *The New Men* (New York: Riverhead Books, 1997), 7.

10. Uwe Siemon-Netto, "Orthodoxy Lures Young Men to Priesthood," United Press International, January 10, 2001.
11. Francis Cardinal Stafford was archbishop of Denver from 1986 to 1996. Since 1996, he has served as the president of the Pontifical Council for the Laity.
12. Peter Droege, "Archdiocese of Denver Experiences Boom in Vocations," *Denver Catholic Register,* September 16, 1998.

Index